WHAT CHRISTIANS BELIEVE ABOUT THE BIBLE

Donald K. McKim

THOMAS NELSON PUBLISHERS
Nashville • Camden • New York

Books by Donald K. McKim

The Authority and Interpretation of the Bible:
  An Historical Approach (with Jack B. Rogers)
The Authoritative Word: Essays on the Nature of
  Scripture, editor
Readings in Calvin's Theology, editor

220.1
M158w
c.1

Published in Nashville, Tennessee, by Thomas Nelson, Inc., Publishers and distributed in Can-
ada by Lawson Falle, Ltd., Cambridge, Ontario.

Printed in the United States of America.

Library of Congress Cataloging-in-Publication Data

McKim, Donald D.
  What Christians believe about the Bible.

  Bibliography: pp. 153-189
  Includes index.
1. Bible—Criticism, interpretation, etc.—History-
20th century. I. Title.
BS500.M35   1985   220.1   85-18846
ISBN 0-8407-5968-1

To Jack B. Rogers

Incomparable colleague
Superb scholar
Foremost of friends
with whom I first studied the doctrine of Scripture.
Dedicated with gratitude, appreciation, and affection.

PREFACE

This book has grown out of a long-standing interest in the doctrine of Scripture. In teaching theology at The University of Dubuque Theological Seminary, however, I found there was no one volume that explained the basics of the various contemporary views about the nature of the Bible. As I considered this, an unpublished paper by Jack Rogers and Gary Watts, "Six Theological Models of the Early 1980s: Their Theological Methods with Special Reference to Their Use of Scripture" helped clarify a method of approaching this topic and outlined certain trajectories of thought. Thus the idea for the book was born. I am grateful to Ronald E. Pitkin who, when he was Executive Editor of Academic and Reference Books, presented my proposal to the Academic Books Editorial Committee of Thomas Nelson Publishers. Paul Franklyn as my editor has been most supportive throughout the project.

My family endured several months of my sustained writing, and I express my appreciation to them. LindaJo, Stephen, and Karl have been very supportive. Also, they gave up their own time on the home computer so I could use it to write.

This book is dedicated to Jack Rogers. He has been a model to me in countless ways. He has shown me how faith, scholarship, and caring can all go together. He has demonstrated how a Christian scholar can be continually a person of faith seeking further understanding.

Donald K. McKim
University of Dubuque Theological Seminary
Easter, 1985

CONTENTS

INTRODUCTION

Many theological options are available today. Numerous theological positions are found within Christian churches. Each has its own style and approach as well as its distinctive perspective that sets it apart from others.

Many different views about the Bible are present today as well. The different theologies have their own ways of understanding the nature of Scripture and its appropriate interpretation. What a Christian theology says about the Bible will significantly affect its concerns and the rest of its approach in general.

This book was written to sort out the varieties of beliefs about the Bible. What follows tries to show the basic views of major contemporary theologies about Scripture. The first two chapter deal with significant ecclesiastical traditions, while the remaining ones cover important theological positions.

For each position a caption or "bumper sticker" is given. This blurb tried to capture the essence of that theology's views about Scripture. These are not the only slogans that could be used, but they seem appropriate in light of the way Scripture is viewed in each instance.

Theological doctrines, to be well understood, need to be set in contexts. Each chapter presents an initial description of the theology at hand. Then attention is given to backgrounds, with concentration on important historical, philosophical, or cultural contexts from which the theology arose. This sheds light on the position and its major beliefs. It also helps explain why Scripture is viewed as it is.

Since the doctrine of Scripture is closely connected with other theological issues and methods of doing theology, these are considered when they are particularly relevant. Since each position has its own history and development, the categories through which they view Scripture differ. In a broad way one can say what each theology believes about topics such as revelation, or the authority, or inspiration of the Bible. But these categories may not be specifically developed in themselves. Thus the special focus of each position must be seen. Some views elaborate one aspect of the nature of Scripture, such as "inspiration," to a more detailed degree. Others may generally assume such a concept and work in very different arenas. So each position must be examined in itself.

The following expositions cannot be exhaustive treatments. In some cases representative figures are chosen and citations made from a number of different works. Other times, one major figure is targeted and that person's work made the central concern. This is the case with neo-orthodox and existential theology, where the works of Barth and Tillich are used. Other theologians could have been chosen as well. In the chapter on liberation theology, the focus is on South American liberation theologians, though black theology and Asian liberation theology movements could also have been explored.

There has been no room here to deal much with hermeneutics or the process of biblical interpretation in these theologies. Such a study could enhance our understandings of the varied views of Scripture. Then we could see how the nature of Scripture in these theologies is incorporated in the practice of exegesis and interpretation for specific biblical texts.

It is hoped that this volume can introduce in a neutral fashion, these basic beliefs about the Bible and the theological movements themselves. The chapters can be read separately or together to gain either a specific look or a general overview of what Christians believe about the Bible.

I

ROMAN CATHOLICISM
Classic and Contemporary

The issue of Scripture in Roman Catholicism touches on a variety of theological topics. Related to the Roman Catholic understanding of the Bible are Catholic views of authority, tradition, the church, and papal infallibility. The church's views have developed explicitness through the centuries. Chiefly, the official positions of the church about the Bible are found in the pronouncements of popes and church councils.[1] Among these are the statements from the Council of Florence (1442), the decrees of the Council of Trent (1546), the decrees of Vatican Council I (1870), and particularly the *Dogmatic Constitution on Divine Revelation (Dei Verbum)* of Vatican Council II (1965). Important papal biblical encyclicals are *Providentissimus Deus* by Leo XIII (1893), *Spiritus Paraclitus* by Benedict XV (1920), and *Divino afflante Spiritu* by Pius XII (1943).[2] Responses and instructions by the Pontifical Biblical Commission and the Holy Office have also been issued since 1905. Not all of these documents are accorded the same weight of authority in Catholic tradition. The decrees of the last three ecumenical councils (Trent, Vatican I, and Vatican II) are of highest import. Anathemas are attached to some canons of the Council of Trent and Vatican I making them of more juridical force than other statements by councils. Vatican II did not pronounce new dogmatic definitions nor issue sanctions against those who reject its teachings.[3]

While official Catholic teachings are contained in the types of documents mentioned, these do not set forth a comprehensive and systematic doctrine of Scripture. The theologians of the church are those charged with synthesizing data and producing a full dogmatic treatment. As long as theologians and individual Catholics do not move against the established doctrines of the church, they may proceed as they deem best in their systematic work. The ecclesiastical magisterium, the body that formulates official Catholic

9

doctrine, usually plays a supervisory, judicial role and intervenes only when a serious crisis, error, or controversy arises. Thus, in a sense,

> one cannot fairly set forth *the* Catholic teachings concerning Scripture. The church leaves its members free to follow any theological theories within the bounds of orthodoxy. Orthodoxy itself provides not so much a doctrine as a set of negative norms which serve as guidelines for theological speculation.[4]

This position is possible because

> except for several brief but important statements issued by Trent and Vatican I, the Roman Catholic Church has not issued any infallible or irreformable pronouncements in regard to the Bible. With these exceptions, official Catholic teachings on Scripture may be regarded as fallible and therefore subject to challenge.[5]

In order to gain perspective on how these views developed as well as to see what the Church's teachings are and how they are interpreted, it is necessary to survey certain background dimensions.

BACKGROUNDS

Sources of Authority

In the year A.D. 434, the theologian Vincent of Lerins wrote his *Commonitory* to attack the predestination teachings of Augustine and his successors. Vincent claimed they were innovations and deviated from the tradition of orthodoxy. In this work Vincent described the authority of the church's tradition when he wrote that it consisted of that which had been believed "everywhere, always, by all."[6] One century later in the treatise *On the Christian Faith* attributed to Boethius, the principle enunciated by Vincent was affirmed: "The catholic church, then, spread throughout the world, is known by three particular marks: whatever is believed and taught in it has the authority of the Scriptures, or of universal tradition, or at least of its own and proper usage."[7]

In these statements, the requirement of "universality" meant that in order for a doctrine to be recognized as a teaching of the church, it must be recognized by all the churches (catholic—universally). This distinguished the teaching from the private theory or viewpoints of individuals or single theologians. For it was the catholic church that was "the repository of truth, the dispenser of grace, the guarantee of salvation, the matrix of acceptable worship."[8]

The authoritative status of the church had been supported in its earliest period by several sources of authority. Christians believed that final authority for salvation and the life of faith rested in God who embodied this authority in Jesus Christ. The authority of God in Christ was fundamental as Christ exercised Lordship over the church.

With the spread of Christianity, the church recognized the authority of Christ was exercised through apostles and in the Christian community. Apostolic authority was not inherent in apostles themselves, but was authorized by God. With the death of the apostles, however, questions about the locus of apostolic authority became important. How would God continue to exercise authority in the post-apostolic church? Two possibilities arose. First, God could work through the apostolic writings that could be added to the church's use of the Old Testament as a "canon" of Scripture. Secondly, God could work through the ongoing activity of the church. Pastors and teachers could be seen as having special authority on the basis of the apostolic message they preached and taught.[9]

A related issue had to do with how the church could respond to the variety of interpretations of the faith that arose. Some of these appeared to endanger the essence of the faith. Early "heresies" such as Judaizing Christianity, Gnosticism, Marcionism, Montanism, and Monarchianism made it crucial for the church to understand where the locus of its authority rested.[10]

In the early centuries, the church came to recognize several sources as the bases of its authority.

(1) *Canon.* With the death of the apostles, the church knew it no longer had the personal reminiscences of the apostles from which to draw. Apostolic teachings, however, were preserved and passed on to following generations through traditions. The original Christian gospel was the message of Christ spoken and transmitted by apostolic witnesses. The term to describe this "handing over" or "delivery" refers both to the process of its communication (Gr. *paradidomai*) and its content (Gr. *paradosis*).[11] The content of this body of Christian teaching was called "tradition."[12]

Until well into the second century, the Christian church looked to the Old Testament for its "canon" or collection of sacred, authoritative writings.[13] Traditionally the date of the fixing of the Old Testament canon has been connected with the so-called Council or Synod of Jamnia, *ca.* A.D. 90-100[14] These writings were the Christian Bible. They were read from the Christian perspective of faith.[15] From these, "the apostles of the first century and the apologists of the second century drew their basic texts as they proclaimed and defended the gospel; the reading of them and was sufficient to convince educated pagans of the truth of Christianity."[16]

During the early decades of the church, apostolic writings were produced which eventually became the New Testament Scriptures.[17] "Lists" of books appeared to designate bodies of authoritative writings for Christians.[18] In the second and third centuries the process of ascertaining authoritative writings intensified until the first official document, which delineated the present New Testament canon, was written. This was the Thirty-Ninth Festal Letter of Bishop Athanasius at Easter in A.D. 367. It listed the twenty-seven books of the New Testament, which became the church's official New Testament canon. The Synod of Hippo in 393 and the Third Synod of Carthage in 397 followed and ratified the list of Athanasius.[19] Thus the church turned to its Scriptures as a source of Christian instruction and understanding in the early centuries.

(2) *Creeds.* A second source of authority for the early church rested in the creeds that emerged in Christian communities. Within the first Christian generation, brief summaries of the apostles' preaching developed.[20] When new converts came into the Christian faith, there was a need to instruct them in Christian beliefs. These summary statements served that purpose and were used in the context of baptisms and public professions of faith.[21] In the second century, Irenaeus referred to these summary statements as "the rule [canon] of truth."[22] Tertullian in the third century regularly referred to the "rule of faith" or *regula fidei.*[23]

The rise of various Christian teachings, some later called "heresies," also made it imperative for the church to have authoritative statements of its beliefs. Fixed, traditional formulas of faith became "a key to what the church thought the Scriptures came to, where it was, so to speak, that their weight fell, what was their drift."[24] Gradually, creeds developed as confessions of this faith. At times when differing opinions on theological issues or biblical interpretation arose, the church met in councils to discuss the issue of faith. The first such council was the council of Nicea in A.D. 325, from which emerged the Nicene Creed.[25] The Apostles' Creed, with its origins in the Old Roman Symbol of the second century, gradually became the most widely used confessional statement of the Western Church and took its final form in the ninth century.[26] These two creeds, along with the Athanasian Creed from the end of the fourth century, were the first three ecumenical creeds of the church. They provided statements of Christian beliefs for the instruction of believers and witnessed to the church's faith in the face of varieties of theological positions.

(3) *Church Leadership.* Along with the canon of Scripture and the creeds and confessions, the church recognized apostolic tradition as continuing through the leaders of the churches. The first century "offices" of the church as found in the New Testament continued. These included apostles, prophets, teachers, *episcopoi* (bishops; overseers), deacons, presbyters and evangelists.[27] From this time there developed "an idea of 'succession to the apostles,' which has been interpreted as succession in doctrine, or as succession in office, or both."[28]

With the rise of the variant opinions in the second century, particularly gnosticism, the faithful transmission of apostolic teaching became crucial. The church believed the Holy Spirit would ultimately protect the truth of the gospel. But to recognize how the Spirit protected the gospel, the church linked its reliable transmission to the "seats" or "sees" (Lat. *sed*) of bishops. These sees were considered to have been founded by the apostles. The teachings from these episcopal sees "became important for the councils, which endeavored to set forth authoritative interpretations of 'the faith...delivered to the saints' (Jude 3)."[29]

Through these three channels of authority—canon, creed and church leadership—the early church carried out its mission in the world. The interplay among these three was to have significant consequences for the subsequent history and development of the Roman Catholic church. Because of these interactions, Catholic views on Scripture cannot be isolated from other theological doctrines.

Development of Papacy

The see at Rome came to gain special significance as a seat of authority. Roman bishops were mostly aloof from early doctrinal controversies in the Eastern churches. However, by the middle of the third century, "they seem to have assumed special responsibility for preserving and interpreting the faith of 'antiquity' because of the prerogative of the See of Peter (*cathedra Petri*)."[30] Rome became in many ways the pre-eminent see and the bishop of Rome the pre-eminent bishop.[31] Thus the papacy began to develop.

The position of the pope in the Roman church and throughout Christendom in the coming centuries is a long and complex story.[32] It was "characteristic of the papacy, as it had already been much earlier of the episcopacy, that it was not only a practical system of ecclesiastical governance subject to adjustment and compromise, but also a doctrine that was to be believed, taught, and confessed by the church on the basis of the word of God."[33] Crucial to the doctrine of the papacy was the belief that, as Pope Innocent I expressed it, from Rome "the other churches, like waters proceeding from their natal source...(like) pure streams from an uncorrupt head, should take up what they ought to enjoin."[34] By the sixth century the Formula of Pope Hormisdas (515) stated that in Rome "the catholic religion has always been preserved immaculate."[35]

Roman Catholic understandings of the primacy of the bishop of Rome (the pope) and his special position rest on the interpretation of New Testament texts related to the apostle Peter and the "Petrine function." Chief among these is Matthew 16:18 when Jesus said to Peter: "And I tell you, you are Peter [Gr. *Petros*], and on this rock [Gr. *petra*] I will build my church, and the powers of death [Gr. gates of Hades] shall not prevail against it" (RSV). As interpreted by Pope Gregory I in one of his letters:

> To all who know the Gospel it is obvious that by the voice of the Lord the care
> of the entire church was committed to the holy apostle and prince of all the
> apostles, Peter....Behold, he received the keys of the kingdom of heaven, the
> power to bind and loose was given to him, and the care and principality of the
> entire church was committed to him....Am I defending my own cause in this
> matter? Am I vindicating some special injury of my own? Is it not rather the
> cause of the Almighty God, the cause of the universal church?...Certainly[sic],
> in honor of Peter, the prince of the apostles, [the title 'universal'] was offered to
> the Roman pontiff by the venerable Council of Chalcedon.[36]

Other important texts have been John 21:17 and Luke 22:31, 32. Peter is
seen as the "rock" on which the church is to be founded (Matt. 16:18). It is
for Peter that Jesus prays so his faith will not fail (Luke 22:32). Peter has
been given power and authority in receiving the "keys of the kingdom"
(Matt. 16:19) so that he with others has the task of "binding and loosing"
(Matt. 18:18) as well as "strengthening the brethren" (Acts 15:32).

The primacy of Peter and the growing powers of the bishop of Rome as
pope are expressed in numerous theological statements such as that of Am-
brose Autpert who said Peter was "the bearer of the person of the church."[37]
For Isidore of Seville, the pope as supreme pontiff was "the chief of
priests...the highest priest" for he appointed all other priests in the church
and had all ecclesiastical offices at his disposal.[38] For Hincar, archbishop of
Reims in the ninth century, the "solicitude for all the churches has been committed to the holy Roman church, in Peter, the prince of the apostles."[39]

During the early Middle Ages (600-1050), churches of the West recognized the "vicar of St. Peter" with honor but Eastern churches nearly
never consulted him.[40] During the High Middle Ages (1050-1500) the papacy
became the central focus of Western Christendom. Struggles between papal
power and secular rulers had been a feature of Western society until Pope
Gregory VII (1073-1085) declared the papacy free from secular rulers. His
Gregorian reforms, summarized in twenty-seven *dicta* (*Dictatus Papae*;
1075) announced among other things that the pope had the power to depose
emperors.[41]

In 1198, Innocent III became pope (1198-1216). His pontificate is often
considered "the apogee of the medieval papacy, the culmination of the hiero-
cratic tendencies for which Gregory VII had fought."[42] Of the papal office Innocent wrote:

> To [the pope] is said in the person of the prophet: 'I have set you over nations
> and over kingdoms, to root up and to pull down and to waste and to destroy and
> to build and to plant.' [Jer. 1:10] To me also is said in the person of the apostle: 'I

14

will give to you the keys of the kingdom of heaven....' Thus, others were called to a part of the care, but Peter alone assumed the plenitude of power. You see then who is the vicar of Jesus Christ, successor of Peter, anointed of the Lord, a God of Pharaoh, set between God and man, *lower than God but higher than man*, who judges all and is judged by no one.[43]

In the following centuries, the medieval papacy went through a series of crises including attempts at reforms by the conciliar movement, a great schism, and "Babylonian Captivity" with rival popes in three locations vying for power.[44] By the opening of the sixteenth century, demands for institutional an doctrinal reform in the church were being heard.[45] In the face of the Protestant Reformation, the Roman church responded at the Council of Trent (1545-1563) by further defining its faith and instituting ecclesiastical changes through the powers of the papacy.

Scripture in Roman Catholic Theology

Canon and Inspiration

The term "canon" means a rule or standard by which something is judged. By accepting a canon of biblical writings, "the Catholic Church implicitly declares that these writings have special authority for and in the church."[46] As noted above, by the fourth century the church had settled the books of the Christian canon. In the history of the Catholic church, the Council of Hippo in 393 (Canon 38) officially listed the church's canonical writings. This same canon was endorsed by the Third Council of Carthage in 397 (Canon 47) and repeated by the Fourth Council of Carthage in 419 (Canon 29).[47] Several popes in the fifth century and the Council of Florence in the fifteenth century further reasserted it, and the Council of Trent reinforced it by imposing "anathema" on those who reject the canonical Scriptures.[48] In 1870 the First Vatican Council stated, as Trent said, that the books "contained in the ancient Latin edition of the Vulgate" are held by the Church "to be sacred and canonical."[49]

Perhaps the usual interpretation of the significance of the canon is that "in drawing up the canon, the church vouches for the fact that these books *and no others* are sacred, inspired, and divinely authoritative." But as Avery Dulles goes on to note, "canonization also can be interpreted to mean that these books, *and perhaps others*, are sacred, inspired, and divinely authoritative. In the latter case, the church would leave open the possibility of adding to its canon."[50] While he finds it "very unlikely that the list will be changed in the future," he also states that "to the best of my knowledge, the canon never has been defined in an exclusive sense. Thus it seems possible, at least in theory, that a new book could be added."[51]

At the time of the Protestant Reformation, the Reformers followed the Hebrew Bible and its thirty-nine books of the Old Testament as constituting the Protestant canon of Scripture. The Hebrew Scriptures omit seven books (and parts of two others) that are retained in the forty-six books of the Latin Vulgate, which forms the Catholic Old Testament.[52] The Vulgate, translated in the fourth-century by Jerome, is cited in Catholic pronouncements as the Bible containing the approved canon. Yet the Vulgate has not been as an inspired text in and of itself. It is rather a 'substantially reliable translation, free from doctrinal error.'[53] The Council of Trent, while approving the Vulgate translation, also called for a critical edition of the Vulgate text.

It is been the Catholic understanding since the time of the early church that the Scriptures are inspired by God.[54] However, it was not until the First Vatican Council issued the decrees of its third session on April 24, 1870 that as assertion was made by an official Catholic body on the nature of Scriptural inspiration. Earlier documents had spoken of Scripture's inspiration. The Decree of the Council of Florence (1442) professed

> one and the same God as the author of the Old and New Testament, that is, of the Law and the Prophets and the Gospel, since the saints of both Testaments have spoken with the inspiration of the same Holy Spirit, whose books, which are contained under the following titles it accepts and venerates.[55]

But Vatican I went on to add that

> the Church holds [these books] to be sacred and canonical, not because, having been carefully composed by mere human industry, they were afterwards approved by her authority, nor merely because they contain revelation with no admixture of error, but because, having been written by the inspiration of the Holy Spirit, they have God for their author and have been delivered as such to the Church herself.[56]

This statement of Vatican I spoke positively of inspiration in that by "the inspiration of the Holy Spirit" (*Spiritu Sancto inspirante*) the Scriptures are documents that have "God for their author." At the council of Trent (also quoted by Vatican I), the statement on Scripture said that church belief

> is contained in the written books and unwritten traditions which have come down to us, having been received by the apostles form the mouth of Christ Himself, or from the apostles themselves by the dictation of the Holy Spirit [Spiritu Sancto dictante], and have been transmitted as it were from hand to hand.[57]

While Trent's statement on inspiration uses the image of "dictation" to describe the inspiration of Scripture, Vatican I speaks only of God as the "author" of Scripture.[58] A further description of the mode of inspiration was provided in the papal encyclical letter *Providentissimus Deus* issued by Pope Leo XIII on November 18, 1893. Leo's view of biblical inspiration was that

> by supernatural power, He [God] so moved and impelled them to write—He so assisted them when writing—that the things which He ordered, and those only, they, first, rightly understood, then willed faithfully to write down, and finally expressed in apt words and with infallible truth. Otherwise, it could not be said that He was the Author of the entire Scripture.[59]

For Leo, this view of the inspiration of Scripture also entailed Scripture's inerrancy, its depiction of truth on the matters with which it dealt. As Leo wrote:

> For all the books which the Church receives as sacred and canonical are written wholly and entirely, with all their parts, at the dictation of the Holy Spirit; and so far is it from being possible that any error can coexist with inspiration, that inspiration not only is essentially incompatible with error, but excludes and rejects it as absolutely and necessarily as it is impossible that God Himself, the supreme Truth, can utter that which is not true.[60]

For Leo, "the formula of divine authorship was understood in a literary sense: author-writer *simpliciter*.[61] By the laws of logic, if God is the "author" of Scriptures and God is perfect, without error, humans as the "writers" of Scripture would also share in this perfection of "inerrancy" when writing.

The formulations of Vatican II are contained in the *Dei Verbum* ("Dogmatic Constitution on Divine Revelation"). The main features of Vatican I's teachings on inspiration were reiterated with the statement:

> To compose the sacred books, God chose certain men who, all the while he employed them in this task, made full use of their powers and faculties so that, though he acts in them and by them, it was as true authors that they consigned to writing whatever he wanted written, and no more.[62]

Dulles has noted that Vatican II's statement affirmed that "the human writers were not mere secretaries but true authors, thus by implication repudiating certain 'dictation' theories."[63] Contemporary Catholic theologians, he observes, generally

> reject the idea that by inspiration, God directly infused words or ideas into the minds of the biblical writers. Inspiration does not relieve its recipients of the necessity of applying their own powers to the research and composition from which books result. It assures only that those powers are so effectively assisted that the resulting books serve as God intends for the guidance of the church.[64]

In light of the Vatican II insistence on the human writers as true authors, Dulles as a contemporary Catholic theologian suggests that a rethinking of

17

the sense in which God is the "author" of Scripture should be made. His full statement is illuminating:

> The term *auctor* in Latin (or *archegos* in Greek) does not necessarily mean *literary author*, but rather *originator*. Thus it is possible to say that God is author of the Bible in the sense that God initiates and controls the process whereby it is written, even thought he does not dictate or miraculously infuse the ideas and the words. In this view God would be, in the first instance, the author of the people of Israel and of their faith, and of the development of that faith through Jesus Christ. Inasmuch as God personally involves himself in salvation history, God could be called the author, indirectly, of the documents whereby the people of God express their faith in a divinely guided and reliable fashion.
>
> Thus conceived, biblical inspiration results in a body of traditional literature which represents the faith of the people of God at various stages of development. In a special way, it expresses the faith of the prophetic and apostolic leaders who helped to shape the faith of Israel and of the church. A sufficient deposit of that inspired literature has survived to allow the church of subsequent centuries to constantly test its own teaching and piety against that of the recipients of the Jewish and Christian revelation.[65]

Other contemporary Catholic theologians besides Dulles such as Raymond E. Brown and Bruce Vawter note the Vatican II document states that "the books of Scripture, firmly, faithfully and without error, teach that truth which God, for the sake of our salvation, wished to see confided to the sacred Scriptures."[66] The significance of this from their perspective is that the term "inerrancy," which had been present in the earliest (1962) draft of the document, "eventually disappeared from the text of the conciliar discussion if not from the discussions themselves."[67] Vawter writes:

> "Without error" is predicated of the Scripture specifically in respect to the truth that God willed to be present there for the sake of our salvation. The Bible is no longer seen as automatically inerrant in virtue of its being the work of an inspired writer. A certain truth only is ascribed to it, and that only as it is the vehicle of a divine salvific intention.[68]

As Raymond Brown explains this, "it is not as if some parts of Scripture teach without error 'truth for the sake of salvation,' and other parts do not. Everything in Scripture is inerrant to the extent to which it conforms to the salvific purpose of God."[69] In this way, contemporary Catholic theologians can uphold the classical teachings of the church on issues of canon and inspiration while at the same time being open, receptive, and in many cases frontrunners of current biblical scholarship.[70]

Scripture and Tradition

Roman Catholic statements about Scripture and its nature are always made—whether by individual theologians or ecclesiastical councils—within the context of the church. The issue of the authority of Scripture and its right interpretation is an issue that in Catholic theology is related to the wider questions of the relation of Scripture and tradition, the nature of the church, and specifically the primacy and functioning of the pope. In the late Middle Ages, various reform movements within the Roman Catholic church raised the issue of where ultimate authority in the church was to be found. Focused most sharply, this was the question of how Scriptural authority functioned in relation to the authority of the traditions of the church. Two opposing currents of thought developed. Both were "concerned with the authority of Tradition, but Tradition conceived in two radically differing fashions."[71]

One stream, following the lead of Thomas Bradwardine (1290-1349) of Oxford, stressed the "exclusive and final authority of Holy Scripture."[72] Bradwardine argued for "the sufficiency of Holy Scripture as understood by the Fathers and doctors of the Church. In the case of disagreement between these interpreters, Holy Scripture has the final authority."[73] The tradition of the church is the means by which the faith or truth contained in Holy Scripture is received. Implicit in this position was "a sharp distinction between the word of God in 'Scripture alone,' which was the only authority deserving of total credence, and the word of 'all the saints except for Christ,' whether popes or church fathers or even apostles, apart from Scripture."[74]

The second stream, following the views of William of Occam (1285?-1347), argued that "there are many catholic truths that neither are contained explicitly in Sacred Scripture nor can be inferred solely from its contents.[75] For Occam there were ultimately two sources from which doctrines may be derived. One source is Scripture which contains the truth of God. The second is through the approval of the pope who does not invent but rather "formulates what truth is in a particular respect since truth is eternal."[76] Thus in this stream authority is given to both scriptural and extra-scriptural revelation. Ecclesiastical traditions, including canon law, were seen to have an authority equal to that of Scripture.

Up to the Reformation period, both traditions viewed the authority of Scripture as the primary source for Christian faith. Neither rejected the authority of the church nor treated Scripture in isolation from the Catholic church. The question between the two views was

> whether the church, in exercising this doctrinal authority, had the right to promulgate as apostolic doctrines even some beliefs that could not find explicit warrant in what was 'written in the Bible' or in what was 'deduced from this

alone by an obvious conclusion,' but that were rather purported to have 'come down to us through the successive transmission of the apostles and others, as equivalent to the canonical Scripture' in authority and apostolic authenticity.[78]

The tension between the two views had major consequences throughout the period of the Reformation. What was at stake ultimately was whether church tradition provided only an authoritative interpretation of Scripture or whether it also had the authority to expand the scriptural revelation. The Protestant Reformers with their stress on *sola Scriptura* argued for the primacy of Scripture over the church and rejected traditions not explicitly biblically grounded. The Roman church claimed that "the very Scripture whose 'sole' authority was being pitted against that of the church depended for its authentication on the church."[78] Since the church was the authenticating body, no truth for Catholic faith could ultimately lie completely "outside" Scripture. Going back to Augustine's dictum: "For my part, I should not believe the gospel except as moved by the authority of the catholic church," it could be argued as Gabriel Biel (d. 1495) did: "the truth that holy mother church defines or accepts as catholic is to be believed with the same veneration as if it were expressed in Holy Writ."[80] Without the authority of the church and its tradition, even the Scriptures could not be trusted.

At the Fourth Session of the Council of Trent (April 8, 1546), the Catholic church clarified its views in light of the challenge of the Protestant Reformers. Trent decreed that the source (Lat. *fons*) of

> all salutary truth and moral disciplines [is] the gospel promised before by the prophets in the holy Scriptures, promulgated by the very mouth of our Lord Jesus Christ the Son of God, then to be preached by his Apostles to every creature [and that] this truth and discipline is contained in written books and unwritten traditions which were received by the Apostles from the mouth of Christ himself or by the Apostles themselves under the inspiration of the Holy Spirit [*Spiritu Sancto dictante*].[81]

Interpreting Trent, George H. Tavard has written that the source of all truth and Christian behavior is the gospel of Christ which comes through the power of the Holy Spirit. The Spirit uses

> two sets of vessels: Holy Scripture and traditions. In as far as they convey the same Gospel of Christ, in as far as they channel the original impetus whereby the Spirit moved the Apostles, both Scriptures and traditions are entitled to the same adhesion of faith. For faith reaches Christ and the Spirit whatever the medium used to contact us....The touchstone of a Scripture as of a tradition is the Gospel, 'kept in the Catholic Church in a continuous succession.'[82]

The question of how Scripture and tradition are interpreted becomes one of major concluding interest. During the late thirteenth and early fourteenth centuries in a controversy over poverty, the term "infallibility" came to be associated with the papal *magisterium* or teaching authority.[83] Guido Terreni, a Carmelite theologian of the fourteenth century was one of the first to speak explicitly of the "infallible" truth of the Roman pontiff speaking on matters of faith. He wrote that "in the determination of the things that pertain to faith the pope is directed [*dirigatur*] by the Holy Spirit and the Holy Spirit speaks in him." Guido claimed on the basis of biblical and patristic statements about the indefectibility of the church that "the immutable and invariable authority of the catholic church...resides universally, after Christ, solely in the supreme pontiff and not in any private person." This meant to him that "the lord pope, to whose authority it belongs to determine and declare the propositions that belong to the faith, cannot [*non possit*] err."[84] thus the term "infallibility" (Lat. *infallibilitas*) took on a highly technical meaning.[85]

Controversy about this view of the pope's authority continued in the Catholic church for four centuries. Conciliarists, those who sought to locate the church's teaching authority in church councils, resisted attributing this authority to the pope. On July 18, 1870, Vatican I Council gave formal definition to the dogma of papal infallibility. The canon declares that

> the Roman Pontiff, when he speaks *ex cathedra*–that is, when in the discharge of the office of Shepherd and Teacher of all Christians, he defines in virtue of his supreme Apostolic authority a doctrine of faith or morals to be held by the universal Church–enjoys, through the divine assistance promised to him in Blessed Peter, that infallibility with which the divine Redeemer willed to equip his Church when it defines a doctrine of faith or morals; and therefore such definitions of the Roman Pontiff are irreformable of themselves, not however from the consent of the Church.[86]

Catholic theologians have explicated the specific meanings of this dogma of infallibility that were implicit in the Vatican I teaching.[87] Briefly, some of the important aspects are:

(1) The pope must act as universal pastor and teacher. His goal must be to "define" (to impose on believers a precisely formulated truth in the name of fidelity to divine revelation)[88] a truth contained either explicitly or implicitly in divine revelation. The pope thus must be acting in his capacity as pastor and teacher of the church.

(2) The pope must employ his supreme apostolic authority. The Pope must invoke the full force of the doctrinal authority of his office for what he says.

(3) Papal infallibility refers to a personal act of one pope. Since "the definitions of the Roman pontiff are irreformable because of their very nature and not because of the consent of the Church" (*ex sese, non autem ex con-*

sensu ecclesiae—DS 3074), there is no external procedure of the church a pope must follow before his utterance can be infallible. His act must be a free act and must flow from his understanding. Due to this, the basic rule for interpreting infallible papal statements is to discover "the mind of the pontiff."

(4) The pope must intend to define for the whole church. An intent to teach the faithful that which is a universal, binding obligation must be present.

(5) The pope's intention to define must be manifest. As the Code of Canon Law puts it: "Nothing is to be considered as dogmatically declared or defined unless that intention is manifest." This has the effect of establishing that the other conditions must be clear to the church if its members are to be bound be pope's infallible definition.[89]

These are conditions implicit in the pope's speaking *ex cathedra* (from the chair of Peter) on matters of faith and morals. Among the further properties of infallible statements are that they agree with Scripture and tradition, with the present faith of the church, with the universal episcopate and that sufficient investigation be made to ascertain that "his definition in fact conforms with the Christian revelation."[90] As *Lumen gentium* of Vatican II stated, the pope "strives painstakingly and by appropriate means to inquire into that revelation and to give apt expression to its contents" (Art. 25).[91]

Only two papal pronouncements have been generally recognized as having been promulgated by papal infallibility. These are the dogma of the Immaculate Conception (1854) and the Assumption of the Blessed Virgin (1950).[92] In recent times, the concept of papal infallibility has been questioned by Catholics such as Hans Küng and led to his debates with other theologians, most notably Karl Rahner.[93]

Scripture and Tradition Today

The teachings of Vatican II specifically tried to avoid the implication that the tradition of the Roman church contained any truth that is not also found revealed in Holy Scripture. The implication of the *Dogmatic Constitution on Divine Revelation* is that Scripture and tradition are a single source for divine doctrine. Article 9 says:

> Sacred Tradition and sacred Scripture, then, are bound closely together, and communicate one with the other. For both of them, flowing out from the same divine well-spring come together in some fashion to form one thing, and move towards the same goal.[94]

Scripture is called "the speech of God" (Art. 9) and the "written Word of God" (Art. 24). Tradition is never called the Word of God, but "transmits in its entirety the Word of God" (Art. 9).

22

This does not mean Scripture is all that is needed and that tradition is superfluous. According to Vatican II, it is tradition that helps assure the correct interpretation of Scripture: "Thus it comes about that the Church does not draw her certainty about all revealed truths from the holy Scriptures alone. Hence, both Scripture and Tradition must be accepted and honored with equal feelings of devotion and reverence" (Art. 9). Specifically, it is by tradition that "the full canon of sacred books is known to the Church" (Art. 8). This recognition of the place of Scripture in the church shows how Scripture and tradition coinhere.[95]

II

PROTESTANTISM
LUTHERAN, REFORMED, AND ANABAPTIST

The Protestant Reformation produced a number of far-reaching religious changes throughout Europe during the sixteenth century. The Protestant movement was anticipated by earlier movements for church reform reaching back to the fourteenth century. The Waldensians and Hussites (followers of John Hus; 1373-1415) in central Europe and the Lollards (followers of John Wycliffe; *ca.* 1329-1384) in England attacked the hierarchical and legal structures of the Roman Catholic church. In particular, the strongest criticism was made against the papacy for what was perceived as its worldliness, corruption, and abuses of the Christian gospel. By the beginning of the sixteenth century, further social, economic, political, and intellectual factors combined with the theological leadership of prominent Reformers to launch a reformation of the church which lasted until the mid-seventeenth century in Europe.[1]

BACKGROUNDS

The Protestant Reformation began in Germany in 1517. Martin Luther (1483-1546), an Augustinian monk who was a professor of Biblical Theology at Wittenburg University, launched an attack against the Roman Catholic practice of selling indulgences. Luther questioned the church's authority to forgive the temporal punishment due to sin when a person bought an indulgence since the guilt of that sin was already forgiven by God. This occasioned an immediate controversy with Johann Tetzel (ca. 1465-1519) who was selling indulgences in a neighboring town for the purpose of raising money to rebuild St. Peter's Cathedral in Rome.

On October 31, 1517 Luther issued Ninety-five Theses for debate among theologians.[2] In them he questioned a number of theological points, particularly that any penance or works prescribed by the church can produce forgiveness. Instead Luther argued that it was through the merits of Jesus Christ alone that divine forgiveness comes and "the true treasure of the church is the most holy Gospel of the glory and grace of God."[3] Luther's study of the works of Augustine had led him to reject the emphases in late medieval theology on the necessity of "good works" for salvation.[4] His study of the biblical texts, the writings of the early church theologians, and other historical studies done by Renaissance humanists such as Lorenzo Valla (c. 1406-1457) led Luther to question the claims of the Roman pope to be the proper supreme authority for the church.[5] Instead, for Luther the supreme authority for the Christian and the church was Jesus Christ as Christ is known through the Holy Scriptures. This led Luther to rediscover what he believed to be the teaching of New Testament Christianity: that salvation comes by the grace of God through faith in Jesus Christ and not by performing works of righteousness. This emphasis was captured by Luther's watchwords for the Protestant Reformation: *sola fide* (faith alone), *sola gratia* (grace alone), and *sola Scriptura* (Scripture alone).[6]

One of the first to be influenced by Luther's teachings was Ulrich Zwingli (1484-1531) of Zurich. Zwingli was ordained a Roman Catholic priest and served two parishes until he was called to be the people's (or preaching) priest at the Zurich Great Church in 1518. Zwingli had been trained as a Christian humanist and as such had turned to the Bible as the foundational document of the Christian faith.[7] In 1516 he had diligently studied the Greek New Testament published by Erasmus (1466?-1536) and caused tremendous excitement in Zurich when early in 1519 he announced his intention to preach continuous exegetical sermons beginning with the gospel of Matthew.[8] Zwingli led the Reformation in Zurich and was actively involved in giving theological leadership through drafting church confessions (e.g., the Ten Theses of Berne, 1528) and conversing with other theologians, especially Luther on the Lord's Supper and with the Anabaptists. He also dealt with various domestic and diplomatic problems as well. Zwingli was killed in the battle of Kappel while serving as a chaplain for the troops of Zurich as they fought with other Swiss cantons.[9]

Zwingli may be said to have begun the "Reformed" as contrasted to the "Lutheran" and "Anabaptist" traditions of the Reformation. But it was from John Calvin (1509-1564) of Geneva that the Reformed tradition took its most definite shape. The theology of Calvin spread from Geneva and became a powerful force in the Protestant Reformation, particularly in Switzerland, western Germany, France, the Netherlands, and Scotland. To a lesser degree Calvinism was prominent as well in England, eastern Germany, Hungary, and Poland.[10]

Like Zwingli, Calvin was trained as a Christian humanist. His earliest published work was a *Commentary on Seneca's 'De Clementia'* (1532) through which he became adept at interpreting an ancient text with the tools of the Renaissance humanists.[11] His major theological work was his *Institutes of the Christian Religion* which expanded from six chapters in the first edition (1536) to eighty chapters in the 1559 edition.[12] Calvin also wrote biblical commentaries on nearly every book of the Bible as well as polemical pieces, theological tracts, and thousands of personal letters and sermons.[13] His legacy, like Luther's in Lutheran churches, continues in Reformed churches throughout the world.

LUTHERAN AND REFORMED CONFESSIONS

Both Lutheran and Reformed churches since the sixteenth century have been *confessional* churches. That is, these churches have looked to various confessions or declarations of faith as their norms or sources for doctrine. The confessions define what the churches believe.

In the Lutheran tradition, the confessions of the churches are found in *The Book of Concord*.[14] This work is sometimes called *The Confessions of the Evangelical Lutheran Church* (German) or *Concordia* (Latin) and contains those documents most generally accepted as "symbols" (from the Greek *sumbolos* and the Latin *symbolus* meaning "sign" or "mark") or confessions of the churches. *The Book of Concord* was published in 1580 and today includes: the three ancient creeds of the Christian church (Apostles', Nicene, and Athanasian); Luther's *Large and Small Catechisms* (1529); the *Augsburg Confession* (1530) written by Philip Melanchthon (1497-1560), Luther's colleague and successor as the leader of the emerging Lutheranism; the Apology of the Augsburg Confession (1531), written by Melanchthon against the Roman Catholics who rejected the *Augsburg Confession;* the *Smalcald Articles* (1537), written by Luther as a summary of Christian doctrine; the *Treatise on the Power and Primacy of the Pope* (1537), written by Melanchthon to supplement the *Smalcald Articles*; and the *Formula of Concord* (1577), written by a number of theologians to settle numerous doctrinal controversies that affected Lutheranism after Luther's death in 1546. The *Formula of Concord* is composed of an Epitome and a Solid Declaration, each containing twelve articles.

Churches in the Reformed tradition, on the other hand, have not consolidated their confessional standards into any one book as the Lutherans have done. Instead, as the Reformation became indigenous throughout Europe, Reformed churches in various nations, cities, and local communities often drafted their own doctrinal statements. Thus among the many confessions of the Reformed tradition there are those named from the areas of their origination: The *Ten Theses of Berne* (1528); the *First Confession of Basel* (1534); the *Geneva Confession* (1536); the *French Confession of Faith* (1559); the *Scots Confession* (1560); and the *Second Helvetic Confession* (1566) among many confessional statements.[15] Of particular significance for American churches in the Presbyterian branch of the Reformed tradition has been the *Westminster Confession of Faith* (1647), written in England by English and Scottish Calvinists during the time of the English Civil War. In the twentieth century, two important Reformed Statements of Faith have been *The Theological Declaration of Barmen* (1934) written by Karl Barth (1886-1968), in which the German Confessing Church confessed its faith in the face of the threats of Nazism and Adolf Hitler. The Confession of 1967 was written was written as part of *The Book of Confessions* of the United Presbyterian Church in the United States of America [now the Presbyterian Church (USA)] and represents a statement of some aspects of the Reformed faith in contemporary times.[16]

Scripture in the Lutheran and Reformed Confessions

The basic beliefs about the Bible of the Lutheran and Reformed traditions can be found through their confessional statements.[17]

Similarities and Differences

Both of these confessional traditions adopt similar stances regarding the Bible. Usually these views are set in contrast to Roman Catholic positions since the Protestant churches emerged out of the conflict with the Roman church. Yet despite their basic similarities, there are three major ways in which the sixteenth- and seventeenth-century Lutheran and Reformed Confessions differ in their approach to Scripture.

Frequently in the Reformed Confessions of this period, a list of canonical books which record the documents of Scripture is found at or near the beginning of the Confession. These books of Scripture are described as "the Word of God," which is given to the church by "the inspiration of the Holy Spirit." Lutheran Confessions, however, give no such listings of the canon.[18]

The second and third differences are that Lutheran Confessions give no doctrine of the inspiration of Scripture nor do they make any mention of a special activity of the Holy Spirit in how the process of the canonization of biblical books took place. It has been suggested that the reason for these omissions from Lutheran documents may be that "the interest of Lutheran theology was not in a book as such but in the redemptive content" of the Bible.[19] The thrust of Lutheran Confessions is toward hearing the gospel of

Jesus Christ. It is the inspiration of the hearer, not primarily of the book (the Bible) that is primary. Since an explicit doctrine of Scripture is not found here, "the implicit doctrine of Scripture must be gleaned from the actual use of Scripture (in confessional documents) and from the expressed attitude to other sources of knowledge that might lay claim to being norms of church doctrine."[20] From the Reformed point of view, such omissions mean that the doctrine of the inspiration of the Bible must be developed from theological sources outside the Confessions. From the Lutheran perspective, however, the omission of explicit statement of the inspiration of Scripture put the focus where it should rightly be: not in the giving of a canon on Scripture but in the giving of saving faith to those who believe the gospel of Jesus Christ.

Both the Lutheran and Reformed Confessions speak of the relation of the Symbols to Scripture. Both traditions agree that the authority of Scripture stands supreme over all human confessions of faith. The Reformed French Confession of 1559 confessed the Apostles', Nicene, and Athanasian Creeds "because they are in accordance with the Word of God."[21] The Scots Confession of 1560 in its Preface urged its Confession to be judged to see "if any man will note in our confession any chapter or sentence contrary to God's Holy Word."[22] On the Lutheran side, the Epitome of the Formula of Concord said: "We believe, teach, and confess that the prophetic and apostolic writings of the Old and new Testaments are the only rule and norm according to which all doctrines and teachers alike must be appraised and judged."[23]

Canon and Authority

On the issue of the canon, the question between the Protestants and Roman Catholics was: Did the church create the canon or did the canon create the church? Roman Catholic theologian John Eck wrote that "Scripture is not authentic without the authority of the church." To this the Protestants compared the church with the Samaritan woman of whom it is said in John 4:39 that "many of that city believed in Christ because of her saying." But then in 4:42 they say to her: "It is no longer because of your words that we believe, for we have heard for ourselves, and we know that this is indeed the Savior of the world." The Protestants claimed that the church bears witness to its Savior and through its witness men and women are introduced to the Christ of Scripture.[24] Similarly, John Calvin argued on the basis of Ephesians 2:20, where Paul wrote that the church is "built upon the foundation of the apostles and prophets, Christ Jesus himself being the cornerstone," that the message of God through the prophets and apostles existed *before* the church itself was called into being. The church is founded on the gospel message.[25]

For both Lutheran and Reformed traditions, the Confessions are clear that the ultimate authority in the church belongs to Jesus Christ. But the church knows Christ through the Scriptures of the Old and New Testaments. Thus the Scriptures are authoritative for the church. In this the Protestants were standing against the Roman Catholic insistence that the tradition of the church should be received on a par with Scripture as a source of authority. For the Protestants, Scripture alone (*sola Scriptura*) is the sole source of authority for the church. As the Geneva Confession of 1536 put it: "We affirm and desire to follow Scripture alone as rule of faith and religion, without mixing with it any other thing which might be devised by the opinion of men apart from the Word of God."[26] The Formula of Concord calls Scripture "the only rule and norm."[27]

LUTHERAN CONFESSIONS

The main emphasis throughout the Lutheran Confessions is on the authority of Scripture. In the Augsburg Confession, Scripture is appealed to but is not made an article of faith in itself. The Preface states the Confession seeks to be

> a confession of our pastors' and preachers' teaching and of our own faith, setting forth how and in what manner, on the basis of the Holy Scriptures, these things are preached, taught, communicated and embraced in our lands, principalities, dominions, cities and territories.[28]

The second part of the Confession deals with "matters in dispute." Here the doctrine is brought forth similarly when the Confession states: "From the above it is manifest that nothing is taught in our churches concerning articles of faith that is contrary to the Holy Scriptures or what is common to the Christian Church."[29] In the conclusion, the Confession again stresses its appeal to Scripture as *the* authority. It reemphasizes that it "introduces nothing, either in doctrine or in ceremonies, that is contrary to Holy Scripture."[30]

Melanchthon's Apology of the Augsburg Confession makes frequent appeals to Scripture throughout its articles. In it Melanchthon claims he will show readers what the opponents have said and how they "have condemned several articles in opposition to the clear Scripture of the Holy Spirit." He is confident he can show his opponents have not "disproved our contentions from the Holy Scriptures."[31]

In the Smalcald Articles, Luther dealt in Part II in a section on the Mass and Purgatory with the Roman Catholic citation of passages from Augustine and the early Church Fathers who are "said to have written about purgatory." Luther questioned this interpretation and then declared:

> It will not do to make articles of faith out of the Holy Fathers' words or works. Otherwise what they ate, how they dressed, and what kind of houses they live in would have to become articles of faith—as has happened in the case of

relics. This means that the Word of God shall establish articles and no one else, not even an angel (Gal. 1:8).[32]

Luther made the same appeal in the "Treatise on the Power and Primacy of the Pope" when he sought to refute the claims of the papacy by referring in the first article to "The Testimony of the Scriptures." Throughout his Catechisms Luther made frequent references to the Word of God, though he did not present a doctrine of Scripture in itself.

The Formula of Concord is the Lutheran document that deals most fully with Scripture. Its Epitome begins with the statement that Scripture is "the only rule and norm according to which all doctrines and teachers alike must be appraised and judged." All "other writings, ancient and modern teachers, whatever their names should not be put on a par with Holy Scripture." These writings are subordinate to Scripture and are valued only insofar as they witness to the doctrine of the prophets and apostles. After listing the documents Lutherans accept as being faithful witnesses and expositions of the Christian faith, the Formula declares Scripture as the "only judge, rule, and norm according to which all doctrines should and must be understood and judged as good and evil, right or wrong."[33] Thus, "the Scriptures contain the *credenda*, the things to be believed; the Symbols the *credita*, the things that are believed."[34] This same principle is affirmed in Part II, "The Solid Declaration" where allegiance is pledged to "the prophetic and apostolic writings of the Old Testament as the pure and clear fountain of Israel, which is the only true norm according to which all teachers and teachings are to be judged and evaluated."[35]

In the Lutheran Confessions, then, strong emphasis is placed on the role of Scripture as the supreme authority from which doctrine is derived and by which all teaching and belief are to be judged and tested.

REFORMED CONFESSIONS

As noted, Reformed Confessions make their understanding of the nature of Scripture more explicit than do Lutheran standards. Among the numerous Reformed documents, the following emphases from certain Confessions stand out.[36]

Zwingli's Sixty-seven Articles (1523) declared that the basis of Zwingli's doctrine was "the Scripture which is called *theopneustos* ("inspired by God"). But though he affirmed Scripture's inspiration, Zwingli did not propound a theory about *how* the Scriptures were inspired. His emphasis throughout was on the message of the Gospel that is transmitted *through* the Scriptures and which calls people to faith in Jesus Christ (Art. XV).[37]

The emphasis on the purpose of Scripture for salvation was also struck by the First Helvetic Confession (1536). Here the purpose or *scopus* of Scripture was related to humans' understanding that "God is kind and gracious" and that God has "publicly demonstrated and exhibited His kindness to the whole human race through Christ His Son" (Art. 5). Knowledge of God comes through "holy, divine Biblical Scripture inspired by the Holy Spirit and delivered to the world by the prophets and apostles" (Art. 1). This Scripture is called "the Word of God."[38]

The French Confession of 1559 spoke of a revelation of God "in his works, in their creation, as well as in their preservation and control." Yet this source of knowledge of God does not stand alone, for the Confession goes on immediately to add that "secondly, and more clearly," God is revealed "in his Word, which was in the beginning revealed through oracles, and which was afterward committed in writing in the books which we call the Holy Scriptures" (Art. II). This Scripture is not validated as canon by church councils but "by the testimony and inward illumination of the Holy Spirit" (Art. IV). The Holy Spirit is active both in guiding the acceptance of biblical books as God's Word (Art. IV) and in enlightening people in faith to believe the Christian gospel (Art. XXI).[39]

In the Scots Confession (1560), the Scriptures are said to be "the written Word of God" (Ch. XVIII) with their "authority to be from God" (Ch. XIX) for the purpose of instructing and perfecting the people of God. It is the Spirit of God who is the proper interpreter of Scripture. In controversial issues, Scripture should be interpreted by other passages of Scripture (Art. XVIII). Biblical interpretation should seek always the "plain text of Scripture" and should be carried out by "the rule of love" (Art. XVIII).[40]

The Second Helvetic Confession (1566) composed by Heinrich Bullinger (1504-1575) dealt substantially with the doctrine of Scripture. No list of canonical Scriptures was provided but the books of "both Testaments" were designated "the true Word of God" and has having "sufficient authority of themselves" (Ch. I). In the Scriptures, the "universal Church of Christ has the most complete expression of all that pertains to a saving faith, and also to the framing of a life acceptable to God." Thus Scripture's purpose is both theological and ethical. It is God through the Holy Spirit who illumines humans to be believers through the ministry of the preached Word. God may use means other than the preaching of the word to produce faith. But this Confession cites Scripture to show that no "inner light" apart from preaching should be sought since Scripture commands the preaching be done. Both the preached Word and the written Word were sufficient for the church and "no other Word of God is to be invented nor is to be expected from heaven" (Ch. I). The Confession strongly asserts that "the preaching of the Word of God *is* the Word of God."[41]

Sixteenth-century Reformed Confessions acknowledged the authority of

Holy Scripture as the written Word of God. They occupied a middle ground between the position of the Roman Catholics who sought a blend of Scripture and tradition and various Anabaptist groups were stressed the illumination of the Spirit as the only source of religious authority. Scripture is said to be inspired but no formal description of how inspiration was accomplished is offered. The Confessions speak of the Scriptures carrying the evidence of their divine origins "in themselves" (Gr. *autopiston*). Scripture is thus self-authenticating as the Word of God. The Holy Spirit serves several functions in relation to the Word of God in Scripture. The Spirit *inspired* the biblical writers. The Spirit *illuminates* those who hear the Word to come to faith in Jesus Christ. The Spirit *interprets* Scripture in the present day in the church. Scripture's purpose in these Confessions is to bring people to faith and to instruct them for living a life acceptable to God. The Confessions see Scripture as "infallible" in achieving its purpose of proclaiming salvation in Christ. Scripture is not cited as a source for authoritative teachings for science or other worldly matters. The written and the preached Word are the means God uses to make the Gospel known to the world.[42]

The foundations of the sixteenth-century Reformed Confessions on Scripture were built upon through the next centuries. The Westminster Confession of Faith (1647) produced in England during the English Civil War devoted its first chapter in ten sections to discussing the authority and interpretation of the Bible.[43] Westminster affirmed, as had its predecessors, that the written Word of God receives its authority from God. How humans accept this authority is indicated when the Confession said that "our full persuasion and assurance of the infallible truth, and divine authority thereof, is from the inward work of the Holy Spirit, bearing witness by and with the Word in our hearts" (Ch. I, sec. 5). According to Westminster, the content of Scripture is "the whole counsel of God concerning all things necessary for His own glory, man's salvation, faith and life" (Ch. I, sec. 6). Scripture was clear about matters of salvation. It was so clear that "not only the learned but the unlearned, in a due use of the ordinary means, may attain unto a sufficient understanding of them" (Ch. I, sec. 7). The Confession acknowledged that "in all controversies of religion the Church is finally to appeal unto them [the Scriptures]" (Ch. I, sec. 8). But it urged the use of scholarship in these matters and the careful study of Scripture in its original languages. Thus in the Westminster Confession, Scripture can be approached on two levels—on the level of scholarship and on the level of spiritual need. In all cases though, Scripture interprets Scripture (Ch. 1, sec. 9) and "the Supreme Judge by whom all controversies of religion are to be determined ...can be no other but the Holy Spirit speaking in the Scripture."[44]

Two other contemporary Reformed Confessions with their emphases may also be cited.

In 1934 against the backdrop of the rise of Adolf Hitler and Nazism in Germany, Reformed Christians (with some Lutherans and members of the United Church) produced "The Theological Declaration of Barmen." Article I of this Declaration states that "Jesus Christ, as it is attested for us in Holy Scripture, is the one Word of God which we have to hear and which we have to trust and obey in life and death."[45] This stand clearly rejected any notions that a person without the revelation of Christ known through Scripture, could perceive the purposes and plans of God in nature or history. In the context of the times, this was a powerful rejection of the propaganda of Hitler and the Nazis.[46]

In 1967 the United Presbyterian Church in the United States of America (now the Presbyterian Church [USA]) adopted "The Confession of 1967."[47] Consistent with sixteenth-century Reformation Confessions, Scriptures are "the word of God written." They are said to be "not a witness among others, but the witness without parallel" to "the one sufficient revelation of God," who is "Jesus Christ, the Word of God incarnate." To Christ "the Holy Spirit bears unique and authoritative witness through the Holy Scriptures." The Confession of 1967 also recognizes that "the Scripture, given under the guidance of the Holy Spirit," are nevertheless human words written by humans who shared the "views of life, history, and the cosmos which were then current." Thus the church, says this Confession, "has an obligation to approach the Scriptures with literary and historical understanding" (see 9.27—9.30). In this way the Confession affirms both the gospel of the Scripture and Scripture's human cultural context.[48]

THE ANABAPTIST MOVEMENT

As the Reformation movement developed, a third stream in addition to the Lutheran and Reformed was formed. This was the so-called "left wing of the Reformation" or "radical Reformation."[49] From the perspective of the sociology of religion, Ernst Troeltsch distinguished between the "churches" and the "sects" of the Reformation era and the "sects" divided between "Anabaptism" and "mysticism."[50] Others have variously pointed to Anabaptists, Spiritualists, and Protestant Rationalists[51] or Anabaptists, Spiritualists, Enthusiasts, and anti-Trinitarians.[52] Other opt for seeing Anabaptism as "one general phenomenon, albeit with a great many different manifestations."[53]

Anabaptists wanted "reformation as re-formation."[54] While Luther's doctrines appealed to people of all classes, "many of these were not content to move slowly as he, and fundamental differences soon appeared. Some sought to substantiate social, political, and economic views by reference to the Scripture."[55] Varieties of biblical interpretation arose. Some such as Thomas Muenster and the "Zwickau prophets" visioned a new society based on beliefs in continuing revelations by the Spirit. They were confident God would intervene in history, destroy evil, and establish the millennium on earth. Others, turning to Scripture, desired a complete separation of church and state with the faithful living in strict obedience to biblical commands. Still others questioned the received doctrines of the churches and called for a religion based on ethics instead of dogmatics.[56]

Backgrounds

The backgrounds of the Anabaptist movement can be traced to the dispute between Zwingli and Conrad Grebel (1498-1526) which resulted from an adult baptism. In January, 1525 Grebel baptized Georg Blaurock (1480?-1529) in the home of Felix Manz (d. 1527) in Zurich. This led to the designation "Anabaptist" derived from the Greek term for "baptizing again."[57]

Grebel, like Zwingli, had been trained in humanism and was a friend of Zwingli's in Zurich. Zwingli had instructed him in the Reformation faith. Initially Grebel and his friends split with Zwingli over the issue of baptism. But the deeper issue was soteriology (salvation). Zwingli recounted that the future Anabaptist leaders came to him wishing to form "a church in which there would be only those who knew themselves without sin,"[58] which meant the nature of Christian commitment was of fundamental concern. For the Anabaptists, "to be a Christian meant a voluntary and deliberate decision, which expressed itself in reception of adult Baptism and separation from the 'ungodly.' "[59]

The baptism administered by Grebel was a violation of the criminal code of Zurich. Those involved, instead of fleeing, decided to defy the authorities. After a religious disputation on January 17, 1525 in which Zwingli and the Zurich city council ruled that Anabaptists must conform or be exiled, the offenders were arrested and those who did not recant were imprisoned and later expelled from the Zurich territory. But they spread their message. Persecutions followed throughout Europe, yet Anabaptism spread into southern Germany, Upper Austria, Moravia, Hungary, the Low Countries, and elsewhere. Among the major leaders of the movement were Jacob Hutler, Balthasar Hubmaier (1485-1528), Hans Denck (d. 1527), David Joris (1501-1556), Menno Simons (1496-1561), Pilgrim Marpeck (d. 1556), Melchior Hoffman (d. 1543), and the mystically inclined Sebastian Franck (1499-1543).[60]

The first major attempt to bring all Anabaptists together came in a gathering at Schleitheim. The *Brüderliche Vereinigung* or Schleitheim Confession of Faith was the result. The seven articles of this Confession "more succinctly than any other document sum up the distinctive convictions of

Evangelical Anabaptism."[61] The Confession dealt with baptism, excommunication, communion, separation, the ministry, the sword and the oath.[62] It presented alternatives to the positions of the Lutherans and Reformed on major issues. In particular it designated infant baptism as "the highest and chief abomination of the pope" as well as of the Protestant churches."[63] For Anabaptists, "inward baptism" by the Holy Spirit had to precede "outward baptism" with water.

H. Bender has argued for three main views as the bases of Anabaptist views. These were "first, a new understanding of the nature of Christianity as discipleship; secondly, a new conception of the church as the brotherhood of believers; and thirdly, a new ethics of love and defencelessness."[64] Some analysts have stressed the central concept of the church for the Anabaptist movement. They have identified this as a concern for "primitivism," that is, the view that an ideal state existed in the early church which can be established again in the present.[65] Others present the concept of "discipleship" as the key idea. They cite the "motto" of Hans Denck: "No one can truly know [Christ] unless he follows [nachvolge] Him in his life."[66] While Anabaptists were not "perfectionists," they did expect their followers "to obey the commands of God and lead lives of holiness."[67]

Scripture in the Anabaptist Tradition

It is sometimes said the Anabaptists devalued Scripture and put in its place a sole reliance on the Holy Spirit. While it is true that the Anabaptists emphasized the work of the Holy Spirit, they did at the same time rigorously uphold their view of the Bible. For Anabaptists this meant that Scripture was supremely authoritative. It was this concern for the authority of Scripture, as interpreted by the Swiss Brethren, that led them to separate from Zwingli and flee Zurich. In their concern to be biblical Christians the Anabaptists were concerned to "carry through consistently the demands of the New Testament, and especially of the Sermon on the Mount, as they understood them."[68] This is seen too in their responses to the charges made against them by appealing to biblical texts. Yet as Reventlow has noted:

> the reference to Scripture was made in direct association with reference to the Spirit. Among the authentic Anabaptist the two cannot be separated (and in this respect the old identification with Spiritualists has proved inaccurate), but in such a way that the 'inner word' provides the legitimation for reference to the outward word.[69]

It is here the relation of Scripture and the Spirit is found. For the Anabaptists, "God's Spirit, which the Anabaptists believed themselves to possess, is the ultimate authority which first gives authority to the written word of the Bible."[70] In their stress on the "outer" and "inner" Word, the Anabaptists were saying that "a biblical text without the penetration and testing of personal appropriation is a dead letter."[71] When Hans Denck, perhaps the first Anabaptist to use the "inner"/"outer" word pairs, drew up a list of contradictory Scripture passages, he did so not to show that Scripture should not be authoritative. Rather he wanted to point out that "in order to reconcile seemingly contradictory understandings, there must be a deeper personal penetration of what the texts are all about."[72]

In many respects, the Anabaptists shared large areas of agreement with Lutheran and Reformed Christians, not only on doctrines—such as the message of salvation by grace and the exalting of the authority of God—but also with regard to their understanding of the Bible. Among points of agreement between the Anabaptists and other Protestants were:

(1) The Bible holds a place of authority in the church.

(2) The Bible is meant to be understood. Scripture is understandable.

(3) The Bible has some parts that are difficult to understand.

(4) Special techniques for understanding are necessary to interpret these parts.

(5) Scripture interpretation should be undertaken in freedom from the structure of church authorities who restrict interpretations.

(6) The Bible should be obeyed.[73]

If these areas of broad, general agreement about Scripture had been the only perspectives of the Anabaptists, they could have perhaps worked well with the other Reformation Protestants. But disagreements were to be found too. Among these may be listed:[74]

(1) The extent to which the Bible's authority was applicable, particularly to public life. This surfaced in the theological disagreements over church and state, the use of oaths, etc.

(2) The sharp distinction between the Old and New Testaments. For Anabaptists, the Old Testament was "promise"; Jesus was "fulfillment." The Old Testament was "shadow"; the New was "reality." This was a basic principle of interpretation for the Anabaptists. To a large part this was behind, for example, Calvin's rejection of the theology of the Schleitheim Confession. With each article, "the critical issue is the hermeneutical one."[75]

(3) The pre-understanding of the Anabaptists that Jesus must be followed was a crucial condition placed upon the understanding of Scripture. As has been said for Menno Simons,

> the prerequisites of understanding are seen to lie in the attitude of the one who comes to the Scriptures. Very briefly this attitude must be marked by obedience..., a willingness to be instructed both by the Spirit and by the brethren and a personal application in seeing the truths as they apply to everyday life. ...Wrongdoing...blinds people so that they do not understand.[76]

(4)That anyone who has made the commitment to obedience and has the Spirit of God can read Scripture with understanding. This belief led to a basic mistrust of the tools of biblical scholarship to come to ultimate meanings. Instead, Anabaptists often looked to the community of faith as the locus for biblical interpretation. For "the text can be properly understood only when disciples are gathered together to discover what the Word has to say to their needs and concerns."[77] From the Anabaptist perspective, "this process is designed to save Christians from the tyranny of the specialized knowledge and equipment of the scholar, as well as from the tyranny of individualist interpretation and of the visionary."[78]

For many Anabaptists, "the Word of God was broader than the Bible, although the Bible is always viewed as the chief medium for the sharing of God's Word" with humanity.[79] The Word of God can also come directly to the heart through no intermediary. This direct act of God can be the source of one's "blessedness" or "salvation." As Hans Denck wrote in 1528:

> I hold Holy Scripture above all human treasures, but not so high as the Word of God, which is living, powerful and eternal...for it is as God himself is, Spirit and not letter...Therefore salvation, too, is not tied to scripture, however useful and good Scripture may be to that end. The reason is that it is not possible for Scripture to make an evil heart better, though it may become better informed. But a pious heart, that is, a heart with a true ray of divine zeal, is improved by all things...Thus a man chosen by God may find salvation through preaching and Scripture.[80]

The predominant emphasis in Anabaptist writers is that the Bible is written by people of faith with the purpose of inspiring faith in others. This led them to a "hermeneutics of obedience" or "hermeneutics of discipleship" which was based on certain theological assumptions.[81] In most instances they looked directly to the literal interpretation of a biblical text. But they also recognized that Scripture functioned on another level, on the level of the Spirit. It was only as the Spirit was operative, particularly in the gathered Christian community (church) that the true meaning of the Scripture could be found. In their desire for biblical fidelity, they sought not complicated theories of interpretation but an emphasis on Scripture's basic authority for all life. As Melchior Hofmann put it: "Therefore I warn all lovers of truth they do not give themselves over to lofty arguments which are too hard for them, but that they hold themselves solely to the straightforward words of God in all simplicity."[82]

III

LIBERAL THEOLOGY
SCRIPTURE AS EXPERIENCE

On the day after the death of Friedrich Daniel Ernst Schleiermacher (1768-1834), his colleague in the theological faculty of the University of Berlin told his students of Schleiermacher: "From him a new period in the history of the Church will one day take its origin."[1] In retrospect, one hundred years later Karl Barth applied to Schleiermacher what Schleiermacher said of Frederick the Great: "He did not found a school but an era."[2] Schleiermacher is often called "the father of Protestant Liberalism."[3] But his influence extended beyond the liberal movement even to those who reacted against liberalism itself.[4]

Protestant liberalism became the dominant theology in Europe during the nineteenth century and maintained this position until challenged by the emerging neo-orthodoxy of Barth and Brunner in the 1930s.[5] In America, while it continues in modified forms as a theological force today, "it was during the first thirty-five years of this century that liberalism achieved its most pervasive influence among the leading thinkers of the day."[6]

During the last quarter of the nineteenth century, liberalism gained a foothold in America as it challenged the dominant Protestant orthodoxy. It gradually replaced the modified Calvinism of Jonathan Edwards, Samuel Hopkins, Nathaniel Emmons, Timothy Dwight, Nathaniel W. Taylor, and Edward A. Parker under the name "the new theology."[7] Through this rubric its adherents saw themselves as seeking a reconstruction of orthodox Christianity in a way that was congruent with the advances of the sciences, especially the natural sciences.[8] In America, the "Fundamentalist-Modernist" controversy highlighted the tensions on the American theological scene and dramatized the differences between those holding to orthodox doctrine and those seeking to "modernize" Christian theology. The liberal argument was that "the world...has changed radically since the early creeds of Christendom were formulated; this makes the creeds sound archaic and unreal to the modern man. We have to rethink Christianity in thought forms which the modern world can comprehend."[9]

BACKGROUNDS

European Development

The theological impetus for the emergence of liberal theology came with Schleiermacher's reorientation of Christian theology.[10] Schleiermacher was one of the first theologians to respond to the critical philosophy of Immanuel Kant.[11] For Schleiermacher, religion is not a matter of belief or of practical action. As he said, "Piety cannot be an instinct craving for a mess of metaphysical and ethical crumbs."[12] Instead, true religion is a feeling or intuition. It is an affection. To find one's true religion one's own consciousness must be examined."[13] Religion is a "sense and taste for the Infinite, and of all temporal things in and through the Eternal."[15] One's religion is thus based on one's experience, on a "feeling of utter dependence" on the ground of nature—God.[16] This sense of the immediate certainty of God thus replaces the traditional arguments for God's existence. Theology's task, according to Schleiermacher, is to explicate the specific content of this divine consciousness.[17]

Schleiermacher's reorientation of Christian theology provided a way to establish religion's independence from philosophy and science. Since it was based on one's own experience, it carried its own proof and was not dependent on the arguments of philosophers nor the findings of science. By shifting the focus of religious authority away from the traditional source, the Bible, to an individual's religious experience, one is not held hostage to the findings of "the scientific study of the Bible" or biblical criticism. Critical biblical studies for Schleiermacher could be a positive help since they aided in understanding the Bible more fully.[18]

A second significant figure in the emergence of theological liberalism was Albrecht Ritschl (1822-89).[19] Ritschl elevated ethics to a place equal in importance with religion. For Ritschl, the Christian faith is an ellipse with two foci. One is the redemption accomplished by Jesus Christ. The second is the kingdom of God. The kingdom is defined as "the moral organization of humanity through love-prompted action."[20] Christ and the kingdom are inseparable. Redemption in Christ (justification) takes shape historically and communally. Thus the church as the community of believers is crucial for Christian existence. Religion for Ritschl was based on value judgments and was sharply distinct from science that is based on facts.[21] There was no need for conflict between Christian faith and science as long as each kept to its own realm. Biblical criticism was a welcomed tool in order to establish the facts on which the Christian religion is based. But biblical criticism cannot go on to make the value judgments on which Christian faith ultimately rests.

The major popularizer of Ritschl's views was Adolf von Harnack (1851-1930).[22] Harnack was an historian of Christian dogma whose lectures, published as *What is Christianity?* (1901), did much to publicize and popularize the emerging liberal theology. Harnack used historical and critical tools in his quest to isolate "the real religion of Jesus." He wished to focus particularly on "the essence of Christianity," which he defined as meaning "one thing and one thing only: Eternal life in the midst of time, by the strength and under the eyes of God."[23] Harnack's simplified view of Christianity reduced it to three essentials:

> If...we take a general view of Jesus' teaching, we shall see that it may be grouped under three heads. They are each of such a nature as to contain the whole, and hence it can be exhibited in its entirety under any one of them.
> *Firstly, the kingdom of God and its coming.*
> *Secondly, God the Father and the infinite value of the human soul.*
> *Thirdly, the higher righteousness and the commandment of love.*[24]

To Harnack, the story of the development of Christian doctrines in the early centuries was the story of the "acute Hellenization" of Christianity—a Hellenization that was detrimental in that it obscured the simple teachings of Jesus himself.

American Backgrounds

At the beginning of the twentieth century theologians in the tradition of Schleiermacher, Ritschl, and Harnack believed that orthodox theology needed reconstruction in light of the modern world. In the midst of new intellectual, social, moral, scientific, philosophical, and religious climates liberal theology arose as an attempt to give a new mode of expression to the Christian faith.

One historian of this period has analyzed three types of influences that were significant in the development of liberal Protestant thought.[25] These factors centered on that which led to an emphasis on continuity rather than discontinuity in the world; those which focused on the autonomy of human reason and experience instead of on an authoritative divine revelation; and those forces that stressed on dynamic rather than the static nature of the world and human life.[26]

In brief, these influences can be summarized as follows.

(1) *Continuity.* Whereas the older orthodoxy had stressed the many sharp

contrasts in reality, particularly between the natural and supernatural, new forces turned the emphases toward the continuities of life and thought. One such force was science. Mechanical causation was seen as the law of the universe and "miracles" in the traditional sense were severely questioned. The theory of evolution and other developmental theories emphasized the unitary process of which nature and human existence emerged and continued to exist. Positively, this prepared a way for an emphasis on the immanence of God.

In a similar way, the philosophies of the Enlightment served to reject traditional sharp distinctions between reason and revelation. They also emphasized the inherent goodness of humanity and the possibility of its perfectability. Philosophical trends, such as pantheism, the absolute idealism associated with Hegel who taught that reality consisted of the divine Spirit unfolding itself in history through a dialectical process, and Romanticism, which stressed the presence of God in nature and in human beings, also contributed to the motif of "continuity."

The rise of the study of comparative religious fanned the hopes of discovering a universal religion that would unite all people. Movements stressing God's immediate presence in religious experience such as pietism in Germany, the Wesleyan movement in England, and American revivalism were also prominent in this period. Against the emphasis of seventeenth-century scholastic orthodoxy and eighteenth-century rationalism on the remoteness of God, these experiential movements stressed God's presence in the inner life.

The results of this emphasis on continuity were widespread. For this theme

> reduces the distinction between animals and men, men and God, nature and God, Christianity and other religious, nature and grace, the saved and the lost, justification and sanctification, Christianity and culture, the church and the world, the sacred and secular, the individual and society, life here and hereafter, heaven and hell, the natural and supernatural, the human and divine natures of Christ, etc.[27]

As a leading liberal theologian put it, continuity was "the major positive principle of the liberal mind."[28]

(2) *Autonomy*. In distinction from orthodoxy, with its stress on religious knowledge that comes through divine revelation given by God and stands above the reason and experience of humans, liberalism emphasized religious knowledge based on reason and experience. The emphasis in liberal thought was on the autonomy of human reason. In this sense

the principle of autonomy means that liberal theologians rejected any arbitrary appeal to external authority and insisted that all religious affirmations must be grounded in, or at least subject to confirmation by, the data of religious experience or the conclusions of reason.[29]

In science, discoveries increasingly contradicted biblical statements about history and "scientific" matters. The empirical method, which stressed the place of observation and experimentation, lessened the emphasis on authority and also led theologians to try to interpret experience objectively. Theology itself became an empirical science. A scientific world view which stressed the mechanistic nature of the universe—that it operated as Newton said through fixed, inexorable laws—made this world seem to be a machine with no human or God-given values built into it. Reactions against mechanism surfaced in various philosophies in which attempts were made to distinguish the external, law-bound world from the internal, spiritual world of faith.[30]

A related influence in the stress on human autonomy was the rise of the historical-critical method in biblical studies. Literary and historical research opened new avenues for biblical interpretation and the understanding of how the Scriptures were formed. For many this development necessitated an alternative view of the authority and relevance of the Bible from the inherited traditions of orthodoxy. The shift for the locus of authority from the "external" Scriptures to the "internal" religious experience represents a reaction to the way in which the Scriptures were understood in light of the modern biblical research of the period.[31]

(3) *Dynamism*. In traditional orthodoxy, religious truth consisted of a variety of propositions or doctrines that were to be believed. The world was believed to have been created at a definite time and humans created originally in the form in which they exist at the present time. The categories were static in nature. In the nineteenth century, an alternative view arose. Reality was perceived as developmental or evolutional. As one writer put it, since the eighteenth century, the "one conception that all sorts and conditions of thinkers have accepted is that, whatever else the world may be, it is not a static and finished thing, but is itself, as a whole and in each of its parts, in a process of change and growth."[32]

The philosophies of the Enlightenment era fostered views of social progress as guided by the use of reason and the spread of science. Individuals and societies were seen as able to ascend to perfection. This evolutionary view produced a climate of optimism. This "combination of evolution and immanence goes a long way toward providing the basic context out of which liberalism came and in which it grew."[33]

Literary developments in the Romantic movement stressed the view that the world is vital and growing. History, according to philosophers such as Hegel, is the arena in which human thought, social institutions, and the world itself are in a process of "becoming." In biblical studies, the religious ideas of the Hebrews were seen as having developed over a long period of time. The Bible itself was viewed as containing a religion that was marked by many stages, theologies, and even ethical stances so that the Scriptures were perceived as "a record of the progressive discovery of God in human experience, not as a static body of theological dogmas all equally inspired and all of equal religious value."[34] In light of this growing perception of dynamism as the basic category or reality, traditional views and orthodoxies were challenged and reconstructed. In this context, Protestant liberal theology emerged.

Leading Figures

In an attempt to formulate Christian theology and to bridge the gap between ancient doctrines and contemporary cultures, the central task of liberal theologians was to make it possible for a person "to be both an intelligent modern and a serious Christian."[35] Thus, liberalism "can best be understood in terms of its effort to harmonize Christ and culture under the conditions set by the late nineteenth and early twentieth centuries."[36] Yet the varieties of approach among liberals differed.

Henry P. Van Dusen has pointed to two basic types of liberalism. One is *evangelical liberalism*, comprised of people standing within the Christian tradition who accepted the tradition as the way by which Christianity is best understood. Their intentions were to reconstruct the Christian faith in continuity with Christian orthodoxy in a way that was appropriate to the modern world. The norm of religious truth for these liberal theologians was Jesus Christ. The need was to reinterpret traditional doctrines while maintaining the meaning of the religious experiences to which these doctrines originally witnessed. In Fosdick's words, there are "abiding experiences and changing categories."[37] Among the theologians who fit this pattern were William Adams Brown (1865-1943), Harry Emerson Fosdick (1878-1969), Walter Rauschenbusch (1861-1918), A. C. Knudson (1873-1953), and Eugene W. Lyman (1872-1948).

A second type of liberal theology may be called *modernistic liberalism*. The term "modernistic" here refers to a determination to be oriented in outlook by twentieth-century thought. The empirical sciences often provided these theologians with their most promising source for a method that could establish theology in a place of respectibility in the modern world. Since "modernists" had abandoned traditional beliefs in God's revelation in Scripture, the Bible itself did not function as their norm nor did Christ or the Christian tradition. Their aim was "to discover a source and standard of religious truth independent of the historic faith. Hence, the search for a new methodology became a prime consideration and often overshadowed the efforts to define the content of religious truth."[38] This modernist trend developed after liberal theology had begun and is represented by people such as Shailer Matthews (1863-1941), Douglas Clyde Macintosh (1877-1948), Henry Nelson Wieman (1884-1975), and G. A. Coe (1863-1951).

SCRIPTURE IN LIBERAL THEOLOGY

Revelation

Liberal theology reacted sharply against the traditional orthodox view of the revelation and authority of the Bible. In orthodoxy, propositions or doctrines were seen as the content of God's revelation. Liberal theology tended to focus on revelation as Jesus Christ and "in a wider sense revelation includes the preparation for the revelation in Christ and the results of his influence in the lives of individuals and in the church since the time of Christ."[39] By conceiving revelation in this way, liberal theologians were able to speak about God's disclosure in history and also to use the tools of biblical scholarship and science to help in reconstructing theology.[40]

For liberal theology, God's revelation is the event in which God speaks God's word. This revelation took place supremely in Jesus Christ and, more widely in these "great, cumulative series of divine acts to which witness is borne in the Bible."[41] But since every communication must have both one who speaks and one who hears, or one who writes and one who speaks and one who hears, or one who writes and one who reads, "the effectiveness of communication generally depends clearly on both the one who makes known and the one to whom something is made known."[42] In God's revelation, humans who receive the communication of God have the freedom to be either open or closed to God's revelation. So in the present day, "at every moment, our own decision affects the actual success or failure of the divine-human communication."[43]

This leads to the emphasis in liberal thought that the Bible as a revelation of God was written by human authors. The mystery of revelation, declared C. H. Dodd who represents this view, is "the mystery of the way in which God uses the imperfect thoughts and feelings, words and deeds, of fallible men, to convey eternal truth, both to the men themselves and through them to others."[44]

The Nature of Scripture

Since the Bible was penned by human authors, liberals argued that "strictly speaking, the Bible itself is not the pure Word of God."[45] Similarly,

God's word spoken to us through the Bible depends for the clarity and purity of its reception both upon our own open and understanding minds and also upon the reception and expression given his word by the ancient men who wrote the words of the Bible and, in some instances, others who related orally the messages later written down in the Scriptures.[46]

Thus, "the Bible shows clearly the fallible men have written, edited, copied, and translated it."[47]

When liberal theologians approached Scripture, they pointed out various phenomena that showed how Scripture was conditioned by the culture in which it was written. This included what was considered contradictions or mistakes in Scripture, both of historical and religious natures.[48]

Thus in Scripture, "the level of truth varies greatly in different parts of the Bible."[49] It is sometimes the case, in this view, that people of later times will be prepared to receive new and higher revelations on the basis of earlier writings.

Inspiration

One is led to conclude that there are varying degrees of "inspiration" in the Scriptures. Some writings may indicate a maximized "divine element" while others display a minimal divine element.[50] As humans were "prepared through progressive stages of understanding, obedience and humble spiritual sensitiveness," God was able to show "increasing measures of His truth to humanity."[51] The writings of Scripture are by humans

conditioned and limited by their times and their individual peculiarities, though also rising frequently to great heights of expression under the illumination of God's self-disclosing presence. The reader who would hear the true word of God in the reading of the Bible must be prepared to discriminate between the word of God and the words of men.[52]

This sharp distinction between the word of God and human words leads to a definition of "inspiration." As Harold DeWolf defines it:

The Bible as a whole was accomplished by an extraordinary stimulation and elevation of the powers of men who devoutly yielded themselves to God's will, and sought, often with success unparalleled elsewhere, to convey truth useful to the salvation of men and of nations.[53]

The biblical writers were often described as "religious geniuses" on the basis of their inspiration. The writers recorded their understanding of the ways of God with humanity on the basis of their special religious experience.[54] Yet since even their record or witness displays the marks of their own cultural conditioning, some have seen the Bible as nothing more than the ancient religious writings of an ancient people not varying significantly from other such ancient writings. Scripture had thus only a human origin.[55] But insofar as the biblical writers were "inspired" and their natural powers were stimulated and evaluated to an extraordinary degree so that the Bible is a book of exquisite spiritual beauty, power, and dignity, Scripture possesses its own uniqueness as a witness to God's revelation.

Biblical Authority

As one proponent of liberal theology has written:

> When the Scriptures are understood as human documents, they then are susceptible to all the canons of modern historical and literary analysis. To the liberal theologian, there is a considerable difference between viewing the Bible primarily through the eyes of faith and being equally open to a cultural and historical perspective. Historically, the resurrection of Jesus and the virgin birth are at best ambiguous as concrete of occurrences. From the perspective faith, however, they may have quite a different significance. But one should never conclude that the Scriptures are unimportant for the liberal Christian. Quite the contrary, they are central to the Christian faith. The fact that more attention is given to them as symbolic documents than as historical documents does not distort their importance.[56]

For liberal theologians, "at least one basepoint for all reflection and meditation is the symbolic forms present in Scripture and the traditions of the church."[57] Scripture functions as an "authority" insofar as "in the study of Scripture one learns, or refreshes one's acquaintance with, those stories which make reference directly or indirectly to all the grand questions surrounding human existence."[58] The value of Scripture as a "religious" book is separate from the questions of biblical scholarship in which the Scriptures are sent to be conditioned by historic time and culture. As Bishop James A. Pike noted:

> Therefore, in the Scriptures we have quite a mixed bag of truth, of error, of sound ethics, unsound ethics, of myth in the best sense of the word, and legends—some useful, some apparently not so useful. The worldview of the time of writing and the public of the particular writer very much influenced what was said.[59]

But "what makes the Bible important is neither literalness nor historicity, but rather the images, as represented in story and parable and example, that challenge the moral imagination."[60] For

> the authority of the word of God resides precisely in those teachings through which God speaks now to the living faith of the reader.... The reading of its [the

Bible's] pages renews our understanding of the faith by which we live as Christians. The teachings of the Bible, as tested in the life of the church, and in the open, critical thinking of innumerable devout scholars, call us back to the events through which the power of God came uniquely into human history for our salvation. By present study of the Scripture we correct our understanding of our faith and we renew our faith itself.[61]

SCRIPTURE AS EXPERIENCE

Liberal theology attempted to reformulate traditional orthodoxy in a way that would be acceptable to modern thought and persons. It did so by following the lead of Schleiermacher and focusing the locus of religious authority on religious experience. This experience was centered on one's appropriation of the teachings of Jesus which Harnack summarized very succinctly.

In liberal thought, "experience" became a controlling feature. It was through the Bible that one's religious experience could come. The Scriptures themselves were the religious experiences of those who witnessed to their encounter with God. The Bible was a very "human" book and was not seen as "perfect" in matters of truth. The tools of biblical criticism could help establish fuller understandings of Scripture.

With the recognition of the humanness and culturally conditioned nature of the Bible came the question of how the thought forms and categories of the ancient writings could be meaningful to contemporary people in a modern and scientific world.

One liberal response to this was suggested by Fosdick who spoke of "abiding experiences and changing categories."[61] Fosdick suggested that some basic human experiences always remain the same. But these are expressed in a variety of concepts and frameworks that change from time to time and place to place. The theologian, according to Fosdick, must search out these "abiding experiences" which stand underneath the categories of the Bible and then reinterpret and reformulate the meaning of these experiences in forms that are intelligible and meaningful to contemporary persons. The nature of these "abiding experiences" was defined by Pike who wrote: "What is true in the Scriptures, or what seems to ring true, whether a matter of fact or principle or ethic or inspiration or insight, is made true by its correspondence to what would seem to be plausible inferences from experienced reality."[63]

For liberal theology, the principle of autonomy is seen in this view because Christianity continues in the world not through a body of objective propositions or even in an institution but in the "abiding experiences" which are repeatable for each new generation. These experiences exist independent of any received authorities such as church or Scripture.

The principle of dynamism is also seen in this view of Scripture as experience. The religious truth to which abiding experiences point will always be developing. These experiences will constantly need to be placed in "changing categories" thus being interpreted and reinterpreted again and again.[64]

With this shift to the category of "experience," liberal theology in the tradition of Schleiermacher opened a new way of perceiving the Bible and thus began a new era.

IV

FUNDAMENTALIST THEOLOGY
SCRIPTURE AS PROPOSITION

Two of its leading adherents have recently said that "Fundamentalism is the religious phenomenon of the twentieth century."[1] This American religious movement, which has at times identified itself with the "establishment" and at other times with the "outsiders," is a movement that its supporters say is "here to stay."[2] As the two spokespersons continue to write:

> For years it was ignored, criticized, and relegated to the backwoods of Appalachia. But like a rushing mighty wind, it has moved across the tide of secularism in America and left its sweeping imprint on virtually every level of society. The movement that was once despised and rejected has now resurged as the religious phenomenon of the 1980s.[3]

It is estimated that fundamentalism involves some ten to twenty million Americans.[4] Commenting on the use of current technology, one historian has noted that

> militant fundamentalists control a large percentage of the 1,400 radio and 35 television stations that make up the Protestant media network....Moreover, fundamentalist leaders like Jerry Falwell and Pat Robertson—who take in more money than the Republican and Democratic parties—are mastering the mails.[5]

From its inception, Falwell's publication *Moral Majority Report* had a greater circulation than any of the traditional "old-line" denominational magazines.[6]

The "identity" of fundamentalists has been variously described. But at its base, they see themselves as

> the legitimate heirs of historical New Testament Christianity. They see themselves as the militant and faithful defenders of biblical orthodoxy. They oppose

Liberalism, communism, and left-wing Evangelicalism. True Fundamentalists hold strongly to the same basic tenets that they were debating seventy-five years ago. These defenders of the faith range from well-educated professors to back-woods preachers.[7]

BACKGROUNDS

Historical Interpretations

Historians of the movement known as fundamentalism have painted varying pictures of the movement at different times. In 1931 the early historian of the movement Stewart Cole interpreted fundamentalism as a form of social maladjustment. He wrote: "For a half century the church has suffered a conflict of social forces about and within it that accounts for the present babel of witnesses to Christian truth and purpose."[8] H. Richard Niebuhr writing in the mid-1930s set the "social sources" of fundamentalism in relation to "the conflict between rural and urban cultures in America."[9]

In the 1950s the "anti-intellectual" nature against evolution and other modern thought was emphasized.[10] Richard Hofstadter claimed that fundamentalist anti-intellectualism and paranoid style were "shaped by a desire to strike back at everything modern—the higher criticism, evolutionism, the social gospel, rational criticism of any kind."[11]

In the late 1960s revisions of these portraits began to be made. Paul Carter argued that fundamentalists were not anti-intellectual, just intellectual in a different way from their opponents.[12] Ernest Sandeen saw the roots of the fundamentalism of the twentieth century as reaching back to the alliance in the nineteenth century between the Old Princeton theology of Princeton Seminary Calvinists and advocates of millenarianism.[13]

The most detailed and persuasive vision of the nature of fundamentalism has been offered by George M. Marsden. His capsulized definition of fundamentalism is worth citing in full.

> Fundamentalists were evangelical Christians, close to the traditions of the dominant American revivalist establishment of the nineteenth century, who in the twentieth century militantly opposed both modernism in theology and the cultural changes that modernism endorsed. Militant opposition to modernism was what most clearly set off fundamentalism from a number of closely related traditions, such as evangelicalism, revivalism, pietism, the holiness movements, millenarianism, Reformed confessionalism, Baptist traditionalism, and other denominational orthodoxies. Fundamentalism was a 'movement' in the sense of a tendency or development in Christian thought that gradually took on its own identity as a patchwork coalition of representatives of other movements. Al-

though it developed a distinct life, identity, and eventually a subculture of its own, it never existed wholly independently of the older movements from which it grew.[14]

These varying historical interpretations of the fundamentalist movement showed

> a much more complex phenomenon than previously imagined. It is urban and rural, sophisticated and simplistic, intellectual and anti-intellectual, moderate and militant. In short, fundamentalism is much more diverse—geographically, socially, politically, educationally, and theologically—than its negative public image portends.[15]

Historical Developments

The immediate context out of which the fundamentalist movement arose was the American scene from the 1870s to the 1930s. These decades were marked by rapid change and the rise of various new "philosophies of life" (such as "pragmatism"). More Americans were attending college and strides in science were substantial.

At the beginning of this period evangelical Protestantism was "the dominant religious force in American life."[16] But the changing social and intellectual scene presented new theological problems.

One such challenge was that of evolution. In 1859 Charles Darwin had published his *The Origin of Species*. This work presented the theory of the process of "natural selection" which came to be described as the "survival of the fittest." In its theoretical form this theory of "evolution" suggested that only natural forces are involved in determining which species will be able to adapt to world conditions and thus perpetuate themselves as a species. In 1871 with Darwin's *The Descent of Man*, the developmental hypothesis was extended to include humans. All of these ideas were unsettling and troublesome to those who understood the Bible to teach (as in Gen. 1:25) that God had made "the beast of the earth after his kind." The "argument from design" which had been a traditional proof for God's existence was thus called into question since the new theory seemed to rule out the need for a God through whose design the whole world itself was created and sustained.[17]

Another major challenge to traditional Protestantism was the rise of biblical criticism and the "scientific study" of religion. As the views of European "biblical critics" (most often Germans) began to spread in America, increasing controversies in seminaries and denominations developed.[18] Under attack by the "Higher Critics" and historians of religion were the views of Christianity as a unique religion founded on supernatural revelation; the miracles as recorded in the Bible; the historicity of various biblical characters such as Abraham or Moses; and the historical accuracy of biblical accounts since they were written from the perspectives of believers in Jesus. With the spread of these kinds of questions in America, traditional Protestantism faced another major challenge.[19]

A third major difficulty for American Protestantism from 1870-1930 was the rapid social change in America itself. During this period

> America was changing rapidly from a culture dominated by small towns and the countryside to one shaped by cities and suburbs. Waves of 'uprooted' immigrants, together with rapid industrialization, created virtually insurmountable urban problems. Industrialization, with the drive for efficiency, usually overcoming traditional moral restraints, created ethical, social, labor, and political problems beyond the capacities of traditional solutions.[20]

With these challenges in front of them, American Protestants had much to be concerned with and much to ponder.

Theologically, another force was making itself felt at this period. With the spread of biblical criticism and the "scientific" study of religion in America, an alternative theological force to the dominant American evangelicalism came to the fore. This was liberal theology, later called "Modernism."[21] Liberalism sought to integrate the findings of science, biblical criticism, and historical studies within its structure and refashion Christian doctrine accordingly. But did scientific discoveries and "the assured results of higher criticism" offer a truth more secure than that of the Bible itself? For liberalism they did. For traditional Protestants they did not. But now, "for the first time in American history a broad and influential theology developed which was not evangelical."[22] To this challenge taking shape in the form of an organized theology, conservative American Protestants felt the need to respond.

RESPONSES

A three-fold task may be seen as the agenda for "evangelical" American Christians at the beginning of the twentieth century:

> (1) to defend the name of Christianity against the Modernists who wanted the sanction of Protestant tradition without the substance of Protestant faith, (2) to maintain the validity and integrity of evangelical theology in the face of the great changes in American life, (3) to make a convincing response to new forms of thought, particularly evolutionary science.[23]

One significant response to liberalism was the publication of twelve paper back books from 1910-15 for a project called *The Fundamentals: A Testimony of the Truth*.[24] These books were financed by Lyman and Milton Stewart who owned the Union Oil Company of Los Angeles. Approximately three million copies were distributed free to Christian leaders throughout the English-speaking world. They sought to defend the basics of traditional Christian faith and in that way to answer the charges of liberalism. While some 200,000 reported letters of support were received, however, only a small number of religious journals reviewed the books or gave them notice.[25]

The writers of these volumes represented a broad coalition of denominational and theological affiliations. Included as authors were Methodists, Baptists, Presbyterians, Episcopalians, and ministers of Independent churches. One-fourth of the authors were British. An indication of the breadth of participation can be seen in that the writers included the staunch Calvinist B. B. Warfield of Princeton Seminary as well as C. I. Schofield, the leading exponent of dispensationalism; a theological position that differed on many crucial points from the reformed orthodoxy of Warfield.[26] The editor of the series was A. C. Dixon, a prominent evangelist and author who was then pastor of the Moody Church in Chicago. He was succeeded by Louis Meyer, a Jewish-Christian evangelist and Reuben Torrey, another well-known evangelistic preacher.

Approximately one-third of the articles concerned Scripture and sought to answer the attacks of the liberal theologians. Another third were devoted to traditional Christian doctrines while the final pieces included polemics against modern "isms" (such as Russellism, Mormomism, Eddyism, and Romanism), personal testimonies, and articles on mission and evangelism. Political causes and issues were avoided. *The Fundamentals* represent a symbolic "starting point" for identifying a "Fundamentalist movement." It represents the movement "at a moderate and transitional stage before it was reshaped and pushed to extremes by the intense heat of controversy."[27]

From 1917-20 many conservative American Protestants found themselves shifting from a moderate to a more militant stance. In that period many were drawn to the desire to save American civilization from the perceived dangers of "evolutionism." With the social experience of World War I, a heightened interest in millenarian thought behind them, and the decline of the German civilization in front of them, many linked attacks on the Bible to the potential total collapse of civilization. Christian concern for the spiritual and moral welfare of the nation merged with the theological concern for the place of the Scriptures as supreme authority to cause many to seek a return to the time when an evangelical theological consensus was the controlling factor in American life.[28]

In 1919 the World Christian's Fundamentals Association met in Philadelphia with 6000 people in attendance. Other similar meetings were held throughout the country. Out of these meetings emerged what later became the "five points of Fundamentalism," which were to serve as an antidote to liberalism. Reflecting the fundamentals of Christian doctrine, they emphasized: (1) the inerrancy of Scripture, (2) the Deity of Christ, (3) the substitutionary atonement of Christ, (4) Christ's bodily resurrection and (5) Christ's literal [premillennial] second advent.[29]

From 1920-25 fundamentalism took shape as a definite movement. Active on two fronts they sought to gain control of the major denominations and to recover these bodies from their driftings towards liberalism. In 1923 J. Gresham Machen of Princeton Seminary wrote a book entitled *Christianity and Liberalism* in which he argued that modern religious liberalism was a separate religion from historic Christianity.[30] During this period, the Presbyterian Church underwent an ecclesiastical struggle over fundamentalism and modernism centered around the sermon preached by the Baptist Harry Emerson Fosdick, who was supply preacher for the First Presbyterian Church in New York City in 1922. His sermon was entitled, "Shall the Fundamentalists Win?" In the Arch Street Presbyterian Church in Philadelphia, Clarence Edward Macartney preached a rejoinder: "Shall Unbelief Win?"[31]

Secondly, fundamentalists sought to influence American culture by stopping the teaching of evolution in the public schools. This effort was dramatized in the famous Scopes trial at Dayton, Tennessee in 1925, which pitted William Jennings Bryan against Clarence Darrow in the courtroom. The case concerned John Scopes, a biology teacher who was charged with violating a Tennessee law against the teaching of Darwinism in any public school. In this arena, the two lawyers represented the two sides of the "Fundamentalist-Modernist controversy."[32]

This "Scopes monkey-trial" was a severe test for the fundamentalist movement. Though Scopes was eventually cleared of the charge, the effect of the trial was to discredit fundamentalism intellectually to many Americans. As Marsden has analyzed it:

> Before 1925 the movement had commanded much respect, though not outstanding support, but after the summer of 1925 the voices of ridicule were raised so loudly that many moderate Protestant conservatives quietly dropped support of the cause rather than be embarrassed by association.[33]

Yet while fundamentalism as a movement receded from the center stage of American cultural life, it took further root through other means. In local congregations, independent agencies, Bible schools, and mission organizations as well as through various media, fundamentalist theology and values continue to thrive.[34] The movement in the last fifty years can be seen as taking form within three major bodies: (1) major denominations such as the Southern Baptist Convention which self-consciously identify themselves with fundamentalism, (2) fundamentalist influence within non-fundamentalist denominations, and (3) separate fundamentalist denominations.[35]

Thus through churches, theological schools, publishing houses, magazines, radio and television media, and vigorous leaders, fundamentalist theology remains an important force in American religious and cultural life.[36]

FUNDAMENTALIST VIEWS OF SCRIPTURE

As fundamentalism developed historically, its views of Scripture owed much to the formulation of the doctrine of Scripture made by the theologians of Princeton Seminary in the nineteenth and early twentieth centuries.[37] In a famous formulation of this view, A. A. Hodge and B. B. Warfield of Princeton presented what they considered to be "the great Catholic doctrine of Biblical Inspiration, *i.e.* that the Scriptures not only contain, but *are the Word of God*, and hence that all their elements and all their affirmations are absolutely errorless, and binding the faith and obedience of men."[38] For them, "every element of Scripture, whether doctrine or history, of which God has guaranteed the infallibility, must be infallible in its verbal expression." Since "infallible thought must be definite thought, and definite thought implies words," one is led to believe in "the truth to fact of every statement in the Scriptures."[39]

This doctrine of Scripture stressed the "inerrancy" of Scripture, which meant that the Bible is completely accurate on all matters of science, history, and geography about which it teaches. Today this doctrine of inerrancy is often said to be the "evangelical badge" by those who identify themselves as "evangelicals" and who stand in the tradition of American fundamentalism.[40]

From the 1940s to the present, American fundamentalism has had two streams. A "new evangelicalism" has emerged which stands in basic continuity with much fundamentalist doctrine but rejects the name "fundamentalist."[41] The second stream is that of those who maintain the name "fundamentalist." This latter group is often marked by a separatist stance towards those who do not agree with their doctrine.[42]

Those who throughout the entire period persisted in calling themselves fundamentalists were marked by continued militant separatism. They were mostly dispensationalists and maintained a steadfast refusal to cooperate with apostates and even sometimes with friends of apostates. Some of their leading evangelists often preached anticommunism and American patriotism...others were more consistently separatist and apolitical.[43]

Thus "fundamentalism" today is a varied grouping and includes different ecclesiastical bodies, differing emphases especially in eschatology, and different theological structures.[44] One strain of fundamentalism is influenced

by evangelical pietism and expresses itself in missionary and Bible confer-
ences.[45] Another strain is more confessional or scholastic in orientation; it is
this group particularly who perpetuates the Old Princeton theological formulation of the doctrine of Scripture.[46] Thus fundamentalism draws together diverse groups, even those with differing fundamental theological
assumptions, such as dispensationalist and covenant theologians.[47]

The Nature of Scripture

As indicated, fundamentalist views of the Bible often stem from the doctrine of Scripture and its nature and authority as formulated by the Old Princeton theology.[48] Part of this view is capsulized in the statement of a
contemporary fundamentalist theologian, Charles C. Ryrie:

> Today, "in order to affirm clearly a belief in the full inspiration of the Scrip-
> ture," it has become necessary to say, "I believe in the verbal, plenary, infallible,
> unlimited inerrancy of the Bible."[49]

To gain a perspective on this fundamentalist view of the nature of Scripture, these terms may be defined.

(1) *Verbal inspiration.* According to Ryrie it used to be enough to say, " 'I
believe in the inspiration of the Bible.' That said it all. Everyone understood
those words to mean that the Bible was from God, completely accurate and
reliable, and therefore authoritative."[50] But now it is important to emphasize
"verbal inspiration" to say that "the very words were inspired, not only the
thoughts....God must have guided the very words used by the writers, or
the Bible is less than inspired."[51] This view is also emphasized in "The Chicago Statement on Biblical Inerrancy" which affirms that "the whole of
Scripture and all its parts, down to the very words of the original, were given
by divine inspiration."[52]

(2) *Plenary inspiration.* Ryrie defines the term "plenary" as meaning "full"
or "complete." This term assures that "no part of the Bible would be omit-
ted" with regard to inspiration[53] and counters a view that "the inspiration of
Scripture can rightly be affirmed of the whole without the parts, or of some
parts but the whole."[54]

(3) *Infallible.* With regard to inspiration, Ryrie writes that the term "infallible" affirms that "the words were exactly the ones God wanted in the text,
and therefore every word was authoritative."[55] In a wider sense, as the "Chicago Statement" says, Scripture is "infallible, so that, far from misleading us,
it is true and reliable in all the matters it addresses."[56] A fuller definition follows: "*infallible* signifies the quality of neither misleading nor being misled
and so safeguards in categorical terms the truth that Holy Scripture is a sure,
safe and reliable rule and guide in all matters."[57]

At this point it may be noted that most fundamentalists reject the charge that their view gives them a "mechanical" or "dictation" mode of inspiration. How did God inspire human authors to record God's Word? The "Chicago Statement" declares that "the origin of Scripture is divine. [But] the mode of divine inspiration remains largely a mystery to us."[58] Yet, a leading fundamentalist preacher and writer John R. Rice appears to argue in favor of the dictation theory when he writes that "God raised up men, prepared the men and prepared their vocabularies, and God dictated the very words which they would put down in the Scriptures."[59] Rice also writes:

"Dictation," says someone, "dishonors the men who wrote the Bible." Shame! Shame! So you want big prophets and a little God, do you? You do not want a man simply hearing what God says and writing it down, do you? Well, then, your attitude is simply the carnal attitude of the unbelieving world that always wants to give man credit instead of God, whether for salvation or inspiration. A secretary is not ashamed to take dictation from man. Why should a prophet be ashamed to take dictation from God?[60]

While owning the term "dictation," Rice says it was not "mechanical dictation": "Face it honestly, if God gave the very words and men wrote them down, that is dictation. It was not *mechanical* dictation."[61]

(4) *Inerrancy and unlimited inspiration.* For Ryrie, "inerrant inspiration" focuses on "the necessary relation between accuracy of the words and authority of the message."[62] Put positively, he says, "the inerrancy of the Bible means simply that the Bible tells the truth."[63] This quality is further defined in the "Chicago Statement" as meaning "the quality of being free from all falsehood or mistake and so safeguards the truth that Holy Scripture is entirely true and trustworthy in all its assertions."[64] Article XII of the "Chicago Statement" states both "positive" and "negative" dimensions to inerrancy:

We affirm that Scripture in its entirety is inerrant, being free from all falsehood, fraud, or deceit.

We deny that Biblical infallibility and inerrancy are limited to spiritual, religious, or redemptive themes, exclusive of assertions in the fields of history and science. We further deny that scientific hypotheses about earth history may properly be used to overturn the teaching of Scripture on creation and the flood.[65]

In this view, the terms "infallible" and "inerrant" may be "distinguished but not separated."[66]

For the fundamentalist a distinction is sometimes made between what the Bible "says" and what it "teaches." When critics of inerrancy look at the book of Job and see the recorded speeches of the "comforters" of Job who espouse a wrong theology and thus conclude that the Bible teaches "error," inerrantists respond. Their argument would be that "these 'errors' are *recited* rather than *asserted*. The literary form permits us to distinguish between the fact that they said this (the *veritas citationis*) and the truth of what they said (the *veritas rei citatae*)."[67] This distinction does not in the minds of fundamentalists diminish the concept of "unlimited inerrancy." For it is "where Scripture explicitly teaches truth about history and nature [that] it is wholly reliable."[68] Or, as Harold Lindsell has described it:

> This Word is free from all error in its original autographs....It is wholly trustworthy in matters of history and doctrine. However limited may have been their knowledge, and however much they may have erred when they were not writing sacred Scripture, the authors of Scripture, under the guidance of the Holy Spirit, were preserved from making factual, historical, scientific, or other errors. The Bible does not purport to be a textbook of history, science, or mathematics; yet when the writers of Scripture spoke of matters embraced in these disciplines, they did not indite error; they wrote what was true.[69]

Where "problem passages" such as apparent discrepancies, conflicting numbers, differences in parallel accounts, or purportedly unscientific statements occur in the Scriptures, inerrantists would respond that these were "due to errors in the transmissions of manuscripts over time, modern misunderstanding of what the texts really mean, or temporary confusion that would clear up with more time and scholarship."[70] Or, as Ryrie put it:

> The inerrantist, on the other hand, has concluded that the Bible contains no errors. Therefore, he exercises no option to conclude that any of those same problems is an example of a genuine error in the Bible. His research may lead him to conclude that some problem is yet unexplainable. Nevertheless, he believes it is not an error and that either further research will demonstrate that or he will understand the solution in heaven.[71]

It is this view of the nature of Scripture that underlies the sole doctrinal basis for the Evangelical Theological Society founded in 1949: "The Bible alone, and the Bible in its entirety, is the Word of God written and is therefore inerrant in the autographs."[72] On this foundation the conclusion is drawn that "because the Bible is God's Word, he originally gave it to us in a form that was without error and that spoke truthfully on whatever subject it treated. God is true, and therefore his Word sets forth the truth without any admixture of falsehood."[73]

SCRIPTURE AS PROPOSITION

Behind the fundamentalist views of infallibility, inerrancy, and authority lies a specific view of the nature of God's revelation in Scripture. For fundamentalists and those in the fundamentalist tradition, Revelation is considered as "a set of propositional statements, each expressing a divine affirmation, valid always and everywhere."[74] Carl Henry urges that God is revealed "in the whole canon of Scripture which objectively communicates in propositional-verbal form the content and meaning of all God's revelation."[75] Further, Henry writes: "God's revelation is rational communication conveyed in intelligible ideas and meaningful words, that is, in conceptual-verbal form."[76]

Since it is believed that "the biblical position is that the mighty acts of God are not revelation to man at all, except in so far as they are accompanied by words to explain them," the words of Scripture are seen as revealed by God and inspired by God."[77] These Scripture propositions themselves reflect the character of God since they are God's Word. Thus, since God is perfect and cannot lie or deceive, God's Word in its propositional form also cannot lie or deceive. Put in syllogistic form, Ryrie proposes:

(1) *Major Premise*: God is true (Rom. 3:4).

(2) *Minor Premise*: God breathed out the Scriptures (2 Tim. 3:16).

(3) *Conclusion*: Therefore, the Scriptures are true (John 17:17).[78]

As Ryrie concludes, "A God-breathed Bible must be a *true* Bible."[79]

V

SCHOLASTIC THEOLOGY
SCRIPTURE AS DOCTRINE

The movement that may be termed "scholastic theology" can be associated with a distinctive theological movement that was particularly powerful in America in the nineteenth century. This movement is often called the "Old Princeton" theology. It is associated with a line of professors who taught at Princeton Seminary from its founding in 1812 until the seminary was split by a theological dispute in 1929. Throughout the nineteenth and into the twentieth century the "Princeton Theology" was very influential in the intellectual life of American.[1] It sought to maintain a continuity with the Reformation theology of John Calvin and his successors in the period of seventeenth century reformed orthodoxy.

One of the hallmarks of the Princeton theology was its developed doctrine of Scripture. In the 1920s and later many Americans adopted the formulations of Old Princeton on Scripture as their own.[2] Both fundamentalists and Old Princeton adherents were united in their opposition to liberalism and modernism. However they disagreed sharply on other points of doctrine such as the covenant, predestination, and eschatology.

Contemporary controversies over the nature of Scripture and its authority have focused special attention on the doctrine of Scripture as formulated by the Old Princeton school.[3] In particular, the view of the inerrancy of Scripture which was a crucial component of the Princeton position is today carefully scrutinized and debated.[4]

BACKGROUNDS

Four Princeton Theologians

Princeton Seminary was founded in 1812. Until that time in America, the Presbyterian Church had no centralized location for providing theological training for its pastors. In 1808, the Rev. Archibald Alexander (1772-1851) preached a sermon to the General Assembly of the church lamenting this fact. Alexander who had been moderator of the church in 1807, found himself in 1811 as the chair of a committee that was to construct a plan for a theological seminary. In 1812, he was elected as the first professor of the church's first seminary located in Princeton, New Jersey. On August 12, 1812 he was inaugurated to this post.[5]

Archibald Alexander was to play a significant role in the shaping of what became the Princeton theology.[6] It was his task to construct the curriculum for the new institution, and the course of study for many years was directed largely by Alexander's own interests and concerns. Prior to assuming his position, Alexander had been pastor of the Third Presbyterian Church in Philadelphia and also President of Hampton-Sydney College in Virginia. His earlier pastorates were in Charlotte County, Virginia, and he had been for a time a "circuit-rider" preacher along the frontiers of Virginia and Ohio.[7]

Alexander's early education was received through his tutor William Graham, a graduate of Princeton College who studied there under its famous president, John Witherspoon. Graham conveyed Witherspoon's influence to Alexander, particularly Witherspoon's commitment to the Scottish Common Sense philosophy. Alexander's religious experience was also shaped by his exposure to various revivals in the Blue Ridge region which he visited with Graham. Through Graham, Alexander also became familiar with the writings of Calvinist theologians such as Jonathan Edwards, John Owen, and Francis Turretin.[8]

It is well said that "in Dr. Alexander is to be found, in germ, the entire Princeton theology."[9] This is true not only with regard to various doctrines but also in terms of the "grand motifs" of the Princeton theology. These have been summarized as: devotion to the Bible, concern for religious experience, sensitivity to the American experience, and full employment of Presbyterian confessions, seventeenth-century Reformed systematicians, and the Scottish philosophy of Common Sense.[10]

One of Archibald Alexander's earliest and most brilliant students was Charles Hodge (1797-1878). Hodge was the son of a surgeon who was born in Philadelphia and entered the sophomore class of Princeton College in the fall of 1812. From 1815-19 Hodge attended Princeton Seminary where he studied theology with Alexander. The first Princeton professor had become nearly a father to Hodge who had lost his own father early in life.[11]

After graduating from the seminary, Hodge followed the course suggested by Alexander and made a special study of biblical Hebrew while also being licensed to preach. In June, 1820 Hodge returned from his home in Philadelphia to become an instructor in the biblical languages to Princeton seminary students. He was to remain on the faculty for fifty-eight years during which time he taught approximately three thousand students.[12] Hodge became Professor of Didactic Theology in 1840. From 1826 to 1828 Hodge toured German theological institutions and gained appreciation for the benefits of the German approach to theology. Meanwhile he also saw the dangers of "rationalism," "mysticism," and "ritualism."[13]

Charles Hodge elaborated on the groundwork laid by Archibald Alexander and provided the Princeton theology with its most comprehensive systematic statement. In 1872, Hodge's 2000–page, three-volume *Systematic Theology* replaced the *Institutio Theologiae Elenticae* of Francis Turretin as Princeton's principal textbook of systematic theology.[14] This text became one of the most widely used seminary textbooks and remains in print to the present day. Hodge's influences were substantial through his voluminous writings, which are marked by his unchanging commitment to orthodox Calvinism, his emphasis on logic as a tool of Christian theology, and also a concern for the personal and spiritual dimensions of theological doctrine.[15]

In 1877, one year before Charles Hodge died, he was joined at Princeton by his son Archibald Alexander Hodge (1823-86), who became his assistant and then his successor as Princeton's third Professor of Theology.[16]

A. A. Hodge was named in honor of Archibald Alexander and graduated from the seminary in 1847. He had served three pastorates in Maryland, Virginia, and Pennsylvania prior to becoming a Professor of Theology at Western Seminary in Allegheny, Pennsylvania (now Pittsburgh Theological Seminary) in 1864.

Benjamin Breckinridge Warfield (1851-1921) was a close friend and colleague of A. A. Hodge as Professor of New Testament Language and Literature at Western Seminary in Pennsylvania. When A. A. Hodge died suddenly and without warning in 1886, Warfield was chosen to take his place. He served as Professor of Didactic and Polemical Theology at Princeton for thirty-three years.

B. B. Warfield entered Princeton College the same years James McCosh (1811-94) became its President. McCosh was the last great proponent of Scottish Common Sense realism on the American intellectual scene.[17] After initial interests in science, Warfield entered Princeton Seminary in 1873 where he studied under Charles Hodge until 1876. When he graduated, Warfield traveled and studied in Europe, became an Assistant Pastor of First Presbyterian Church of Baltimore, in 1878 went to Western Seminary in Allegheny, Pennsylvania to teach New Testament. When the call to Princeton came, Warfield switched to the field of theology in the same way that Charles Hodge had.[18]

B. B. Warfield was a prolific writer who was a vigorous defender of the Princeton theology on all fronts. In particular he worked to refine the Princeton doctrine of Scripture to meet the rising tides of liberalism and the continuing assaults of biblical criticism. This took particular focus in Warfield's defense of the Princeton doctrine against the criticisms of Charles Augustus Briggs (1841-1913), who questioned its doctrine of inerrancy and charged the Princeton theology with deviating from the teachings of Calvin and the Westminster Confession.[19]

THE OLD PRINCETON TRADITION

The four theologians from Alexander to Warfield were the major shapers of the Old Princeton theology, but others made important contributions as well. The last major defender of the old Princeton theology at Princeton Seminary was J. Gresham Machen (1881-1937). Machen became a student of Warfield's in 1902 and from 1906-29 taught New Testament at Princeton.[20] In 1923 Machen published a book entitled *Christianity and Liberalism*, in which he argued that Christianity and liberalism were two completely different religions. In 1929 the General Assembly of the Presbyterian Church gave its approval to the reorganization of Princeton Seminary. Under the leadership of president J. Ross Stevenson (president since 1914), the seminary was moving in the direction of including a variety of theological positions among its faculty.[21] When the seminary was reorganized in 1929, Machen and three other faculty members, Oswald T. Allis, Robert Dick Wilson, and Cornelius Van Til left to found Westminster Seminary in Philadelphia to carry on the Old Princeton tradition. In its first semester, fifty students enrolled at the new seminary.[22] Today the Old Princeton tradition is self-consciously carried on in a variety of forms at Westminster Seminary, Covenant Seminary in St. Louis, the Reformed Seminary in Jackson, Mississippi, and Faith Seminary in Philadelphia. In addition, individual professors in other theological institutions may be found who self-consciously adhere to the Old Princeton theology.[23]

SCRIPTURE IN THE OLD PRINCETON THEOLOGY

The Princeton theologians were deeply committed to traditional Calvinism. As American Presbyterians each professor at Princeton took a subscription vow to the Westminster standards.[24] In this they confessed their belief that there was a system of doctrine taught in Holy Scripture which has been accurately systematized in the Westminster Confession of Faith. As professors at Princeton, they promised not to teach anything contrary to this system of doctrine.

The particular sources of the Princetonians' doctrine of Scripture has been studied and debated in recent years.[25] Some scholars have argued that the Princeton doctrine with its emphasis on the "inerrancy" of Scripture, particularly in the original (now lost) autographs, owes its origin to the scholastic theology of seventeenth-century Reformed orthodoxy and especially to the writings of the Swiss theologian Francis Turretin (1623-87). It is further argued that Turretin's theological method was a Protestant version of the approach of the medieval Roman Catholic Thomas Aquinas (1225-74) in which reason is given a priority over faith and reason leads to faith. In this and in Reformed scholasticism's development of the concept of inerrancy, by which the Bible is said to provide technically accurate information on all subjects about which it teaches, some have seen a departure from the views of Calvin and of the Westminster Confession.[26] In this view, Calvin and the Westminster Confession stand in a tradition that stretches back to Augustine (354-430) and emphasizes that faith leads to understanding as a theological method. Scripture is seen as providing guidance for the life of Christian faith. Scripture is infallible for that purpose. Technical inerrancy is not required for this purpose to be accomplished.[27]

Others have stressed elements of continuity between the Reformers and Reformed orthodoxy. In their view, the orthodox developed the theology of the reformers to meet the challenges of their own context and times, and in many instances merely drew out the logical implications of what was already to be found in, for example, Calvin's teachings. In this view, the "inerrancy" of Scripture is seen as Calvin's own teaching with its roots in the earlier history of the church as well.[28] Scholars of this persuasion, while recognizing that Turretin was a "major influence at Old Princeton," do not see that Turretin and Reformed scholasticism were "dominant in the sense of determining the scope and sweep of their theology."[29]

Despite these scholarly disputes, it is possible to delineate the distinctive features of the Princeton theology's view of Scripture. Variations and developments from Archibald Alexander to B. B. Warfield can be discerned. But these took shape in the context of the new questions and issues with which the Princeton theologians had to deal.[30]

Reason and Revelation

From its inception, the Princeton theology placed a heavy emphasis on the powers and capacities of human reason. The original "Plan" of the theological seminary was concerned to train theologians who could combat Deism.[31] Deists believed that human reason could discover the moral law that was inherent in nature as the only revelation humanity needed. Princeton professors sought to demonstrate the proper use of reason in religion and the need for biblical revelation. As Archibald Alexander wrote:

> Without reason we can form no conception of a truth of any kind; and when we receive any thing as true, whatever may be the evidence on which it is founded, we must view the reception of it to be reasonable. Truth and reason are so intimately connected that they can never with propriety by separated.[32]

Reason was also a useful tool with which to interpret Scripture. Again Alexander wrote: "it is reasonable to believe whatever God declares to be true."[33]

For all the Princeton theologians, there were two sources of the knowledge of God. "Natural revelation" was God's revelation in the course of nature and history. "Special revelation" was God's revelation in Scripture. The theistic proofs of God's existence, developed particularly by Aquinas and his followers, were logically valid for the Princeton theologians and thus through rational arguments one could come to a knowledge of God's existence.[34] As Warfield wrote of the relationship between general and special revelation:

> Without special revelation, general revelation would be for sinful man incomplete and ineffective....Without general revelation, special revelation would lack that basis in the fundamental knowledge of God as the mighty and wise, righteous and good, maker and ruler of all things, apart from which the further revelation of this great God's interventions in the world for the salvation of sinners could not be either intelligible, credible or operative.[35]

Thus reason and revelation went together. Both were necessary for a knowledge of God and both in their own ways produced a reliable knowledge of God.

The Nature of Faith

Due to the presence and power of human sin, the Princeton theologians believed that humans could not come to a *saving* knowledge of God on their own. For this the "internal testimony" or "internal witness" of the Holy Spirit was needed.[36] This was the act of "regeneration" which occurs when the Spirit grants the gift of the faith in Jesus Christ to sinners.

But for the Princeton theologians, particularly Warfield, the means the Holy Spirit used were the methods of causing the human reason to acquiesce to logical "reasons for faith." Charles Hodge defined faith as "assent to the truth, or the persuasion of the mind that a thing is true.[37] For him, "The Scriptures teach that faith is the reception of truth on the ground of testimony or on the authority of God."[38] As Warfield developed this notion that faith is grounded in evidence, he taught that "the action of the Holy Spirit in giving faith is not apart from evidence, but along with evidence; and in the first instance consists in preparing the soul for the reception of the evidence."[39] Thus faith is not "unreasonable." It is indeed *the* most "reasonable" action since the "testimony" on which one's faith rests is the testimony of God by the Holy Spirit.

But for Hodge and Warfield, this testimony of the Holy Spirit was an action separate from the act of "faith" by which one came to believe in the divine origin of the Scripture. The "evidence" upon which this "faith" rested, Warfield called the *indicia* of the divinity of Scripture.[40] These *indicia* provided the proofs of the divine origination of the Bible. These *indicia* were "coworkers" with the Holy Spirit to bring one to the faith that Scripture was divine.[41]

Authority of Scripture

For the Princeton theologians, Scripture was authoritative because God has spoken through the biblical writers. As Charles Hodge put it: "The Bible claims to be the Word of God; it speaks in his name, it assumes his authority."[42] Warfield wrote:

> The authority of the Scriptures thus rests on the simple fact that God's authoritative agents in founding the Church gave them as authoritative to the Church which they founded. All the authority of the apostles stands behind the Scriptures, and all the authority of Christ behind the apostles. The Scriptures are simply the law-code which the law-givers of the Church gave it.[43]

This meant for Warfield that it was crucial to show that all the canonical books had apostolic sanction and authority.[44]

Verbal Inspiration

In his earliest expression of biblical inspiration, Archibald Alexander had distinguished among three kinds of inspiration: (1) *Superintendence* which was guidance of the authors but no new revelation of facts to them; (2) *Suggestion* which functioned to communicate new information to the author; and (3) *Elevation* which is seen when a biblical writer spoke or wrote in words or ways that were "far more sublime and excellent than they could have attained by the exercise of their own faculties."[45] Later Princeton writers rejected these degrees of inspiration.

Charles Hodge, however, was the first to give systematic expression to the Princeton view of inspiration which was defined in his *Systematic Theology* as:

an influence of the Holy Spirit on the minds of certain select men, which rendered them the organs of God for the infallible communication of his mind and will. They were in such a sense organs of God, that what they said God said.[47]

Earlier Hodge asserted that "the whole end and office of inspiration is to preserve the sacred writers from error in teaching."[48]

B. B. Warfield defined inspiration in his Inaugural Address at Allegheny Seminary in 1880 as the "extraordinary, supernatural influence (or, passive, the result of it) exerted by the Holy Ghost on the writers of our Sacred Books, by which their words were rendered also the words of God, and therefore, perfectly infallible."[49] Both human and divine dimensions were present in inspiration. As Warfield wrote:

> The Church, then has held from the beginning that the Bible is the Word of God in such a sense that its words, though written by men and bearing indelibly impressed upon them the marks of their human origin, were written, nevertheless, under such an influence of the Holy Ghost as to be also the words of God, the adequate expression of His mind and will.[50]

Warfield used the term *concursus* to describe both of these dimensions, defining it as meaning that "every word is at once divine and human."[51]

Inerrancy

Charles Hodge recognized difficulties with what Warfield later described as *concursus*, that is, that God guided the language as well as the thoughts of the biblical writers. When "difficulties" in the biblical text arose, Hodge said the only proper course was "to believe what is proved to be true, and let the difficulties abide their solution."[52] Basically Charles Hodge believed that "the difficulties are so minute as to escape the notice of ordinary intelligence." An example of such, he said would be when one writer might state that "on a certain occasion twenty-four thousand persons were slain; another, a thousand years after, says there were twenty-three thousand." While there may be other more serious objections, Hodge still believed these objections were "pitiful" and "miraculously small." Hodge's view was captured in his famous description:

> The errors in matters of fact which skeptics search out bear no proportion to the whole. No sane man would deny that the Parthenon was built of marble, even if here and there a speck of sandstone should be detected in its structure. Not less unreasonable is it to deny the inspiration of such a book as the Bible, because one sacred writer says that on a given occasion twenty-four thousand, and another says that twenty-three thousand, men were slain. Surely a Christian may be allowed to tread such objections under his feet.[54]

For Hodge, the inspiration of Scripture was seen in the form that it comes to us. It comes to us in verbal forms or words. These words, since Scripture *is* the word of God, are also the *words of God*. Since God is perfect and cannot lie or err, Scripture too must be perfect in this way. Scripture, for Charles Hodge and the Princeton tradition, cannot deceive or err, even on matters of science, geography, and history. As Charles Hodge wrote:

> An inspired man could not, indeed, err in his instruction on any subject. He could not teach by inspiration that the earth is the center of our system, or that the sun, moon, and stars are mere satellites of our globe, but such may have been his own conviction. Inspiration did not elevate him in secular knowledge above the age in which he lived; it only, so far as secular and scientific truths are concerned, preserved him from teaching error.[55]

> Inspiration extends to all the contents of these several books. It is not confined to moral and religious truths, but extends to the statements of facts, whether scientific, historical, or geographical. It is not confined to those facts the importance of which is obvious or which are involved in matters of doctrine. It extends to everything which any sacred writer asserts to be true.[56]

For Charles Hodge, biblical teachings were perfectly congruent with the findings and teachings of nineteenth-century science. As he put it in one example in 1857, "no man now pretends that there is a word in the Bible, from Genesis to Revelation, inconsistent with the highest results of astronomy."[57]

During the next three decades with developments in biblical criticism, the natural sciences, and historical thinking, the Princeton position on Scripture also developed. In the 1879 edition of *Outlines of Theology* A. A. Hodge explicitly introduced the notion that the "original autographs" of Scripture are "absolutely infallible when interpreted in the sense intended, and hence are clothed with absolute divine authority."[63] By careful definition, A. A. Hodge went on to assert that the present copies and translations of Scripture may contain apparent "discrepancies" arising from "frequent transcription." But these "descrepancies" do not damage a view of the plenary or full inspiration of the Scriptures since in the most technical sense "the Church has asserted absolute infallibility only of the original autograph copies of the Scripture as they came from the hands of their inspired writers."[59]

This appeal to the "original autographs" of Scripture became an important part of the Princeton theology's view of Scripture in the writings of Warfield and particularly in the article he jointly authored with A. A. Hodge in 1881.[60] For A. A. Hodge and Warfield, the terms "inerrancy" and "infallibility" were synonymous terms. They each logically implied the other. They both referred to "the complete trustworthiness of Scripture in all elements and in every, even circumstantial statement."[61] For the Bible "in all its parts and in all its elements, down to the least minutiae, in form of expression as well as in substance of teaching, is from God."[62] The Princetonians were not bothered by the argument that we no longer possess the original copies of Scripture. Warfield believed that God had preserved providentially texts that are close enough to the original that through textual criticism the autographic texts were within reach. As he wrote: "God has not permitted the Bible to become so hopelessly corrupt that its restoration to its original text is impossible."[63]

For the inerrancy of Scripture to be *disproved*, A. A. Hodge and Warfield set out their views on what would constitute a "proven error" in Scripture. They wrote:

> (1). Let it be proved that each alleged discrepant statement certainly occurred in the original autograph of the sacred book in which it is said to be found. (2). Let it be proved that the interpretation which occasions the apparent discrepancy is the one which the passages was evidently intended to bear. It is not sufficient to show a difficulty, which may spring out of our defective knowledge of the circumstances. The true meaning must be definitely ascertained, and then shown to be irreconcilable with other known truth. (3). Let it be proved that the true sense of some part of the original autograph is directly and necessarily inconsistent with some certainly known act of history, or truth of science, or some other statement of Scripture certainly ascertained and interpreted. We believe that it can be shown that this never yet been successfully done in the case of one single alleged instance of error in the Word of God.[64]

For Hodge and Warfield it was not the "common text" of Scripture but only "the autographic text that was inspired" and "no 'error' can be asserted, therefore, which cannot be proved to have been aboriginal in the text."[65]

With these criteria for "error" fully established, the Princeton theology's doctrine of the authority, inspiration, and inerrancy of Scripture was firmly in place.[66]

SCRIPTURE AS DOCTRINE

The Old Princeton theology has been explicated as an example of what may be termed "scholastic theology."[67] Generally this view can be categorized as emphasizing that God through the Scriptures has revealed certain doctrines to be believed. The Bible then is, "primarily a source for doctrine, or religious *teachings*."[68]

> Charles Hodge expressed a doctrinalist perspective when he insisted that 'Revelation is the communication of truth by God to the understanding of man. It makes known doctrines. For example, it makes known that God is...that Christ is the Son of God; that he assumed our nature; that he died for our sins, etc. These are logical propositions.'[69]

Similarly for Hodge's successor B. B Warfield it can be said that "Biblical texts, construed as containing a system of doctrine, strike with numinous power so that one's initial responses, as Warfield reports it are awe, trembling, and submission."[70] Thus, "for the doctrinalist understanding of the Bible, the most important and fundamental way in which human beings are to respond to the Bible is with intellectual assent to the 'teaching' propositions asserted therein."[71]

This scientific approach exemplifies the self-understanding of the Old Princeton theology.[72] But it also meant that one of the doctrines of Scripture to be believed was the doctrine of Scripture itself. Thus the Princetonians called the people to believe what may be called the "doctrine of the doctrine of Scripture." One came to believe or have "faith" in Scripture by assenting to the truth of Scripture of which one was persuaded in one's mind by the "evidences" of Scripture that prove its divine origin. Methodologically, "reason leads to faith." When this occurs one comes to believe, said the Princetonians, that "the Scriptures are the word of God in such a sense that their words deliver the truth of God without error."[73] For the Princeton theology, this was seen as the Church's view of the Bible since the earliest times.[74] In the nineteenth and twentieth centuries, those of the Old Princeton tradition dedicated themselves to perpetuating this view of the Bible.[75]

VI

NEO-ORTHODOX THEOLOGY
SCRIPTURE AS WITNESS

The theological movement variously known as neo-orthodoxy, neo-reformation theology or neo-Calvinism reacted simultaneously to contemporary forms of scholastic theology and to the theology of liberalism. Neo-orthodoxy gained impetus with the publication of Karl Barth's (1886-1968) biblical commentary, *The Epistle to the Romans* (1919). This work went through six editions and marked a new approach to biblical scholarship. The movement is chiefly associated with Barth and with Emil Brunner (1889-1966). Together they began what was initially known as "dialectical theology" or the "theology of crisis."[1] Other early figures associated with neo-orthodoxy include Eduard Thurneysen (1888-1974), Friedrich Gogarten (1887-1967), and Rudolf Bultmann (1884-1976).[2] In the broader sweep of the movement, theologians such as Hendrik Kraemer, Dietrich Bonhoeffer, Otto Weber Wilhelm Vischer, Daniel Jenkins, and Thomas Torrence may also be seen as related to it.[3] In America, Reinhold Niebuhr (1892-1971) was also seen moving with its direction.[4]

BACKGROUNDS

The term "dialectic theology" as a designation for the theology of what became also known as "neo-orthodoxy" can be traced back to the second edition of Barth's commentary on Romans, published in early 1922. There Barth wrote that he wished to exegete the Scripture in "a dialectic movement as inexorable as it is elastic," to attain "the *inner dialectic of the subject matter*." Barth's commentary affirms: "The grace of creation, like the grace of redemption, is nowhere present as a given condition among other given conditions. It is the imperceptible relation in which all given conditions

71

stand, and knowledge of it is always and everywhere dialectic."[5]

Barth's association with Gogarten was in part responsible for his re-working the first edition of *Romans* to produce the second. Behind Barth's understandings at this time were thinkers such as Luther and Calvin, Dostoevsky. Blumhardt, Kierkegaard, Nietzsche, and especially Franz Overbeck (1837-1905). Overbeck was a friend of Nietzsche who attacked Christianity and Christendom by arguing that Christianity and history do not belong together. When Christianity takes on an historical form, it is no longer Christian and become demonic.[6] A genuine religion, said Overbeck, must be based on a supernatural revelation that originates beyond history. In the course of Christian history, Christianity has become "historicized." In it, "the original message of Christ and the apostles, a message which spoke of the wholly supernatural kingdom of God, had been betrayed by the transformation of Christianity itself into a social, cultural, and political movement *within* history."[7]

Basic to Barth's thought as it developed into "dialectical theology" was the absolute contrast between God and humanity. The personal potency of this contrast for Barth was strong. As the son of a minister of the Swiss Reformed Church who was born in Basel, Switzerland, Barth was trained in the liberal theology of Adolf von Harnack, who passed on to him the theological approach of Schleiermacher. Schleiermacher's influence was to be prominent with Barth for many years.

In 1911 Barth became pastor of a Reformed church. For the next three years he preached as his theological training had taught him, emphasizing life and experience as the basis for his sermons.[8] When World War I broke out and Barth saw his former theological professors were supporting the war policy of Kaiser Wilhelm II, Barth said that "a whole world of exegesis, ethics, dogmatics and preaching, which I had hitherto held to be essentially trustworthy, was shaken to the foundations, and with it, all other writings of the German theologians."[9]

During the war years, Barth studied with his friend Eduard Thurneysen and was introduced to the thought of Johann Christoph Blumhardt (1805-80). Blumhardt's theology stressed eschatology and commitment to the kingdom of God. Barth sought the "signs" of the "breakthrough" of the kingdom while also "waiting patiently for God as he worked for the Kingdom as he could. During this time he said the one term which summed up his new insight from the New Testament was 'hope.' "[10]

Barth's constant need to preach and to produce sermons eventually led him to discover he could not continue to follow Schleiermacher. Instead of life and experience, Barth began to believe that theology should begin with the Bible and with the God who encounters humans in the strange new world of the Bible....We have found in the Bible a new world, God, God's sovereignty, God's glory, God's incomprehensible love. Not the history of man but the history of him who hath called us out of darkness into his marvelous light! Not human standpoints but the standpoint of God![11]

This approach was seen in Barth's commentary on Romans. There Barth said he wished "to see through and beyond history into the spirit of the Bible, which is the Eternal Spirit."[12] Barth's method clashed with the historical-critical methods of biblical studies, which were taught and practiced by his own teachers, and led to heavy criticism of his book by biblical scholars and theologians such as von Harnack and Adolf Jülicher.[13] While Barth did not want to negate totally the results of recent centuries of biblical scholarship, he did wish, as he was later to write, that criticism stop serving "the foolish end of mediating an historical truth lying behind the texts.' " Instead, scholars should examine Scripture "as it actually is before us."[14] Barth's goal was to turn with "all the more attentiveness, accuracy and love to the texts as such."[15] For Barth this meant "theological exegesis" carried out from the presupposition of the church's basic confession that "Jesus Christ is Lord."[16]

With the second edition of Barth's commentary, the influences of his studies of Plato, Kant, Kierkegaard, and Dostoevsky as well as Calvin and Luther showed clearly and the contours of "dialectical theology" began to take shape.[17] From Kierkegaard, Barth borrowed the phrase the "infinite qualitative distinction" between time and eternity, between God and humanity. In opposition to his liberal training, Barth stressed the *discontinuity* between God and humanity. God's transcendence and majesty meant that God is the "Wholly Other," the "Hidden One." Thus for Barth,

> God *is God*, not man writ large; and he cannot be spoken of simply by speaking of ourselves in a loud voice. He cannot be taken for granted as simply "there" in our religious sense, our spiritual depth, or our moral awareness, for he transcends, he stands over against all of these. He can be met, really met, only in the encounter in which we finite creatures of time and history are confronted by the One who is infinite and eternal, and who remains infinite and eternal and "wholly Other" than ourselves in that meeting.[18]

Yet for Barth at the same time, this God has been revealed in Jesus Christ in whom heaven and earth meet. This is the crisis under which the world stands. For all of history and all of humanity has been brought under judgment by this act of God in Jesus Christ. The Word of God in Jesus Christ is one of both mercy and judgment. It contradicts all human achievement, pride, self-sufficiency, ethics, politics, and even *religion*. All human securities, which the Apostle Paul calls the "righteousness of law," fall before the cross of Jesus Christ. There God speaks a decisive "No!" to all human claims for self and leaves humans with no source of security in themselves. This "No!" from God is only part of the picture, however. This "No!" is spoken so that humans may also hear the divine "Yes!" in Jesus Christ. In trusting Christ by faith, humanity is saved. The divine answer to the predicament of humanity (sin) is God's own righteousness in Jesus Christ. In Christ, "the Word of God is the transformation of everything that we know as Humanity, Nature, and History, and must therefore be apprehended as the negation of the starting-point of every system which we are capable of conceiving."[19] Faith comes from the pure promise and invitation of God and was not for Barth, as for Schleiermacher, a general awareness of "absolute dependence." Instead faith was the response of the "moment" to the Word of God himself, Jesus Christ.[20]

The "dialectic" of Barth's thought made a considerable impact on the theological landscape of Europe for the next years. Later Barth said he was like a man who tripped in the darkness of a church tower, accidentally grabbing out and catching a bell-rope to gain his balance, and then with the sounding of the bell, alarming the whole countryside!

For Barth, as for Kierkegaard, the "dialectic" was in the total contrast between God and humans, the relationship of the "No!" and "Yes!" of God in Jesus Christ, and the implications that stemmed from this. For Barth this meant that no human speech about God could ever contain or even directly or indirectly express the truth about God. All statements by humans needed to be qualified and even negated. Only in this dialectical process may one ever hope to hear the Word of God. For Barth, God is the subject who must be revealed to humankind. Human beings can only "witness" to this wonder.[21]

Barth and his colleagues believed their rediscovery of the essential message of Paul and hence of the whole New Testament stood dramatically opposed to the prevailing liberal theology. For the dialectical theologians, the liberals were seen as having replaced God with humanity and thus having turned theology into anthropology. They saw liberalism as secretly assuming that God and humans were in effect identical. This view meant that liberalism had no adequate doctrine of the revelation of God because it did not take with sufficient seriousness the nature and person of God. From this stemmed other inadequacies of doctrine, from that of Scripture as the vehicle of God's Word to humanity as sinful rather than just 'misguided," to the nature of authentic faith which must be radical in its character. The person of Jesus Christ had been grossly distorted in liberalism according to the dialectical theologians. In liberal theology, Jesus was a spiritual ideal, a "man among men" who set the great example and provided the ethical norms for others to follow. For Barth, Jesus Christ was the Word of God who intersected time and eternity, the finite and the infinite, and who is the One through whom all humanity might become reconciled with God. As Barth said in commenting on Romans 3:21, God in Jesus Christ: "pronounces us, His enemies, to be His friends."[22]

Dialectical theology set out to reverse prevailing theological method. Its first emphasis was the "Godness of God." Its second was the reality of the Word of God in Jesus Christ, and thirdly it stressed the impossibility of building theology on any other foundation.[23]

The year 1921 brought Barth the offer of a teaching post in Reformed theology at the University of Göttingen. In 1922 he was given an honorary doctorate of theology from the University of Münster and immersed himself in preparing lectures. At this time he became thoroughly familiar with the Reformed tradition while he taught courses on Calvin, Zwingli, the Heidelberg Catechism, and Schleiermacher.[24]

In 1925 Barth moved to the University of Münster where he taught until 1930. During this time his *Christian Dogmatics in Outline* appeared in 1927. This work stressed the "Word of God" as the speech or act of God in which God was always the initiator, the "subject." It is the Holy Spirit who makes hearing and responding to God's Word possible. This gave a place for the human, existential situation in which God's revelation occurred. But because of his heavy use of Kierkegaard, Barth's thought was being misunderstood. So Barth began again. This time he reworked his whole theological methodology. He completely rethought the relationship between theology and philosophy. Barth wanted to maintain an emphasis on the knowledge of God, faith, Christian belief, and experience without letting them take on an independent status in themselves.[25]

Barth's new insight came when he taught a seminar in the summer of 1930 on Anselm's classic work *Cur Deus Homo?* (*Why God Became Man?*). There at the University of Bonn, where he now taught, Barth lectured on what later became his book *Fides quaerens intellectum*. The work studied Anselm's proof of the existence of God. For Barth the key was in Anselm's concept of theology proceding through "faith seeking understanding." For Anselm and Barth it was "faith" that summons humans to "knowledge." Theology was the quest for understanding which saw behind all "logical understanding" to the inner meaning of the reality behind the words. God initiates faith in us and from there we move on to further understanding.[26]

For Barth, the "understanding" faith seeks comes from Holy Scripture. Scripture must be read from the perspective of faith. It concerns more than merely trying to understand the meaning of words, paragraphs, and histories in the Bible. "Understanding" when reading the biblical texts comes through illumination by God. Thus theology is the task of the church. The theologian presupposes that God has acted and been revealed.[27]

From this insight, Karl Barth moved on to begin his monumental theological work, the *Church Dogmatics*. This work was never completed but at the time of Barth's death ran to thirteen part-volumes which were published between 1932 (Vol. I/1) and 1967 (Vol. IV/4, Fragment). In his *Dogmatics*, Barth moved away from the influence of Kierkegaard and tried to "rethink everything that I had said before and to put it quite differently once again, as a theology of the grace of God in Jesus Christ."[28] Barth's work was structured around the doctrines of the Word of God (Vol. I), God (Vol II), Creation (Vol. III), and Reconciliation (Vol. IV). Each of these revolved around the trinitarian structure of God's being as Father, Son, and Holy Spirit. Barth's projected volume on Redemption was never begun. Throughout, Barth's beginning and ending points are Jesus Christ as the revelation of God. This emphasis on Christ and the Word of God were to become hallmarks of Barth's theology.

SCRIPTURE IN NEO-ORTHODOX THEOLOGY

The Word of God

Barth's "prolegomena" to his studies called *Church Dogmatics* began with two volumes on "The Doctrine of the Word of God." The term "Word of God" for Barth meant God's "self-revelation."[29] Barth said quite simply: "God's Word means that God speaks."[30] God's revelation and speaking are in Jesus Christ and in the reconciliation of the whole world accomplished in Him. For, to say revelation is to say 'The Word became flesh.' "[31]

A special emphasis for Barth was that the Word of God comes in a threefold way. There is the Word revealed (Jesus Christ), the Word written (Scripture), and the Word proclaimed (preaching).[32] These three forms are mutually interrelated and not isolated from one another. There are not three different "Words" of God. There is only one Word of God—Jesus Christ—who meets us in this threefold way.[33]

For Barth, the Scriptures of the church as the church's "canon" prevented the church from merely proclaiming a human message of its own invention.[34] The canon of Scripture is "self-authenticating" for Barth, in that there are no "proofs" or "reasons" behind it. The content of the canon is what is decisive. As Barth wrote: "The Bible is the Canon just because it is so. It is so by imposing itself as such.[35]

The Bible Becomes God's Word

God has chosen to confront the church through the ages *via* the Bible. This was God's free decision, not humankind's. So "the Bible is God's Word to the extent that God causes it to be His word, to the extent that He speaks

76

through it."[36] This was a confession of faith. It is not that "man has grasped at the Bible but that the Bible has grasped at man."[37] According to Barth

> the Bible, then, becomes God's Word in this event, and in the statement that the Bible is God's Word the little word 'is' refers to its being in this becoming. It does not become God's Word because we accord it faith but in the fact that it becomes revelation to us.[38]

The Bible is the key link between God's revelation in Christ and the church. Barth wrote:

> The decisive relation of the Church to revelation is its attestation by the Bible.... The Bible is not itself and as such God's past revelation. As it is God's Word it bears witness to God's past revelation, and it is God's past revelation in the form of attestation.[39]

As a "witness," the Bible points in a definite direction "beyond the self and on to another."[40] In this respect the Bible as a witness claimed no authority for itself but let "that other than itself be its own authority." For Barth, "we thus do the Bible poor and unwelcome honour if we equate it directly with this other, with revelation itself.[41] The direct identification between revelation and the Bible only takes place as "an event." It happens "when and where the biblical word becomes God's Word."[42] In this "event" it is the revelation which "should be understood primarily as the superior principle and the Bible primarily as the subordinate principle."[43]

In "the event of inspiration," however, biblical writers "become speakers and writers of the Word of God."[44] They told of "the occurrence of God's revelation itself apart from their own existence" which had happened "once and once-for-all." This was nothing less than the fact that "God was with us;" that "His Word became flesh of our flesh, blood of our blood." The "publishers of revelation," the prophets and apostles, witnessed that "this 'God with us' has happened. It has happened in human history and as a part of human history." It was this witness which gave the biblical writers authority. Even though "they seek no authority, even with their fallible human word they can continually claim and enjoy the most unheard of authority."[45]

The biblical writers, according to Barth were "witnesses" to the divine event of God's revelation. Barth said: "Revelation is originally and directly what the Bible and the Church proclamation are derivatively and indirectly, i.e., God's Word."[46] Thus both the Bible and the church's proclamation of the Bible (which is the basis for its preaching and message) "must continually become God's Word." When this happens, it is an act of God's free grace. Insofar as the church's preaching and the Scriptures themselves witness to God's revelation, "one may thus say of proclamation and the Bible that they are God's Word, that they continually become God's Word."[47]

The Authority of Scripture

For Karl Barth, the authority of the Bible was grounded in "the witness of the Holy Spirit."[48] To say this meant that Scripture *becomes* "authentic" and "authoritative" for humans through the work of the Holy Spirit. No reasons or logical proofs lead one to confess the authority of Holy Scripture. One makes this confession through the work of the Holy Spirit. In this sense, Barth was appropriating the theological method he learned from Anselm: "faith leads to understanding." For Barth, "Scripture is holy and the Word of God, because by the Holy Spirit it became and will become to the Church a witness to divine revelation."[49] The Bible is a unique book. God has made it so. The special content of the Bible, as witness to the Word of God through which the Holy Spirit works to create faith and obedience, is what gives Scripture its authority in the church.

The Inspiration of Scripture

The Scriptures claim for themselves that they are witnesses to Jesus Christ, God's incarnate Word.[50] But it is through human beings who were "witnesses" that this revelation in Christ came to the world. These people were

> *witnesses* of the Word. To be more precise, they are primary witnesses, because they are called directly by the Word to be its hearers, and they are appointed for its communication and verification to other men. These men are the *biblical witnesses of the Word*, the prophetic men of the Old Testament and the apostolic men of the New. They were contemporaries of the history in which God established his covenant with men. In fact, they became contemporary witnesses by virtue of what they saw and heard of this history.[51]

These witnesses saw and heard God's revelation and then spoke it.[52] They served in a God-given capacity, unique to them, and what they did in this capacity was inspired by God.[53]

Barth viewed the inspiration of Scripture particularly in light of the biblical passages from 2 Timothy 3:14-17 and 2 Peter 1:19-21.[54] Barth concluded that "the decisive center to which the two passages point is in both instances indicated by a reference to the Holy Spirit, and indeed in such a way that He is described as the real author of what is stated or written in Scripture."[55] For Barth the human authors of Scripture had a direct relationship to God's revelation.

> The special element in this attitude of obedience lay in the particularity, i.e., the immediacy of its relationship to the revelation which is unique by restriction in time, and therefore in the particular nature of what they had to say and write as eye-witnesses and ear-witnesses, the first-fruits of the church.[56]

This view led Barth to criticize early church views of the inspiration of Scripture as limiting the work of the Holy Spirit "in the emergence of the spoken or written prophetic and apostolic word as such."[57] Barth also complained that in the early church there was "a tendency to insist that the operation of the Holy Spirit in the inspiration of the biblical writers extended to the individual phraseology used by them in the grammatical sense of the concept."[58] The Reformers, however, corrected this. For Luther and Calvin inspiration was not "mantico-mechanical" nor "docetic." The Reformers rested Scripture's inspiration directly on the relationship of the biblical witnesses to the special content of their witness.[59]

In the seventeenth century according to Barth, however, orthodox theologians turned the knowledge of the Bible as the Word of God into a part of one's eternal knowledge of God or the knowledge of God which humans can have on their own without the grace of God.[60] Barth asked if, in these theologians when they speak of the biblical writers, there is not "a return to the idea that they are mere flutes in the mouth of the Holy Spirit?"[61] Post-Reformation theologians separated the doctrine of the internal testimony of the Spirit from the witness of the Spirit in Scripture. They went on to justify the Bible as the Word of God by appealing to certain convincing characteristics of the biblical record.[62] To Barth this represented a "docetic" theory because it suppressed the human dimensions of the texts. For Barth, the orthodox had grounded the Bible upon itself "apart from the mystery of Christ and the Holy Ghost." Scripture had become a "paper Pope" and "was no longer a free and spiritual force, but an instrument of human power."[63]

Barth recognized that Christianity as a "book religion" taught that God through the Holy Spirit spoke the divine Word in human words. Thus it is proper to speak of "verbal inspiration" in that it is only in the *words* of Scripture that the *Word* of God is to be found.[64] Yet, said Barth, "the literally inspired Bible was not at all a revealed book of oracles, but a witness to revelation, to be interpreted from the standpoint of and with a view of its theme, and in conformity with that theme."[65]

SCRIPTURE AS WITNESS

Barth recognized that the words of the biblical witnesses were human words and were thus limited in terms of space and time. The Scriptures could not themselves be a substitute for the Word of God. He wrote: "It is quite impossible that there should be a direct identity between the human word of Holy Scripture and the Word of God, and therefore between the creaturely reality in itself and as such and the reality of God the Creator."[66] Scripture, for Barth, was included as part of God's act of revelation. But it in itself was not the central act of revelation. Jesus Christ was. Scripture's function was to point or witness to Jesus Christ. The written Word of Scripture "takes the place of the thing itself (i.e., the Word of God)."[67] The written Word directs its readers to the living Word. Thus, Scriptural statements must not be directly equated with the reality of the revelation in Jesus Christ. Like "the unity of God and man in Jesus Christ," Scripture for Barth was in its own way and degree "very God and very man, i.e., a witness of revelation which itself belongs to revelation, and historically a very human literary document."[68] Scripture's form for Barth was a very *human* form.

Scripture as witness to Jesus Christ written in human words meant that there was not a direct correlation between the Truth and the Scripture's statements about the Truth. In some sense the light of all truth was "refracted" through the lenses of the Scripture writers. This was what Barth meant when he spoke of the extent to which Scripture was the Word of God: "The Bible is God's Word to the extent that God causes it to be His Word, to the extent that He speaks through it."[69] Scripture statements were God's Word only to the degree that God by the Holy Spirit permitted them to witness to God's truth. Since the words of the biblical writers were "human and conditioned by time and space," they could never in themselves be infinite, perfect, or absolute. They could never let the whole truth of God shine through in all its fullness.

For Barth the limits of human language and the biblical writers "can be at fault in any word, and have been at fault in every word." Yet, "according to the same scriptural witness, being justified and sanctified by grace alone, they have still spoken the Word of God in their fallible and erring human word."[70] Barth resisted attempts to overemphasize divine dimensions of Scripture when he wrote that

> every time we turn the Word of God into an infallible biblical word of man or the biblical word of man into an infallible Word of God we resist that which we ought never to resist, i.e., the truth of the miracle that here fallible men speak the Word of God in fallible human words—and we therefore resist the sovereignty of grace, in which God Himself became man in Christ, to glorify Himself in His humanity.[71]

"Verbal inspiration" for Barth

> does not mean the infallibility of the biblical word in its linguistic, historical and theological character as a human word. It means that the fallible and faulty human word is as such used by God and has to be received and heard in spite of its human fallibility.[72]

For Barth there was a pointed "distinction between inspiration and therefore the divine infallibility of the Bible and its human fallibility."

We cannot expect or demand a compendium of solomonic or even divine knowledge of all things in heaven and earth, natural, historical and human, to be mediated to the prophets and apostles in and with their encounter with the divine revelation, possessing which they have to be differentiated not only from their own but from every age as the bearers and representatives of an ideal culture and therefore as the inerrant proclaimers of all and every truth. They did not in fact possess any such compendium. Each in his own way and degree, they shared the culture of their age and environment, whose form and content could be contested by other ages and environments, and at certain points can still appear debatable to us.[73]

Since the biblical writers were "witnesses," there is a "vulnerability of the Bible" since the writers had a "capacity for errors."[74] Yet no one, even in the twentieth century had the right to specify what was an "error" in Scripture and what was not. For Barth when speaking of the biblical writers,

within certain limits and therefore relatively they are all vulnerable and therefore capable of error and even in respect of religion and theology. In view of the actual constitution of the Old and New Testaments this is something which we cannot possibly deny if we are not to take away their humanity, if we are not to be guilty of Docetism. How can they be witnesses, if this is not the case?[75]

But through it all Barth recognized that God could use any particular portion of Scripture through which to speak the Word of God. No one has the right to say which portions of Scripture are more or less fallible:

We are absolved from differentiating the Word of God in the Bible from other contents, infallible portions and expressions from the erroneous ones, the infallible from the fallible, and from imagining that by means of such discoveries we can create for ourselves encounters with the genuine Word of God in the Bible.[76]

For Barth and other neo-orthodox theologians the genuine Word of God in the Bible, the center of Scripture, was Jesus Christ to whom all the witnesses of Scripture point with one accord.

VII

NEO-EVANGELICAL THEOLOGY
SCRIPTURE AS MESSAGE

With the deaths of Harold John Ockenga and Francis Schaeffer (in 1985 and 1984 respectively) two of the most influential leaders of "evangelicalism" in America were gone.[1]

It was Ockenga, in a 1947 convocation address at Fuller Theological Seminary in Pasadena, California, who coined the term "the new evangelicalism."[2] As a distinguishable movement from that time on, Ockenga and Schaeffer along with Billy Graham, Harold Lindsell, and Carl F. H. Henry gave leadership that established "neo-evangelicalsm" as a major force in American religion.[3]

Today "neo-evangelicalism," like the term "evangelicalism," is defined and understood in various ways.[4] Those who accept this name as characteristic of their theological positions may not agree exactly on all or specifically on a few major doctrinal points. This is especially true as will be seen in terms of the doctrine of Scripture.[5] But before these diversities can be appreciated it is necessary to examine some definitions and backgrounds to the current scene.

BACKGROUNDS

The term "evangelical" has been prominent in America in recent years. In 1976, George Gallup Jr., on the basis of a Gallup Poll, called 1976 "the year of the evangelical."[6] Commentators have written of an "evangelical renaissance," an "evangelical resurgence," and a "new evangelical majority."[7] In the Gallup poll, 34 percent of the respondents said they have had a "born again" experience which had been a turning point in life that led to a commitment to Jesus Christ. On a national scale this percentage would mean nearly 50 million Americans fit in this category. Among Protestants, 48 percent and among Roman Catholics 18 percent said they have had a born-again experience.[8] According to Gallup, 30 percent of Americans accept the term "evangelical" to define their religious position.[9] A *Christianity Today* poll put the number at 22 percent.[10]

The statistics naturally raise problems for the definition of "evangelical." James Davison Hunter has provided a broad, contextual definition when he writes that evangelicalism is best understood as

> a religiocultural phenomenon unique to North America though clearly related in intimate ways to other forms of theologically conservative Protestanism in other times and places. The world view of Evangelicalism is deeply rooted in the theological tradition of the Reformation, in northern European Puritanism, and later in American Puritanism and the First and Second Great Awakenings in North America. Indeed, Evangelicalism has striven to remain entirely faithful doctrinally to this general conservative tradition. At the doctrinal core, contemporary Evangelicals can be identified by their adherence to (1) the belief that the Bible is the inerrant Word of God, (2) the belief in the divinity of Christ, and (3) the belief in the efficacy of Christ's life, death, and physical resurrection for the salvation of the human soul. Behaviorally, Evangelicals are typically characterized by an individual and experiential orientation toward spiritual salvation and religiosity in general and by the conviction of the necessity of actively attempting to proselytize all nonbelievers to the tenets of the Evangelical belief system.[11]

From this definition, several considerations can be noted. "Evangelicalism" in America does refer to "a fairly unified tradition." While this tradition over the centuries has

> undergone considerable change, it has nevertheless maintained its identity and looked back to its origins with considerable sympathy and respect. Its origins lie in that revolution in Christendom which the English Puritan movement intended to accomplish. Only in North America, however, where ancient traditions had very little social and economic footing, were the full implications of this revolution borne out.[12]

The backgrounds of English Puritanism led to the Continental Protestant Reformation and to the Protestants who by the 1520s were identifying themselves as "Evangelical" over against Roman Catholicism. In that sense "when the Reformers called themselves Evangelicals, they did not think of themselves as a schismatic group within the church but as representatives of the true church—the church founded by Jesus Christ and based on the biblical gospel."[13]

After the Reformation other movements such as Puritanism and Pietism which later had effects in America through various means further developed the meaning of "evangelical."[14] Looking back to the Greek term *euangelion*, meaning the "evangel" or "good news" or "Gospel," the "evangelical move-ment" of the British Isles in the eighteenth century (whose leaders included John and Charles Wesley, and George Whitefield) stressed the need for reli-gious conversion or "the new birth," being "born again." This emphasis in these figures, however, was not made in isolation from the central theologi-cal theme of the Protestant Reformation: justification by faith. In America the "born again" theme became a hallmark of nineteenth- and twentieth-century revivalism and revivalists/evangelists such as Charles Grandison Finney (1792-1875), Dwight Lyman Moody (1837-99), Rueben A. Torrey (1856-1928), William "Billy" Sunday (1862-1935), and William Franklin "Billy" Graham (b. 1918).[15]

Beyond the historical continuity of an American "evangelical" tradition is the theological or doctrinal basis which defines "evangelicals." In the broad sense as noted, evangelicalism as an American theological tradition looks to the teachings of the sixteenth-century Protestant Reformers as the most faithful expositions of the basic gospel message of Scripture.[16] A further description of this would be that

> if asked to list the key elements in a vital Christian faith, an evangelical in the classical sense might well reply: biblical fidelity, apostolic doctrine, the experi-ence of salvation, the imperative of discipleship, and the urgency of mission. Holding firm to the doctrine taught by the prophets and apostles in Holy Scrip-ture, evangelicals stress the need for personal experience of the reality of Christ's salvation as well as the need to carry out the great commission to teach all peo-ple to be his disciples and to call all nations to repentance.[17]

A specific focus of debate over the meaning of "evangelical" in recent years has been the issue of biblical authority. Particular controversy has centered over the use of the term "inerrancy" to describe Scripture and whether that specific concept must be used to qualify for having an "evangelical" view of the Bible. Harold Lindsell in *The Battle for the Bible* claims that biblical in-errancy (as defined specifically by the theologians of the Old Princeton the-ology) has been the historic position of the Christian church throughout its history and must be maintained as "the badge of evangelicalism."[18] On the other hand, Donald Bloesch argues that

> today, some of the definitions of what it means to be evangelical are too nar-row. To equate evangelicalism with a belief in biblical inerrancy is to leave out many in the past and present who staunchly affirm the gospel in all its breadth and depth and yet who recoil from applying the term "inerrancy" to Scripture.[19]

The debates among "evangelicals" on these issues have produced a great volume of literature.[20]

Among those who define "evangelical" it is possible to see both those who use the term "inerrancy as a guiding criterion and those who do not. Among those in this latter category is the definition by Robert K. Johnston: Those who believe in "(1)the need for personal relationship with God through faith in the atoning work of Jesus Christ, and (2) the sole and binding authority of the Bible as God's revelation"[21] and Richard Quebedeaux: Those who believe in three major theological principles: "(1) the full authority of Scriptures in matters of faith and practice; (2) the necessity of personal faith in Jesus Christ as Savior and Lord (conversion); and (3) the urgency of seeking the conversion of sinful men and women to Christ (evangelism)."[22]

Emerging Evangelicalism

The Fundamentalist-modernist controversy dominated the decade of the 1920s in America.[23] Splits within denominations had occurred within the Presbyterian church with J. Gresham Machen and others continuing the traditions of classical Calvinism at Westminster Seminary and in Methodist, Episcopal, and Church of Christ churches throughout America, particularly in the North.[24]

During the 1930s fundamentalists struggled with "competing desires: they wished to separate themselves from a culture they thought was on its way to Armageddon, yet they still wanted to win that culture for Christ."[25] In the 1930s fundamentalist coalitions sought strength through evangelism and the building of religious communities. The economic depression of the 1930s was accompanied by a "spiritual depression" through which fundamentalism had "the popular support, structural strength, innovative flexibility, and reproductive potential to maintain its vitality."[26] In these times fundamentalism "produced a message that attracted many at a time when Americans were searching for a heritage to remember and conserve. Thus the movement was prepared to play a leading role in the postwar evangelical revival."[27] The three major motifs of fundamentalism during these years were separation, the Second Coming, and revival.[28]

Through a variety of media including radio and marked by the outstanding successes of fundamentalists preachers, such as Charles E. Fuller and "The Old Fashioned Revival Hour," fundamentalists by the beginning of the 1940s began to examine again their place on the American scene. Fundamentalist emphasis on separation had made them "insular and defensive, but now their desire for revival was leading many of them to seek fellowship and cooperation with other evangelicals. Revival would come, many thought, only as evangelicals put aside their quarrels and formed a great united front to accomplish the task."[29]

On September 17, 1941, fundamentalists under the leadership of Carl McIntire, a former follower of Machen who split from Westminster Seminary to establish the Bible Presbyterian Church, founded the American Council of

Christian Churches (ACCC). Their purpose was to attack the Federal Council of Churches and to provide a platform for those who were "militantly pro-Gospel and anti-modernist."[30] On April 7 and 8, 1949, a second group was formed in St. Louis with a more positive purpose in mind. From this emerged the National Association of Evangelicals (NAE), which was "a fundamentalist-initiated but genuinely inclusive fellowship that signaled the formation of a new evangelical coalition."[31] The leaders of this group said they were "determined to break with apostasy but...wanted no dog-in-manger, reactionary, negative or destructive type of organization." They wished instead for an organization "determined to shun all forms of bigotry, intolerance, misrepresentation, hate, jealousy, false judgment, and hypocrisy."[32]

While the ACCC and the NAE were completely united in doctrine, their policies were different. NAE membership was more inclusive with selective membership offered for members of the Federal Council of Churches. The ACCC held the attitude of "no cooperation, no compromise." The NAE adopted the position of "cooperation without compromise."[33] Soon the NAE had become "a major symbol and coordinating center of the evangelical resurgence." By 1947 it represented thirty denominations, totaling 1,300,000 members.[34] Today the NAE represents 30,000 churches and 3 1/2 million Christians.[35]

It was in 1947 that Ockenga called for "the new evangelicalism." According to Ockenga, by 1942 "evangelicalism" had become synonymous with fundamentalism as seen in the choice of the name National Association of Evangelicals. Yet, said Ockenga, "the new evangelicalism differs from fundamentalism in its willingness to handle the societal problems that fundamentalism evaded."[36] He asserted that

> the new evangelicalism embraces the full orthodoxy of fundamentalism, but manifests a social consciousness and responsibility which was strangely absent from fundamentalism. The new evangelicalism concerns itself not only with personal salvation, doctrinal truth and an eternal point of reference, but also with the problems of race, of war, of class struggle, of liquor control, of juvenile delinquency, of immorality, and of national imperialism....The new evangelicalism believes that orthodox Christians cannot abdicate their responsibility in the social scene.[37]

On a variety of fronts ranging through religious radio and television programs, youth evangelistic organizations, periodicals, publishing houses, seminaries, and parachurch organizations, "the new evangelicalism" has emerged as a significant American religious force. Among "the chief symbols of the evangelical establishment" have been, in addition to the National Association of Evangelicals, the Evangelical Theological Society (founded 1949);

Billy Graham, America's foremost evangelist who came to prominence in 1949; and the journal *Christianity Today* founded in 1956 and edited by Carl F. H. Henry and later Harold Lindsell.[38]

Continuing Classifications

The varieties and diversities within evangelicalism have led to numerous attempts at classifying contemporary positions. Some approach the issue on the basis of theological doctrines, others via ecclesiastical traditions, while still others look to a more sociological analysis.

A basic type of distinction is the type made by James Barr who designates "Fundamentalists" and "Evangelicals." Barr bases his distinctions on doctrinal attitudes, particularly attitudes about Scripture.[39]

Hunter has pointed out that generally there are four major religious and theological traditions that are present in contemporary American evangelicalism. These are (1) Baptist, (2) Holiness and Pentecostal, (3) Anabaptist, and (4) Reformational-Confessional traditions. He then provides denominational names for each of the four groups.[40]

Quebedeaux in his *The Young Evangelicals* (1974) distinguished among: (1) separatist fundamentalists, (2) open fundamentalists, (3) establishment evangelicals, (4) the new evangelicals and (5) the young evangelicals. For Quebedeaux these divisions take shape primarily around an assessment of how socially and politically "progressive" each group shows itself to be.[41] In *The Worldly Evangelicals* Quebedeaux designated three "subcultures" within evangelical Christianity as (1) fundamentalists, (2) charismatics and (3) neo-evangelicals whom he describes as "the direct descendants of fundamentalism" but who "broke with what they saw in fundamentalism as theological and cultural excesses—anti-intellectualism, sectarianism, social unconcern, and an almost complete repudiation of the values of the wider society."[42]

Bloesch offers the most comprehensive classifications of contemporary evangelicalism. He distinguishes fundamentalism from evangelicalism when he writes that

> Evangelicalism unashamedly stands for the fundamentals of the historic faith, but as a movement it transcends and corrects the defensive, sectarian mentality commonly associated with fundamentalism. Though many, perhaps most, fundamentalists are evangelicals, evangelical Christianity is wider and deeper than fundamentalism, which is basically a movement of reaction in the churches in this period of history. Evangelicalism in the classical sense fulfills the basic goals and aspirations of fundamentalism but rejects the ways in which these goals are realized.[43]

In this chapter on "The New Conservatism," Bloesch outlines the groups he considers part of the new conservatism in American Christianity today. He notes that

> all of the various strands in the new conservatism would gladly accept the term 'evangelical' with very few exceptions (mainly on the far right). Even pastors and theologians who stand in the theological tradition of Karl Barth and Emil Brunner have no compunction in identifying themselves as evangelical, though the left wing of the neo-orthodox movement might feel uncomfortable with this designation.[44]

Bloesch then describes: (1) fundamentalism, (2) neoevangelicalism, (3) confessionalist evangelicalism, (4) charismatic religion, (5) neo-orthodoxy and (6) Catholic evangelicalism.[45] He recognizes, however, that these categories are "ideal types." For "no one theologial or spiritual leader fits completely into any one type, and most have associations with various types."[46]

Within the category of neo-evangelicalism, Bloesch discerns two distinct strands. As he describes them,

> the first signifies a cautious opening to modern trends which might best be described as neofundamentalism. The second is a more progressive evangelicalism which seeks to move beyond a rigid position on biblical inerrancy. Both these movements wish to be known as evangelical rather than fundamentalist, but only the second is inclined to reject the fundamentalist label.[47]

With these continuing classifications of evangelicalism comes the realization that labels and categories must be used with care. This is why so much time is expended here on the subject. The problem becomes particularly evident also when positions on the nature of Scripture are examined.

Scripture in Neo-Evangelical Theology

The distinctions made by Bloesch between the "right" and "left" wings of neo-evangelicalism are especially helpful in regard to their views of Scripture. As Bloesch puts it: "While the right wing of the neoevangelical movement is particularly insistent on the inerrancy of Scripture, the moderate and left wings prefer to speak of the infallibility of Scripture."[48] He goes on to point out that

> following Hodge and Warfield, the right-wing evangelicals nonetheless qualify inerrancy, claiming that only the original manuscripts or autographs (which are no longer available) are without error. This allows for critical textual work on the various copies and translations. When moderate neoevangelicals employ

the term 'inerrancy' in reference to Scripture, they generally have in mind its teaching or doctrine.[49]

In dealing with the doctrine of Scripture in neo-evangelical theology, attention will be turned to the views of those in the "moderate" and "left" wings of this movement. The views of those on the "right" wing are encompassed in "scholastic theology," which shows the link between fundamentalism and the scholastic view of Scripture. Those who call themselves "neo-evangelical" and are on the "right" wing of that movement have come out of fundamentalism and have basically the fundamentalist view of Scripture as refined by the scholasticism of the Old Princeton theologians. Their primary identification now is "evangelicals" who hold to the Old Princeton view of the Bible, marked by their contention for the term "inerrancy." This, as mentioned above, for some has become the distinguishing mark of an "evangelical."[50]

The preference for the term "infallibility" when applied to Scripture is a distinguishing mark of those in the "moderate" and "left" wings of neo-evangelicalism.[51] Their attempts have been to approach the issue of Scripture without the emphasis on rational arguments to establish the Bible's authority and the attendant apologetic stance to defend the Bible's accuracy in matters of fact and history that are parts of scholastic theology. In this these neo-evangelicals see themselves as returning to the tradition of the sixteenth-century Protestant Reformers, particularly Luther and Calvin. These evangelicals see themselves as carrying on this Reformation tradition which in the nineteenth century was expressed by evangelicals such as T. M. Lindsay (1843-1914) and James Orr (1844-1913) in Scotland and Abraham Kuyper (1837-1920) and Herman Bavnick (1854-1921) in the Netherlands.[52] As these scholars reacted against the inerrancy views of the Old Princeton theologians in the nineteenth century, so now neo-evangelicals see themselves doing the same in the twentieth century. Positively, these evangelicals emphasize the Bible as the Word of God with its central purpose being to proclaim God's message to the world which comes through the human words of Scripture.

Faith and Reason

Many of the neo-evangelicals of this persuasion look also to the Dutch theologian G. C. Berkouwer (b. 1903) of the Free University of Amsterdam as a twentieth-century evangelical whose writings preserve the Reformation emphasis on the doctrine of Scripture.[53] Other significant writers on Scripture in this tradition include Donald Bloesch, Jack Rogers, and Bernard Ramm.[54]

In this view it is emphasized that faith and the knowledge of God are not based on the powers of human reason. This tradition looks back to the theological method of Augustine who saw that "faith leads to understanding."[55] Certain neo-evangelicals believe that the ability of humans to use their reasoning powers was not left untainted by the fall into sin. Since reason is affected by sin, reason itself (through theistic arguments or arguments about the divine origin of the Bible) cannot serve as the foundation on which humans build a knowledge of God. In writing on sin, Berkouwer said that "there is no limit or boundary within human nature beyond which we find some last human reserve untouched by sin; it is man himself who is totally corrupt."[58]

This means too that a "natural theology" which seeks to know God purely from human perceptions of the world and nature is impossible. As Berkouwer wrote:

> What is the background of this conception in which natural reason is considered capable of such knowledge? It is clear that specific anthropology is involved here, an anthropology or view of man which lifts the so-called rational soul out of the sin-depraved life of man, and then by way of this non-corrupt reason considers man capable of knowledge of God.[57]

As Bloesch put it, "any attempt to take the fall of man seriously will radically call into question the capacity of reason to discover or come to the truth."[58] This position does not deny "the possibility of a believing apologetic," says Berkouwer, "but an apologetic will have to begin with faith, not with uncertainty and doubt, if it is to be fruitful and a blessing to anyone."[59] Formal, rational apologetics is thus not first on the theological agenda.

According to neo-evangelicals, Scripture is accepted in faith and then through the use of reason one moves on to further understanding of the message of Scripture. This use of reason is what the Westminster Confession referred to as that which "by good necessary consequence may be deduced from Scripture."[60] Believers use their reason in the service of further obedience and understanding. As Bloesch puts it:

> Reason is not the foundation of faith, but it can be an exceedingly useful instrument of faith. We cannot share Leibniz's view that "faith must be grounded in reason," but we should certainly acknowledge that reason can serve faith. Natural reason can bring much light to bear upon such matters.
>
> It can be said that we reason *in* faith but not *to* faith. We do not arrive at faith by reason, but we can explicate faith by reason. It is not permissible to postulate a "Christian reason" (in the sense of a reason that is inherently Christian), but we can speak of a Christian exercise of reason.[61]

Authority of Scripture

For neo-evangelicals, the purpose of Scripture is to bring people to faith and salvation in Jesus Christ. It is the function of Scripture that is of primary concern.

Technically this is what the Reformers called the *scopus* or "goal" of Scripture, which means that the words of Scripture "are related to and tend toward a definite goal (Phil. 3:14)."[62] The Bible is a book that presents a gospel that does "not come to us as a timeless or 'eternal' truth or idea" but as "a message of salvation received, interpreted, and handed over by men."[63] This "intention and directedness" is made very clear in Scripture itself. There the words of Jesus are focused on a "concrete goal" which is salvation (John 20:31) that produces hope (Rom. 15:4) and is intended to equip the believer for every good work (2 Tim. 3:16).[64]

For Christian believers the Scriptures are authoritative. They are the inspired Word of God and as such present Jesus Christ to us by the work of the Holy Spirit. As Bavinck wrote, "Scripture is the word of God because the Holy Spirit witnesses of Christ in it, because it has the incarnate Word as its subject matter and content."[65] For Bloesch, "the Bible is authoritative because it is centered in Jesus Christ and conveys the truth about Christ."[66] In this the position of Calvin, who wrote that "the Scripture obtain full authority among believers" only when they are regarded as "having sprung from heaven, as if there the living words of God were heard," is reaffirmed.[67]

The authority of Scripture is underlined by the neo-evangelical understanding that "Scripture *is* the Word of God." Berkouwer cites the many instances of Jesus and others using the words "It is written" (Matt. 4:4; 4:7; 10; Mark 1:2; Luke 2:23; Acts 7:42) to indicate the authority of Scripture. These words

> functioned prominently as a last appeal and as a redeeming and blessed limitation of all human meditation and speculation (1 Cor. 4:6). "It is written" points to the source with decisive authority and with the intent to awaken faith in the heart....This arises out of a life with Scripture, to which all his [Jesus'] followers are called because the written Word comes to them with final saving authority.
>
> By its nature, the written Word can never be formally isolated, because precisely that written Scripture testifies of salvation and is directed toward that salvation. And in that context words can become living words (Acts 7:38).[68]

Thus there is an "authoritative function of the written Word."[69]

It is by the work of the Holy Spirit that the authority of Scripture comes to be known and established for believers. As Bloesch puts it, "the truth of revelation can be apprehended through the medium of the human language which attests it but only by the action of the Spirit."[70] For Berkouwer, it is of great importance that the Reformed confessions definitely do not view faith in Scripture as a preparation for true faith, or as a component of it which, if so desired, can be considered independent of it; but they connect faith in Scripture with the testimony of the Holy Spirit.[71]

The Holy Spirit rather than the church or any other "authority" witnesses that the Scriptures are the Word of God.

[For] only God himself is a sufficient witness to himself. The Word of God finds no acceptance until it is sealed by the inward witness of the Spirit, and the heart finds its rest in Scripture only through his inward teaching. Scripture is not subject to human argumentation and proof, and Scripture's own assuring power is higher and stronger than all human judgment.[72]

The witness of the Spirit is tied directly to the content of Scripture—the gospel message itself. Bavinck wrote that

the real object to which the Holy Spirit gives witness in the hearts of the believers is no other than the *divinitas* of the truth, poured out on us in Christ. Historical, chronological and geographical data are never in themselves, the object of the witness of the Holy Spirit.[73]

According by, "our faith in Scripture increases and decreases according to our trust in Christ."[74] Scripture's authority is directed toward its purpose and goal: salvation in Christ.

Inspiration

For neo-evangelicals, Scripture is to be interpreted in light of its central message of salvation. In line with Reformation emphases Scripture is its own interpreter and is to be interpreted in light of the analogy of faith.[75]

One image used to indicate the relationships of Scripture in this regard was expressed by Bavinck in his understanding of inspiration. He spoke of an "organic inspiration" using the picture of the human body to say that there is a center and periphery to Scripture just as in the human organism. For

in the human organism nothing is accidental, neither the length, nor the breadth, nor the color, nor the hue; but all does not therefore stand in the same close connection with the life center. Head and heart have a much more important place in the body than hand and foot, and these again stand in worth above nails and hair.[76]

This did not mean for Bavinck that there were different levels of inspiration in Scripture but rather that each part has its own function. Some parts were more directly related to the central message of Scripture than others. All Scripture is inspired by God (2 Tim. 3:16). God has used human writers to communicate God's Word. There is both a divine and human dimension to Scripture. Yet not all texts of Scripture are related in the same way to the main gospel message God wishes to communicate:

> The hair of the head participates in the same life as heart and hand....It is one Spirit, out of whom the whole of Scripture has come forth through the consciousness of the writers. But there is a difference in the way in which the same life is immanent and active in the various parts of the body. There are varieties of gifts, also in Scripture, but it is the same Spirit.[77]

While neo-evangelicals assert the inspiration of Scripture, they generally avoid speculative theories on how Scripture *is* the Word of God. They do not wish to produce a theory of inspiration. Berkouwer wrote that "The mystery of the God-breathed Scripture is not meant to place us before a theoretical problem of how Scripture could possibly and conceivably be both God's Word and man's word, and how they could be 'united.' It rather places us before the mystery of Christ."[78]

Infallibility

The preference of neo-evangelicals for the term "infallibility" of Scripture rather than "inerrancy" is reflected by their views of faith and reason, Scripture's authority, and inspiration. This theology stresses the central purpose of Scripture to be theological in nature—the revelation or self-communication of God. The authority of Scripture is established not be rational arguments but by the witness of the Holy Spirit. The Spirit witnesses to Scripture's content—Jesus Christ. One does not go to Scripture to answer human philosophical questions or to gain accurate information about ancient history, science, geography, or astronomy. One goes to Scripture to learn how to be related to God and to find how God wants people to live their lives in faithful obedience.

Given these understandings, neo-evangelicals prefer to speak of the "infallibility" rather than the "inerrancy" of Scripture. Infallibility refers to Scripture's complete trustworthiness and its ability to accomplish its purpose. Scripture is infallible, in this view, because it will not deceive humans about matters of salvation. It will not lead them into "error" which according to Berkouwer is biblically conceived as "a swerving from the truth and upsetting the faith (2 Tim. 2:18)."[79]

"Error" in the sense of sin and deception should not be relegated to the same lvele of the concept of "error" as "incorrectness." This "infallibility" position stands in contrast to the "nerrancy" view of scholastic theology which emphasizes the precision and accuracy of the original biblica texts in all matters on which they teach.[80]

SCRIPTURE AS MESSAGE

For neo-evangelicals who seek to stand in the tradition of how they read the Protestant Reformers, Scripture is the inspired Word of God which comes to the church through the words of human writers. Scripture contains a divine message expressed in human words. The thrust of Scripture is not to be a textbook of science nor to offer information on every human topic. As Berkouwer noted, "it is not that Scripture offers us no information but that the nature of this information is unique. It is governed by the *purpose* of God's revelation."[81] Scripture is infallible in accomplishing its purpose. For neo-evangelicals, "the purpose of the God-breathed Scripture is not at all to provide a scientific *gnosis* in order to convey and increase human knowledge and wisdom, but to witness of the salvation of God unto faith."[82] God has used humans to communicate the Word of God. As Berkouwer puts it, "when God speaks, human voices ring in our ears"; yet this "speaking of God through men is not a substitution of God's Word for that of man. It remains man's own speech through the Holy Spirit in the mission to speak words (Jer. 26:5): the authorization of this human speech is found in this mission."[83] Scripture gains its authority by the witness of the Holy Spirit who brings one both to faith in Christ and faith in Scripture. The Bible is God's active, living Word which through a variety of Scriptural forms presents God's message of salvation for the world. Through preaching, "the message of the gospel is expressed in living form."[84] One can live with Scripture "only when the message of Scripture is understood and is not considered 'a metaphysical document,' but a living instrument serving God for the proclamation of the message of salvation."[85]

VIII

EXISTENTIAL THEOLOGY
SCRIPTURE AS LIVING ENCOUNTER

In 1933 a forty-seven year-old man who fled from Nazi Germany began a new career in a new country. His new language was to be English instead of his native German. The man was Paul Tillich (1886-1965). On April 13, 1933 Tillich's name was on the first list of professors to be dismissed from German universities. At that time he was Dean of the philosophical faculty at the University of Frankfurt. Of the twelve suspended at Frankfurt, eleven were Jewish and Tillich was the other. Within one year, 1684 German scholars were removed from their posts. On May 10, 1933 Tillich witnessed the burning of books by Nazis in Frankfurt including the burning of his own book *The Socialist Decision*. By October, 1933 Gestapo members were following him in Dresden and after visiting family and friends, Tillich accepted the invitation to come to the United States to teach at Union Theological Seminary in New York City.[1]

Tillich's experiences helped shape the formation of his theological work. By the time of his death in 1965 Tillich was one of the most well-known and influential American theologians.[2] Tillich taught philosophical theology at Union Seminary until 1955. Then he became University Professor of Theology at Harvard until 1962 and Professor of Theology at the University of Chicago Divinity School until he died.[3] Throughout his career Tillich was concerned to speak to the questions of human existence in a way that was meaningful to contemporary persons.[4] This led him to develop his theology in a philosophical form and in dialogue with historic Christian thinkers as well as secular philosophers.[5]

Tillich's personal development which led him to emphasize both theology and philosophy is but one aspect of how he perceived "the way my ideas have developed from my life."[6] The rubric he used to describe this development was the image of "the boundary." He wrote as early as 1929 that "the boundary is the best place for acquiring knowledge."[7] In his autobiographical sketch published as *On the Boundary* Tillich chronicled his odyssey through a series of "between's" among which were: two temperaments, social classes, theory and practice, theology and philosophy, church and society, religion and culture, and Idealism and Marxism.[8] Thus it is not surprising that Tillich's theological thought is marked by polarities or concepts in tension with each other—a dialectical thinking with Tillich described in Volume II of his *Systematic Theology*:

> In a dialectical description one element of a concept drives to another. Taken in this sense, dialectics determine all life-processes and must be applied in biology, psychology, and sociology. The description of tensions in living organisms, neurotic conflicts, and class struggles is dialectical. Life itself is dialectical. If applied symbolically to the divine life, God as a living God must be described in dialectical statements.[9]

Existential Theology

Tillich's concern to correlate the polarities of human life as expressed in his "boundary" symbol affected all phases of his religious thought.

During World War I Tillich served in the German army as a chaplain. As the war progressed, Tillich faced the horrors of death and devastation, and he suffered a series of collapses. While he had initially been enthusiastic about the German war effort, he became increasingly disillusioned and disturbed by the role of political, ideological, and religious institutions in supporting such wholesale human death.[10] With the collapse of the old orders of German society, Tillich also recognized a collapse of the traditional conception of God. In the midst of a terrible battle Tillich reported he had a personal *kairos* or crisis time in which the philosophical underpinnings under which the war had been waged were destroyed. This was the philosophy of classical idealism which Tillich had imbibed from his philosophical studies of Hegel (1770-1831) and Schelling (1775-1854).[11] According to Tillich, "the idealists claim that their system of categories portrays reality as a whole rather than being the expression of a definite and existentially limited encounter with reality."[12] But in Tillich's war-time experience, this perception of reality was shattered. During this time he reported that he became an *existentialist*. Now he moved "from pure abstraction to a realization of the importance of encounters in living contexts. The war, for example, brought to Tillich the experience of the abyss of existence."[13]

After the war Tillich taught at the University of Marburg from 1924-1925 before moving to Frankfurt. At Marburg both Rudolph Bultmann and Martin Heidegger were lecturing. As Tillich later said, Heidegger's lectures at

Marburg, Heidegger's book *Sein and Zeit* (*Being and Time*), and Heidegger's interpretation of Kant helped him clarify the relationship between theology and philosophy. His further studies on Schelling (on whom he had written two dissertations), Kierkegaard, and Nietzsche led him to a full "acceptance of existential philosophy."[14] For Tillich, "existential philosophy asks in a new and radical way the question whose answer is given to faith in theology."[15] Theologians for Tillich have as their basic attitude a "commitment to the content" they expound for

> detachment would be a denial of the very nature of this content. The attitude of the theologian is 'existential.' He is involved—with the whole of his existence, with his finitude and his anxiety, with his self-contradictions and his despair, with the healing forces in him and in his social situation.[16]

Theological Method

Tillich's concerns and theological method are outlined in the Introduction to his three-volume *Systematic Theology*. Tillich explained that theology moves back and forth between two poles, the "eternal truth of its foundation" and the "temporal situation in which the eternal truth must be received."[17] This is seen in "kerygmatic theology," which emphasizes the unchangeable truth, and "apologetic theology," which is "answering theology"—addressing itself to the questions of the human "situation," humanity's own self-interpretation. Any honest theology must keep both aspects alive and synthesize them using a "method of correlation" to unite both message and situation.[18]

The theologian, Tillich maintained, enters into theological work with a concrete commitment to the validity of the Christian message. This comes by virtue of one's faith commitment in which one declares that the "ultimate concern" is with the Christian message, dealt with "scientifically" but yet nevertheless being acknowledged as unique and universally valid. This approach resolves the conflict between pietists and orthodoxy which in turn stress "faith" and "objectivity." It makes this ultimate concern with the Christian message the criterion for being "inside the theological circle," being a theologian.

At this point Tillich introduced two formal criteria of every theology. These are: 1) that it is the *object* of theology which concerns us ultimately. Thus theological propositions are only those that make the object of theology a matter of concern for us; and 2) "Our ultimate concern," wrote Tillich, "is that which determines our being and non-being." Thus, theological propositions are only those which "deal with their object in so far as it can became a matter of being or non-being for us."[19] "Being" is "the whole of human reality, the aim of existence." These two criteria point to the "boundary" situation between the "scientific" question of ultimate concern and the "faith" question of being.

For Tillich "theology is the methodical interpretation of the contents of the Christian faith."[20] As such it involves the *whole* activity of humans (not just "feeling" as in Schleiermacher) and is grounded definitively in "Jesus as the Christ," the Word become flesh, the union of the absolutely concrete and absolutely universal. This, Tillich argued, is "the only possible foundation for a Christian theology which claims to be *the* theology," for it is the only concept great enough to include *all* of thought and to conquer "cosmic pluralism."[21] If this assertion is accepted, Christian theology infinitely transcends all other theologies.

On the question of theology and philosophy, Tillich acknowledged that every theologian must be a philosopher in that the theologian questions reality as a whole, the quest of being. But there are three differences between the philosopher and theologian. First, the philosopher remains objective and detached toward questions. The theologian become involved in the object of the question and thus has an "existential concern." Secondly, there is a difference in their sources. The theologian is not just concerned with reality as a whole but also with one's ultimate concern, the *logos*. Thirdly, there is a difference in their content. The philosopher deals with categories as they appear in different material. But the theologian relates questions to the quest for new being.[22]

There is also, however, a convergence between philosophers and theologians. Both are concerned with being. But while the philosopher argues in the name of universal *logos* or "reason," the theologian is shaped by the appearance of a "particular *logos*" which reveals the meaning of the whole. Thus, "neither a conflict between theology and philosophy [is] necessary, nor is a synthesis between them possible." For there is no "common basis" for this relationship and no particularly "Christian" philosophy.[23] The Christian claim of Jesus Christ as the *logos* need not "include the claim that wherever the *logos* is at work agrees with the Christian message." Also, "no philosophy which is obedient to the universal *logos* can contradict the concrete *logos*, the Logos 'who become flesh.' "[24]

Tillich's third section deals with the organization of theology in which he considers the difference between historical and systematic theology.[25] In his section on the method and structure of systematic theology Tillich pointed to the three important questions of systematic theology: the question of its sources, the medium of reception, and the norm determining the use of these sources.

The source for systematic theology may be thought to be the Bible but Tillich argued there is more. For the Bible arose out of the church's history and this too must be a source. Included in this for Roman Catholics are the decisions of church councils and the popes. A broader source is the history of re-ligion and culture which interprets theologically the materials of pre-religious and religious humankind.[26] In all this there are degrees of im-portance that correspond in direct and indirect relationship to the central event of the Christian faith which is "the appearance of the New Being in Jesus as the Christ."[27]

But these sources can be so only to those who participate in them. Thus the element of existential or experiential concern is prominent. "Experi-ence" today is used in an ontological, scientific, and mystical sense, said Til-lich. But all of these fail as sources. The first excludes a divine being from its theology because it presupposes "an immediate participation in religious re-ality preceding any theological analysis of reality as a whole "in order to give one a concept of what a religious experience is."[28] Thus, the different philo-sophical conceptions of the nature of this religious experience arise.

The completely "scientific" description of experience fails since the object of theology is not within scientific experience and the object can be found only in acts of surrender and participation. Also, the "mystical experience" is not an acceptable criterion for theology since it is secretly presupposed by the ontological and the scientific and does not mediate anything new in us. The real question is "what does experience by participation reveal?"

If all these fall short of an acceptable criterion of experience, the one true criterion must be the experience of the unique event of Jesus the Christ. For "this event is given to experience and not derived from it. Therefore, experi-ence receives and does not produce."[29]

But the decisive question of the norm of theology is not yet answered. This is "the question of the criterion to which the sources as well as the me-diating experience must be subjected."[30] This norm must grow out of the church, as the church is the home of the systematic theologian and also the place where the theologian works. Tillich maintains that the proper norm, "the material norm of systematic theology today is the New Being in Jesus as the Christ as our ultimate concern."[31] The "new being" is based on St. Paul's concept of the "new creation" as the answer to the present and every human situation. This norm is "the criterion for the use of all sources of systematic theology."[32]

But how for Tillich is this norm to be related to the basic source for theol-ogy—the Bible? While the Bible is the basic source, yet as a "collection of re-ligious literature, written, collected, and edited through the centuries," there must be a theological norm to determine canonicity. This norm must be the collective experience of the church in maintaining as its content the Biblical message which grows within the medium of experience and is at the same time the criterion of any experience.[33]

In all this, systematic theology is not a history but a constructive task. Tillich raised the question of the place of reason or the rational character of systematic theology. The theologian is one who not only participates in the New Being but who can also express its truth in a methodical way. Yet reason is not a source of theology. It does not produce the contents of theology. While the theological norm must be a matter of personal and communal religious experience, it nevertheless must also be a matter of the methodological judgment of the theologian. Thus a problem is created that cannot be solved this side of the kingdom of God.[34]

However, certain directing principles can be brought forth. There is first the semantic principle which points to the need for the language of the theologian not to be "sacred" or "revealed" language. The second principle is logical rationality, which points to the desire to give "logical expression of the infinite tensions of Christian existence." It means that God's actions, while perhaps superseding and transcending finite reason, do not destroy or annihilate it. Thus is born the concept of paradox. Yet for Tillich there is only one genuine paradox in the Christian message. It is "the appearance of that which conquers existence under the conditions of existence. Incarnation, redemption, justification, etc., are implied in this paradoxical event."[35] The third principle is that of methodological rationality, which implies that theology follows a method and "a definite way of deriving and stating its propositions."[36]

The Method of Correlation

For Tillich, the method of correlation is the theological methodology of systematic theology. It is the forming of questions implied by the divine-human encounter and the corresponding answers implied in the divine self-manifestation under the guidance of the questions implied in human existence.[37] Tillich argued that systematic theology has always used the method of correlation

> sometimes more, sometimes less, consciously, and must do so consciously and outspokenly, especially if the apologetic point of view is to prevail. The method of correlation explains the contents of the Christian faith through existential questions and theological answers in mutual interdependence.[38]

Thus the answers of Christian "revelation" are "meaningful" only insofar as they are in correlation with questions concerning the whole of our existence, with existential questions."[39]

For Tillich, theology proceeds by making "an analysis of the human situation out of which the existential questions arise, and it demonstrates that the symbols used in the Christian message are the answers to these questions. The analysis of the human situation is done in terms which today are called 'existential.' "[40] All areas of culture contribute to the analysis of the human situation: philosophy, poetry, drama, the novel, therapeutic psychology, and sociology. The theologian "organizes these materials in relation to the answer given by the Christian message" and may make a more penetrating analysis of existence than that of many philosophers.[41]

In Tillich's view,

> the Christian message provides the answers to the questions implicit in human existence. These answers are contained in the revelatory events on which Christianity is based and are taken by systematic theology *from* the sources, *through* the medium, *under* the norm. Their content cannot be derived from the questions, that is, from an analysis of human existence. They are "spoken" *to* human existence from beyond it.[42]

This theological method of correlation replaces three inadequate methods: supranaturalistic, naturalistic, and the dualistic.

Thus Tillich's whole theological system proceded in a question/answer fashion. Its parts were "Being and God"; "Existence and Christ"; "Life and the Spirit"; "The Kingdom of God"; and an epistemological section as Part I of Volume I of his *Systematic Theology* on "Reason and Revelation."[43]

Scripture in Existential Theology

Reason

The categories of "reason" and "revelation" are major ones in the thought of Tillich and his theology of human existence.

For Tillich reason and revelation may be distinguished but not ultimately separated. There is no chasm between the two but a basic continuity between humans and God, between the "natural" and the "supernatural." Yet these are not identical.[44]

In his *Systematic Theology* (Vol. I) Tillich distinguished among various concepts of reason.[45] At its broadest, reason is the structure by which the mind grasps and shapes reality.[46] The "depth of reason" in Tillich's thought refers to the presence of the absolute (God) in the structures of both mind and reality. This presence is such that the mind never completely grasps the reality toward which it points yet it is never fully separated from it either.[47]

Since humanity has fallen into "existence" where it is estranged from the ground of its being (God), human reason is separated from ultimate union with God. Because of the conditions of existence, "reason in existence expresses itself in myth and cult," which while they "contradict essential reason, they betray by their very existence the 'fallen' state of a reason which has lost immediate unity with its own depth."[48]

For Tillich this implies that religious experience will naturally take expression in symbols. These symbols may participate in the reality to which they point and can unite a person with the depth of one's self and with the depth of all being, God.[49] Therefore, in Tillich's thought:

> all reality, especially the personal, participates in God and points to God symbolically when the ultimate manifests itself through its structures. All reality is thus potentially the material for religious experience and so potentially sacramental. On the other hand, no manifestation of God through created structure can be identified with God, for Tillich's system contains an inherent safeguard against idolatry.[50]

Since humans have fallen into "existence," salvation occurs only when the basic self is reunited with the ground of its being, God. This unity or "essentialization" comes when the content or *essentia*, the "definite power of being" is realized,"[51] In its fallen state of existence, reason needs "essentialization" to come to its true essence.[52] For Tillich this process of "salvation" comes by revelation.

Revelation

For Tillich, revelation is a special kind of knowledge, extraordinary in nature. In revelation, reason is driven beyond itself to "its 'ground and abyss,' to that which 'precedes' reason...to the original fact that there is *something* and not *nothing*."[53] This is the *mystery* of revelation and positively in this mystery one comes in *actual revelation* to recognize that it is God who is the "ground" or "the power of being conquering nonbeing."[54] Thus in revelation God is manifest and one's intellect comes to face the transcendent God. Since humans are fallen into "existence" and their reason can grasp only the finite and objects and since God is not finite nor an object—God is the transcendent source of all being. God

> cannot be reached by ordinary human knowledge. In order to acquire any genuine knowledge of God, therefore, it is necessary for the mind to overleap all finite categories and transcend the ordinary distinctions between subject and object. Extraordinary knowledge of this sort is what Tillich means by revelation.[55]

For Tillich, "revelation is the manifestation of what concerns us ultimately. The mystery which is revealed is of ultimate concern to us because it is the ground of our being."[56] Tillich points out that

> in the history of religion revelatory events always have been described as shaking, transforming, demanding, significant in an ultimate way. They derive from divine sources, from the power of that which is holy and which therefore has an unconditional claim on us.[57]

The "objective" side of revelation is that which manifests the divine as the mysterious ground of being. These events are "miracles." The reception of such occurrences in which the mind "transcends its ordinary situation" is "ecstasy."[58] Thus in Tillich's view

> what is given to us, therefore in revelation is no new body of information. There is no increase in our knowledge of nature, history and man. The insight which comes to us through a miracle and is acquired through ecstasy is perhaps best described as a new awareness of, or a new perspective on, that which is already known. We get knowledge about the revelation of the mystery of being, not just additional information. What we already know is clarified and its experiential value heightened by our discovery of its union with the ultimate.[59]

Revelatory events are united by common symbols. There is an "original" revelatory event in which, for example, a new religion is founded. In this both the "miracle" and the "ecstasy" are new and united for the first time. Specifically, Jesus with his disciples, Buddha with his disciples, or Moses and the people fleeing Egypt at the foot of Mt. Sinai would constitute original revelatory events. Original revelation is "given to a group through an individual. Revelation can be received originally only in the depth of a personal life, in its struggles, decisions, and self-surrender."[60]

A "dependent revelation" occurs in later generations where communities (and for Tillich, revelation always creates a community) find that they experience the power of the revelation for themselves. A dependent revelatory situation exists "in every moment in which the divine Spirit grasps, shakes, and moves the human spirit."[61] The original revelatory event is expressed through religious symbols. The symbols themselves become holy objects and then are the media through which new revelatory events occur. Thus, for Tillich,

> religious symbols provide the continuity among a set of dependent revelatory events and link them all to the original event. In the case of Christianity, the disciples of Jesus created a verbal symbol, the 'biblical picture of Jesus the Christ' which is cast in narrative form to express the fact that the original revelatory event had occurred and that they personally had participated in it. This picture thereafter occasions dependent revelatory events as it is read or preached in church.[62]

In the Christian view, the final revelation is the biblical picture of "Jesus as the Christ."[63] This original revelation was given through Jesus to his disciples but continues to the present day as a dependent revelation in the church and through the church until the end of time. Christianity itself "as Christianity is neither final nor universal. But that to which it witnesses is final and universal."[64] This final revelation in Christ was "not an isolated event. It presupposed a revelatory history which was a preparation for it and in which it was received.[65] This is the "history of revelation." It is "universal" in the sense that it can take place anywhere at any time. The "concrete" revelations related to Christianity were to the Jewish people and are recorded in the Old Testament. In the New Testament are the basic documents relating to the final revelation of God in Jesus Christ. Thus the Bible is a record of God's revelation.

Revelation and Salvation

Crucial to Tillich's thought is that "the history of revelation and the history of salvation are the same history. Revelation can be received only in the presence of salvation, and salvation can occur within a correlation of revelation."[66]

> Salvation is derived from *salus*, 'healthy' or 'whole', and it can be applied to every act of healing: to the healing of sickness, of demonic possession, and of servitude to sin and to the ultimate power of death. Salvation in this sense takes place in time and history, just as revelation takes place in time and history.[67]

While "salvation and revelation are ambiguous in the process of time and history," for Tillich, "the Christian message points to an ultimate salvation which cannot be lost because it is reunion with the ground of being."[68] Salvation is not individualistic in that individuals are isolated from each other. Rather "fulfillment is universal" and in the symbol of "the kingdom of God" there is "complete transparency of everything for the divine to shine through it. In his fulfilled kingdom, God is everything for everything. This is the symbol of ultimate revelation and ultimate salvation in complete unity."[69]

Revelation and the Word of God

Traditionally the doctrine of revelation has been developed as a doctrine of the "Word of God." Tillich points out that in the concept of Jesus Christ as *logos*, "Logos points to a revelatory reality, not to revelatory words." For Tillich "the doctrine of the Logos prevents the elaboration of a theology of the spoken or the written word, which is *the* Protestant pitfall."[70]

The term "Word of God" has six different senses, according to Tillich.[71]

1. The Word is "the principle of the divine self-manifestation in the ground of being itself." The ground of being has "the character of self-manifestation; it has *logos* character."

2. The Word is "the medium of creation." In contrast to Greek philosophical (neo-Platonic) emanations, the *Logos* as the medium of creation points to both the freedom of creation and the freedom of the created.

3. The Word is "the manifestation of the divine life in the history of revelation."

4. The Word is "the manifestation of the divine life in the final revelation." The "Word" is a name for Jesus as the Christ. It is not the words *of* Jesus but

"the being of the Christ, of which his words and his deeds are an expression."

5. The Word is also applied to "the document of the final revelation and its special preparation, namely, the Bible." Yet for Tillich, to use the expression "Word of God" for the Bible will mean that "theological confusion is almost unavoidable." Scripture is the Word of God in two senses. It is the document of final revelation and "it also participates in the final revelation of which it is the document." In Tillich's view, "nothing has contributed more to the misinterpretation of the biblical doctrine of the Word than the identification of the Word with the Bible."

6. The Word is also "the message of the church as proclaimed in her preaching and teaching." Human words and language become "the Word" when they are spoken in power and their content received existentially by listeners.

In conclusion, for Tillich

the many different meanings of the term 'Word' are all united in one meaning, namely, 'God manifest'—manifest in himself, in creation, in the history of revelation, in the final revelation, in the Bible, in the words of the church and her members. 'God manifest—the mystery of the divine abyss expressing itself through the divine Logos—this is the meaning of the symbol, the 'Word of God.'[72]

The Nature of Scripture

For Tillich the Bible is a source of revelation and participates in the revelation because the biblical writers wrote as living witnesses to the revelation they encountered.[73] Their participation was "their response to the happenings which became revealing events through this response." Tillich defined the "inspiration" of the biblical writers as

their receptive and creative response to potentially revelatory facts. The inspiration of the writers of the New Testament is their acceptance of Jesus as Christ, and with him, of the New Being, of which they became witnesses. Since there is not revelation unless there is someone who receives it as revelation, the act of reception is a part of the event itself. The Bible is both original event and original document; it witnesses to that of which it is a part.[74]

The Bible for Tillich, while written in ordinary human words is not merely the communication of information. If it were only "information," it would "not have the power of grasping, shaking, and transforming, the power which is attributed to the 'Word of God.' "[75] Words are the indispensable media of all revelation.

But the word of revelation "cannot be spoken apart from revelatory events in nature, history and man."[76] The words of the Bible would mean nothing apart from the revelatory events in history to which they witness. Thus, since "the knowledge of revelation can be received only in the situation of revelation, and it can be communicated—in contrast to ordinary knowledge—only to those who participate in this situation,"[77] the Bible does not convey new content but a new dimension of ultimate meaning. The nature of Scripture as revelation is such that it enables a person to enter into the same revelatory events described in the Bible and to share in the same ecstatic experiences as the biblical writers who witnessed to God's final revelation in Jesus Christ.

SCRIPTURE AS LIVING ENCOUNTER

The Bible for Tillich presents a collage of religious symbols which express the revelatory events witnessed to by the biblical writers. Revelation and salvation are identical so that through the Scripture one gains "an existential understanding of revelation, that is, a creative and transforming participation of every believer in the correlation of revelation."[78]

Biblical religious symbols are authoritative for Tillich

> because they fulfill two functions: They *express* the occurrence and content of the original revelation in Jesus as the Christ, and they *occasion* dependent revelatory events having precisely the same content as the original one. The continuity of content between the original and dependent events apparently hangs entirely on the fact that the same symbols function in them all. Thereby the symbols, and above all the 'biblical picture,' effectively link us with the healing power mediated to [humans] by Jesus of Nazareth.[79]

The climax of biblical revelation is the symbol of "Jesus as the Christ." For in this symbol the biblical writers witness to revelation by saying that in the unique event of Jesus of Nazareth the power of the "New Being" was present as nowhere else.[80] Through the symbols of the Bible, humans are brought into a living encounter with Jesus as the Christ. This biblical picture can and does mediate the power of new being to sinful, estranged humans today.[81] For Tillich it is "the Christian claim that the biblical picture of Jesus as the Christ does sometimes serve as the occasion for such healing events today."[82] These are "healing events" of "salvation" (*salus*) and thus "revelation." For the power of being is mediated to humans through holy objects (the Bible) which rescue humans in estranged existence from the threat of "nonbeing" and aid in their quest for healing and wholeness.

106

IX

PROCESS THEOLOGY
SCRIPTURE AS UNFOLDING ACTION

One of the most significant contemporary theological movements among professional theologians today is process theology. It has developed from process philosophy and has been evolving into its present sophisticated forms since the 1920s. The emphasis on the dialectical theology of neo-orthodoxy since the 1930s gave way to a host of particularized theologies in the 1960s, such as theologies of race, revolution, ecology, and feminism. But in the return of theologians to the search for a system of theology, process theology has offered a new and comprehensive way of viewing basic realities and theological concepts.[1] Process theology presents "an immanent God who is known by rational reflection on human experience."[2]

BACKGROUNDS

Whitehead

Contemporary process theology is built on the philosophical thought of Alfred North Whitehead (1861-1947). Whitehead taught mathematics at Cambridge University from 1885-1910.[3] From 1911-1924 he taught in London and with his former student Bertrand Russell wrote a three-volume work *Principia Mathematica* (1910-1913) which helped create a new framework for logic. In 1922 Whitehead's *The Principle of Relativity with Applications to Physical Science* presented an alternative to Einstein's theory of relativity.

When Whitehead was 63 years old in 1924, he moved to Harvard University to teach philosophy, though he had previously not taught in that discipline. During the next thirteen years Whitehead produced eight books and a number of articles. His major work *Process and Reality* contained his Gifford lectures which had been delivered at the University of Edinburgh in 1927-1928.[4] During his time at Harvard, Whitehead began to develop a new metaphysic which would present a comprehensive picture of reality. His work *Science and the Modern World* outlined his new views which led him to deal with the nature of God and traditional static views of religion.[5] Other American thinkers such as John Dewey applauded Whitehead's work as offering an important new framework to relate personal values and scientific facts. Whitehead's 1926 book *Religion in the Making* argued that humanity's deepest vision of reality is embodied by religion.[6]

Metaphysics

Whitehead's metaphysic rested on the notion of process. This he spoke of as a "philosophy of organism." For Whitehead, the entire universe was

> a vast, creative movement, a 'process', involving multifarious levels of interrelated elements which he called 'actual entities'. These ranged from God himself at one end of the scale to the slightest 'puff of existence' at the other. Each of these entities was 'bi-polar', with both a 'physical' and a 'mental' aspect—though only above a certain level did the latter attain the intensification which produced 'consciousness'. The mental aspect at all levels enabled what he called 'prehension', by which the different entities linked up with and related to each other. Through the whole network of prehensions and interactions, the universe was integrated as a dynamic, developing whole, a cosmic symphony.[7]

Whitehead believed that

> the temporal process is a 'transition' from one actual entity to another. These entities are momentary events which perish immediately upon coming into being. The perishing marks the transition to the succeeding events. Time is not a single smooth flow, but comes into being in little droplets. A motion picture suggests an analogy: the picture appears to be a continuous flow, whereas in reality it is constituted by a series of distinct frames.[8]

What Whitehead called "occasions of experience" stressed that actual entities arise, become, reach completion, and then are past. Yet

> the things that endure are series of these occasions of experience. Electrons, molecules, and cells are examples of such enduring things. Likewise the human soul, or stream of experience, is composed of a series of distinct occasions of experience.[9]

All experiences are related to previous experiences through a multiplicity of relations. A momentary experience becomes distinct in itself by how it reacts to and is unified with these relations. Thus the ways these relate are called "prehension" and "feeling." The present occasion "prehends" or "feels" occasions that have gone before. The present occasion is "nothing

but its process of unifying the particular prehensions with which it begins."[10]
To summarize this view:

Each of Whitehead's occasions of experience begins, as it were, as an open window to the totality of the past, as it prehends all the previous occasions (either immediately or mediately). Once the rush of influences enters in, the window is closed, while the occasion of experience forms itself by response to these influences. But as soon as this process is completed, the windows of the world are again open, as a new occasion of experience takes its rise. Hence, the next molecular occasion within that series constituting the enduring molecule, or the next moment of human experience within that stream of experiences constituting the soul, is open to the contributions that can be received from others.[11]

This means too that

Whiteheadian process thought gives primacy to interdependence as an ideal over independence. Of course, it portrays interdependence not simply as an ideal but as an ontologically given characteristic. We cannot escape it. However, we can either exult in this fact or bemoan it.[12]

God

This basic view of reality has implications for the process view of God. For Whitehead, "one all-pervasive fact, inherent in the very character of what is real is the transition of things, the passage one to another."[13] Or again, he wrote: "It belongs to the nature of a 'being' that it is a potential for every 'becoming.' This is the 'principle of relativity.' "[14] Thus, "how an actual entity *becomes* constitutes *what* that actual entity is....Its 'being' is constituted by its 'becoming.' This is the 'principle of progress.' "[15]

Process philosophy when it speaks of God is sometimes called "dipolar theism." Charles Hartshorne (b. 1897), Whitehead's former teaching assistant and Professor of Philosophy at the University of Chicago from 1928-1955, describes God as having two "poles" or aspects. One is the abstract essence of God, the other is God's concrete actuality.[16] God's abstract essence is eternal, absolute, independent, and unchangeable. At every moment, the divine existence is marked by these aspects. God's concrete actuality is temporal, relative, dependent, and changing constantly. In God's life each moment produces new, unforeseen happenings in the world. God's concrete knowledge thus depends upon decisions made by people or actualities in the world. Thus God's knowledge is "always relativized by, in the sense of internally related to the world."[17]

Whitehead's description of the nature of God varied from Hartshorne's. Whitehead spoke of the primordial and the consequent nature of God. The "primordial nature" may be defined as the mental pole in God. The primordial nature is God's grasp of all possibilities. This grasp involves an ordering evaluation of possibilities into a harmony which is called the 'primordial vision.'[18]

The "consequent nature" of God according to Whitehead may be said to be "the physical pole in God." This is "God's feelings of the world. It is 'consequent' in a twofold sense: first, it follows from the primordial nature in God, and second, it follows from the actual happenings in the world."[19]

God is intimately related to this world in that God participates in all that happens in the world and all that happens makes an impression on God. For Whitehead "God related entities to each other on a grand order as God integrated the physical feelings of God's consequent nature with the conceptual feelings of God's primordial nature."[20] In contrast to traditional theism which stressed the divine absoluteness and "simplicity," process thought stresses that the divine relativity enters into the world of "feelings." This means that

> the divine relativity is not limited to a 'bare knowledge' of the new things happening in the world. Rather, the responsiveness includes a sympathetic feeling with the worldly beings, all of whom have feelings. Hence, it is not merely the content of God's knowledge which is dependent, but God's own emotional state. God enjoys our enjoyments, and suffers with out sufferings. This is the kind of responsiveness which is truly divine and belongs to the very nature of perfection.[21]

The implication for Christians is that this view of God is also "the ideal for human existence. Upon this basis, Christian *agape* can come to have the element of sympathy, of compassion for the present situation of others, which it should have had all along."[22]

SCRIPTURE IN PROCESS THEOLOGY

Doctrine and Authority

Contemporary process theologians see the compatibility of Whitehead's analysis of reality with basic features of the Christian faith. Religious doctrine is a structured form that is given to beliefs that one consciously holds. For process theologians these beliefs are derived from

> induction, deduction, and authority, as well as from immediate experience, and there is a great diversity among them. Belief at this level must be distinguished from the complex of prereflective beliefs that we all hold in common, since we all immediately apprehend a common reality in every moment of our experience. These deeper beliefs are originally preconscious and prereflective. They may or may not emerge into conscious awareness.[23]

When beliefs emerge into conscious awareness and take the forms of conscious beliefs, they have profound effects on human existence. Christian doctrines

> which are explications of universal aspects of experience have importance in the same way. For example, they lift into consciousness certain aspects of the universal experience of deity, such as divine grace....Christian doctrine, by selecting certain features of experience for conscious emphasis, shapes attitudes, purposes, and commitments, and even the structure of human existence itself.[24]

For process theologians following Whitehead, religious doctrines can be accepted only if they are self-evident.[25] This does not mean that the doctrine will be equally obvious to all people, because not everyone has the same ability to "perceive the previously unformulated factors in experience."[26] When these have been perceived consciously and then verbally expressed, others may recognize them. Whitehead used an analogy of a tuning fork and a piano. The piano responds to the note struck by the tuning fork only because it has a string that is tuned to the same note that the turning fork emits.[27] People may assent to and affirm doctrines as verbal expressions of a universally experienced fact because they have already perceived the fact. The verbal form (doctrine) brings the perception to the conscious level and will make it become more important in one's life. It could in fact become a central principle around which one's whole life might be organized.[28] Theology's task in this view is to state the basics of one's beliefs so they call forth a response of perception from others who find them self-evidently true.

Besides doctrines, other things are self-evident to humans as well. The reality of the external world is one of these. It is thus possible for one's "prethematic" or prereflective view of reality also to become conceptualized. When this happens it may receive validity as an expression of one's experience. In the philosophy of Whitehead, process theologians find an accurate description of the human experience of reality.[29]

The Functions of Scripture

The Bible for process theologians may serve several functions. First, it may be used as a source for doctrine. Since doctrine represents the explication of universal aspects of experience it is entirely possible and likely that the Christian Scriptures may be used as a source for finding data or materials that will help toward the explication of these universal aspects of experience.

One example of how this may work can be seen in process Christology and specifically in the doctrine of the incarnation of Jesus Christ. There are varieties among process theologians with regard to Christology just as there are on other topics as well.[30]

One process Christology proceeds as follows: "Special revelation" may be considered as taking place "through intensifying the image of God in human consciousness. While this may occur in an ultimate sense in Jesus, revelation begins far before that time in the long history of Israel."[31] Through the covenant in the Old Testament, God established a relationship with Adam, Noah and Abraham. Through the covenant,

> God's will toward justice in relationships is revealed; through the people's participation in the covenant, justice in relationships is enacted in society. Faithfully, God lures the people into being a people who will reflect the divine character. Insofar as the people become a society of justice, the image of God is created in human society; insofar as they fall away, the image is distorted. Always the constancy of God is like a goad, pricking the people into relationships which exhibit justice, and therefore fulfill the covenant.[32]

In a process world, "God acts with the world as it is, leading it toward what it can be. The aims of God will transcend the given, but must also reflect the given."[33] Throughout the Old Testament, God's revelation builds and

> Christian history builds upon Israelite history. The richness of Judaism made Christianity possible. The revelation of the nature of God, seen and still seen through a whole people, was also given through the one person, Jesus. Through this one, yet another people are given birth so that they too might reflect the image of God.[34]

In this one person Jesus, according to the process theologian, both the nature of God and the nature of what humanity is called to be are revealed. This person may thus be called "Immanuel, God with us."[35]

In distinction from traditional Christology, however, in process thought,

> if all this it to be achieved by a human person incarnation cannot be a once-for-all happening but must be a continuous process. In process thought a person is not one actual occasion but a series of many, many occasions. For incarnation to occur, there would have to be an assent to incarnation in every moment of existence. Incarnation would have to be continuous.[36]

From this one may examine the gospel accounts of Jesus of Nazareth and see his character. This character also reveals the character of God and thus Jesus becomes the special revelation of God. As Suchocki puts it:

> No matter which gospel text we take to consider the life of Jesus, we are confronted with one who consistently manifests the love to which he calls others. He breaks down all partitions that divide humans from each other; he embodies a love that is just, and a love that therefore variously exhibits judgment, affirmation, service, or sharing, depending upon the context of love. But this is the life

which reveals the nature of God for us; this is the life which offers a concrete vision of the reality to which God calls us; this is the revelation of God to us for the sake of conforming us to that divine image. If we see in Jesus a revelation of God for us, then the way Jesus loves is the way God loves.[37]

In process thought, "to see the life of Jesus as God with us, incarnate in him, is to lift all that we see in that revelation to ultimacy."[38]

It is clear here that the Bible functions as a source for this "doctrine of the incarnation" because Scripture provides the data from which the doctrine springs. But the doctrine itself, as a Christian doctrine, formally expresses what people will find when they encounter the biblical picture of Jesus of Nazareth. In this sense it will confirm what is self-evident.[39]

However, doctrinal statements that originate from Christian Scripture are not to be accepted only through appeals to authority.[40] They must be judged on the basis of their self-evidency. In this case of the doctrine of the incarnation, the question would be about how the nature of God is revealed through God's presence in Jesus and how this perception about Jesus coincides with what process thought believes about God. As such, this doctrine with its source in the biblical data should be presented (as Cobb and Griffin state) "in such a way as to elicit a responsive perception of these as self-evidently true."[41]

In response to these theological questions, Suchocki's statements are relevant. She writes:

> How, then, is the nature of God revealed through God's presence in Jesus? Consider Jesus' openness to others in relation to the sense in which God, through the consequent nature, feels every reality in the universe precisely as that reality feels itself. What is added to the philosophical statement by the biblical revelation is that the openness to all which is stated philosophically is a loving openness. Jesus reveals the character of God as love. In Jesus, openness to the other is in the mode of love; in God, openness to the other which feels the other regardless of place, position, or power is an openness of love. Jesus is open to the other with a will toward the well-being of the other: the openness of God through the consequent nature must therefore be an openness which wants the well-being of the other. Process philosophy requires that every prehension be felt with a certain 'subjective form' or qualifying feeling. The revelation of God in Jesus tells us that God's subjective form in feeling the world is love.[42]

Thus it is clear that the affirmation of God's presence of Jesus which is verbalized as a "doctrine of the incarnation" is a self-evident perception arising from the biblical picture of Jesus of Nazareth and how that figure Jesus exemplified in his life and actions the consequent nature of God. The attitudes and actions of Jesus coincide with the experienced reality of a God who "feels every reality in the universe precisely as that reality feels itself."

The biblical picture adds to the philosophical picture by presenting Jesus acting in the mode of love. This love can then be perceived as the feeling of the prehension or the feeling of the other in the universe. A further development of this model of process Christology occurs when Suchocki goes on to answer how Jesus who "loves with a mutuality which invites giving and receiving" is like God. This is seen in that for Suchocki, "the fullness of the revelation of God does not stop with the life of Jesus, but continues through the crucifixion and resurrection."[43] There is thus an "interplay" between human experience as understood via process modes of expression and doctrines derived from the Bible. In these discussions too, Scripture becomes a source for helping to describe (in doctrines) the unfolding action of God in this world.

A second function of Scripture in process thought is for the Bible to present possibilities of experience that go beyond the experience of a society not informed by Scripture. An example of this would be the Christian experience of the grace of God. Events or modes of relationships may be opened by Scripture even though they have not yet been a particular part of our own experience. In this sense again, the Bible introduces us to the unfolding action of God as people turn and return to the Scriptures and find their returns continuing to bear new insights and inspiration. As Cobb and Griffin write:

> Nevertheless, our immediate experience is the final court of appeal. We have faith in the continued fruitfulness of returning to the first accounts of and reactions to Jesus' life for new insights because of the repeated fruitfulness of this return in the past. But this fruitfulness must finally prove itself in our own experience, or faith in the continuing relevance of Jesus will decline in company with other beliefs that do not ring true for us.[44]

As one turns to Scripture, one's own experience is both confirmed and enlarged by encountering the continual evolution of God and God's relationship with the world.

SCRIPTURE AS UNFOLDING ACTION

From this survey of process theology it is apparent that process theology is closely related to process philosophy. This philosophy is a comprehensive view of reality that stresses "becoming" rather than "being," and this fundamental direction significantly affects the whole of Christian theology. Traditional Christian doctrines are redefined within the process system.

Process theology views of Scripture and its nature are closely related to its views of reality and the nature of God. Scripture may be a source for "doctrine," but it derives its authority from its concurrence with one's own self-evident experience. To interpret Scripture the process view of reality is to be used, which itself is validated by its self-evidence.

Scripture may be seen in this system to be a source among others through which one perceives the unfolding action of God in the world. As one turns to the Bible and finds experience confirmed or enlarged, one may experience a way by which God can be known. By opening new avenues of experience, Scripture provides the means through which humans can relate to God and the avenue by which the "divine relativity" may become real to humans. As a source for insight and inspiration, Scripture opens new possibilities of experience to us. The process view of God presents a deity evolving with creation into the new possibilities of the future, which is much closer, process theologians argue, to the biblical witness of a God who is active in time and history and who relates to humans in responsive love. The traditional picture of God as static and absolute is discarded. The story of the Bible is thus continued in our own "stories" as humans progress into their futures with a God who grows with the world and works together with humanity for a better and more unified world of tomorrow. Scripture may introduce us to this unfolding action of God.

X

STORY THEOLOGY
SCRIPTURE AS MEDIUM FOR METAPHORS

"Story theology" is a general name for a number of contemporary attempts to emphasize the dimension of narrative in theology and Scripture. As one writer has put it: "There is currently a stir among students of religion about 'narrative theology'—the way or ways in which the ideas of religion may be expressed in story form."[1] While there are varieties of approaches, "these 'theologies of story,' or 'narrative' theologies as they are sometimes called, broadly agree that the way toward theological renewal lies in the reconception of theology as story."[2] Put in its widest context,

> narrative theology is discourse about God in the setting of story. Narrative (in its narrow sense) becomes the decisive image for understanding and interpreting faith. Depiction of reality, ultimate and penultimate, in terms of plot, coherence, movement, and climax is at the center of all forms of this kind of talk about God.[3]

It is the contention of these theologians that the most potent and vital religious, theological, and biblical insights are transmitted through narrative structures, especially stories. To those engaged in story theology, significant help and insight can come from a variety of fields of study. Literary criticism is a natural source for learning the structures and flow of narratives. Psychology with its insights into the human mind and perceptions can help in seeing how narratives may function in shaping behavior. Linguistics offers clues on how human language itself is constructed and how it operates when certain semantic forms are employed. Social ethics can examine how stories function in shaping the identities and actions of whole communities or religious groups. Communications theory can probe how stories are transmitted and how they are perceived by their various receptors. So in the study of "story," a number of disciplines can contribute important dimensions.

The variety of approaches for the study of narratives in themselves is seen in the multiple ways by which story theologians operate. Some are more heavily influenced by a particular discipline than are others. It is important to recognize that theology and the study of Scripture in themselves are crucial components for the establishment of narrative or story theology. Within the Christian context, the Bible and Christian tradition provide the basic data both in which narratives are found and from which stories can be constructed or analyzed. Thus a number of background features go into the formation of story theology and the work of theologians who stress "narrative" today.

BACKGROUNDS

Importance of Stories

Contemporary studies of preliterate cultures have well underlined the significance of storytelling in these societies. Through the power of verbal narratives—tribal myths, legends, tales—the intellectual, social, and religious shape of the world was formed. Oral traditions passed from "generation to generation" and included sacred stories about gods and heroes, tales of the cosmos, wisdom about human behavior, nature, and the miraculous. Personal and social identities were shaped by these stories. Leadership roles, systems of kin, social structures, and accepted behavior patterns were transmitted through these stories. In other words,

> these stories served the metaphysical function of linking the individual to the mystery of the universe as a whole, telligible and heuristic image of nature, the sociological function of articulating and enforcing a specific social and moral order, and the psychological function of marking a pathway to guide the individual through the various stages of life. Ritually enacted and socially imposed, these stories patterned the thinking and living of all members within a given tribe or culture.[4]

Yet despite the vast differences between earlier cultures and our own industrialized, technologized society, stories have not disappeared. Television, movies, advertisements, books, magazines, records, and even little children repeatedly tell us stories. Personal and cultural stories are still enacted and transmitted. While they are more fragmented and diverse than those of previous societies, nevertheless, "stories still give the fundamental shape to personal and social identity in the modern world."[5]

Power of Stories

From ancient times the inherent power of stories has been recognized by people in all walks of life. Besides helping to shape personal and corporate understandings, stories have also the power to evoke action. How stories are formed, how they function, and how they are perceived have been extensively analyzed and probed so a clearer view of the power of the story can be established.[6]

In terms of structure, stories can be characterized as to plot, setting, characterization, and point of view. Various types of stories include tragedy, comedy, elegy, etc. The modes of narrative embrace myth, legend, folktale, epic, romance, allegory, fable, chronicle, satire, biography, autobiography, novel, and short story. Yet, "the careful articulation of these various narrative elements has only clarified what the unlettered folklorist and the growing child know—stories have power over human imagination and behavior because they ring true to life."[7] Stories have the uncanny knack of revealing in a moment of time or saturating our consciousness with penetrating truths about our own lives, our cultures, and our world. They convey this power often in moving and memorable ways.

More technically, explanations have been given as to the common features of narrative, why stories generate their power, and how this happens. In summary, today

> many narrative theologians hold that the power of great stories, including the sagas of faith, lies in their resonance with who and what we most essentially are. Robert Roth points to their purposiveness as kindling a universal human hope; Stephen Crites views them as reflecting the 'tensed modalities' of memory, attention, and anticipation; Metz finds them honoring the facts of suffering and conflict; Robert Alter stressed the place they give to human decision. In each case the constituents of story structure appear: cumulative action in all its suspense and tension depicted as moving toward resolution, led there by narrator vision.[8]

The intimate relationship between human language and perceptions of life has led contemporary philosophers, social scientists, and literary artists to see that "the impact of a story is not limited to the life exemplified or the principle illustrated in the story. Stories have the power to shape life because they formally embody the shape of life."[9] As one observer has put it: Stories have their beginning, end and "in-between time" featuring characters interacting through critical and dramatic moments through relationships that progressively unfold. All elements of the story advance this story line. When the themes of the story have run their course, the story ends—either happily or unhappily. The individual stories presuppose others, as parts of larger episodes which shape and color these stories.[10]

Our lives as well begin and end with the times "in-between" spent "making sense" of the people we know and experiences we have. We have "givens"—age, sex, education, and health—as well as personalities and circumstances that frame the limits of life. The patterns that emerge from life may take any shape as we continually fashion them as we wish within the parameters of our situations. Further, "life is always a movement toward completing the life forms we are living, and thus human life is always seen from ending rather than beginning."[11] Our individual lives take their meaning within the context of larger communities: family, society, culture, race, earth, cosmos, and "whatever 'other worlds' there might be."[12]

There seems to be an inherent "narrative quality" underlying all human experience. Thus,

> both time and space are experienced in all their concrete expressions in an inherently narrative way. The human experience of time would be impossible without memory and anticipation. Without memory, experience would lack all coherence. Without anticipation, experience would lose all direction. But memory and anticipation can be held together without dissolving the present into sheer succession only if the remembered past and anticipated future are taken up in stories.[13]

If there is a narrative structure underlying human experience it is entirely understandable why storytelling is a universal method of cultural expression and why it appeals so powerfully to personal experience.

STORY THEOLOGIES

Several typologies or models have been suggested as ways of categorizing various contemporary story or narrative theologies.[14]

(1) *Introduction to Religion.* This approach uses narrative or story as a way to understand the study of religion in general or Christianity in particular. It is represented by a number of contemporary writers. Among these are: Sam Keen, *To a Dancing God*, Harvey Cox, *The Seduction of the Spirit*, Michael Novak, *Ascent of the Mountain, Flight of the Dove*, Robert Roth, *Story and Reality*, Gabriel Fackre, *The Christian Story*, and John Shea, *Stories of God*.[15]

In this approach, "narrative" is used to "describe and explain the location of religion in human experience and the meaning of 'faith' in relation to a person's encounter with other people and the world."[16] Human experience is perceived as having a "religious" dimension which is related with the stories people tell about themselves and those that help structure their worlds.

(2) *Life Story.* The relationship of narratives to human experience is explored by a number of writers. Stephen Crites' "The Narrative Quality of Experience" argued that "the formal quality of experience through time is inherently narrative."[17] In sacred stories, mundane stories, and temporal experience itself this "narrative quality of experience" is expressed with each of these dimensions "constantly reflecting and affecting the course of the others."[18]

Two significant works fit into this category. John S. Dunne in *A Search for*

God in Time and Memory argues that by seeking to bring the past into the present of our consciousness we may find "what God tends to be for us."[19] In Dunne's method of "passing over by sympathetic understanding to others" he claimed one can enter into others' lives and find what is distinctive about one's own life's story. Thus we can "enter into the life stories of Paul, Augustine, and Kierkegaard and discern the different forms a Christian life assumes and in turn come to a new understanding of ourselves."[20] Modern life stories, he said, could function in the same way. For Dunne, the results of the "passing over" process was that a person "discovers the shape of the life story in other ages, the story of deeds, and they story of experience, and coming back from this to his own time is how he discovers by contrast its current shape, the story of appropriation.[21] From these life stories one finds "God's time, the greater and encompassing time which is that of the stories of God and [one] experiences companionship with God in time."[22]

A second important contribution to "life stories" is in the hearing of another's story. This approach is practiced by James William McClendon, Jr. in his *Theology as Biography*. In it McClendon claims that

> by recognizing that Christian beliefs are not so many "propositions" to be catalogued or juggled like truth-functions in a computer, but are living convictions which give shape to actual lives and actual communities, we open ourselves to the possibility that the only relevant critical examination of Christian beliefs may be one which begins by attending to lived lives. Theology must be at least biography.[23]

Thus it is "biography" that provides the primary tools by which the meaning of Christian doctrine may be known. McClendon then examines the lives of Dag Hammarskjöld, Martin Luther King, Jr., Clarence Jordan, and Charles Ives as the biographical "stories" that can give perspective on (in these cases) "atonement" in a way that differs from the traditional Christian doctrinal formulations. This approach links theology and ethics, and it focuses attention on Christian doctrine as lived beliefs that directly affect ethical decisions and judgments.[24]

3. *Biblical narrative.* A third category of "story theologies" focuses specifically on the Bible and on the category of "narrative" in Scripture. Theologians who concentrate on this approach find examples of narrative texts in Scripture and seek to answer how these texts function as "authority" in the life of Christian communities. Biblical scholars have long been aware of the role of historical narratives in Scripture. These help form what some refer to as *heilsgeschichte* or "salvation history" throughout the Bible.[25]

Particular lines of work on biblical narratives have emerged among scholars. Many have been influenced by the work of literary critics such as Amos Wilder, who argued that "the narrative mode is uniquely important in

Christianity" and "when the Christian in any time or place confesses his faith, his confession turns into a narrative."[26] In a highly significant study, Eric Auerbach in *Mimesis* studied the style of biblical narratives. He concluded that

> the text presents the reader with a vision of the way things are, a representation of reality in which Scripture makes an imperialistic claim. The text depicts a world, and it is 'not satisfied with claiming to be a historically true reality—it insists that it is the only real world, is destined for autocracy.' The challenge the biblical text presents to the reader is not whether the reader can appropriate the text and its claims within the reader's world; the challenge is whether the reader can and will enter into the world of the text; 'we are to fit our own life into its world, feel ourselves to be elements in its structure of universal history.'[27]

These insights have led theologians to examine the history of biblical interpretation and to see how in the eighteenth and nineteenth centuries, the distinction began to be drawn between a text's literal sense—the world it claimed to show and its historical reference—what the narrative referred to historically. When this occurred, readers could come to an understanding of the text's original setting and meaning, but (as Auerbach describes the process of fitting one's own life into the text's world) readers did not enter automatically into the realities that the biblical texts claimed to present. In other words, "once meaning was separated from reference it is no longer possible to read the text realistically."[28]

Related also to the study of the functions of narratives has been the recent emphasis by biblical scholars on "canonical criticism." James Sanders has argued that the meaning of any portion of Scripture must be seen in the context of the whole canon itself.[29] Another Old Testament scholar, Brevard Childs, has defined "canonical criticism" as seeking "to understand the peculiar shape and special function of these texts which comprise the Hebrew canon."[30] Childs has emphasized the final form of the biblical text instead of concentrating on how it came to be formed. His views have been challenged by James Barr.[31]

Of closer direct connection to the "story theologies," which function as introductions to religion and life stories, is the work of Sallie McFague.[32] McFague reflects the insights of literary critics and biblical scholars by arguing that "metaphorical thinking constitutes the basis of human thought and language."[33] Human thought worlds are constructed through metaphors. A metaphor most simply is

> seeing one thing *as* something else, pretending 'this' is 'that' because we do not know how to think or talk about 'this,' so we use 'that' as a way of saying something about it. Thinking metaphorically means spotting a thread of similarity between two dissimilar objects, events, or whatever, one of which is better

known than the other, and using the better-known one as a way of speaking about the lesser known.[34]

McFague has argued that "the parables of Jesus are typically metaphorical" in that

> they bring together dissimilars (lost coins, wayward children, buried treasure, and tardy laborers with the kingdom of God); they shock and disturb; they upset conventions and expectations and in so doing have revolutionary potential.[35]

A "metaphorical theology," says McFague, "starts with the parables of Jesus and with Jesus as a parable of God."[36] Parables are extended metaphors that set in tension both the familiar and the unfamiliar and in so doing open up new dimensions of life and fresh visions for us.[37]

Scripture in Story Theology

The Functions of Language

Fundamental to these major views of "story theology" is the emphasis on the shaping power of language. Language shapes human consciousness. Language also defines our boundaries and ourselves as people. McFague pointed this out when she wrote that "the language of a people is their sense of reality; we can live only within the confines of our language."[38] The images that emerge through the language we use is what Dunne referred to as "personal mythos" when he wrote that "out of this feeling for life or this pattern of feelings there emerge images or a coherent set of images which could be called the 'personal mythos.' The personal mythos has all the elements of drama—plot, characters."[39]

The language humans use, metaphorical in character according to the story theologians, is the shaping agent through which new insights arise. For "metaphor is basically a new or unconventional interpretation of reality."[40] Through life experience and language about it, a "grid" is constructed through which one's own existence is interpreted. This set of images, "personal mythos," or grid also becomes the guide for interpreting new experiences.[41] Some story theologians refer to this grid or vision as one's religion. McClendon writes that "By 'religion'...I mean life lived out under the governance of a central vision. I will seek, therefore, some central image, or cluster of images, by which our subject understood himself and his horizons, and through which that vision may be expressed."[42] It is language, specifically metaphor, which enables us to look beyond and to shape our lives. For "metaphor is movement, human movement; without it, we would not be what we are—the only creatures in the universe to our knowledge who can *envision* a future and consciously work toward achieving it."[43]

Story theologians draw on linguistic insights which show that narratives invite response and are thus highly participatory forms. Violence is done to the fundamental nature of the narrative form itself (particularly parables) if one tries to restate the "meaning" of the story in conceptual terms. "Metaphorical language," writes McFague, "conveys meaning through the body of the world. It makes connections, sees resemblances, uniting body and soul—earthly, temporal, ordinary experience with its meaning. But the 'meaning' is not there to be read off conceptually; we only get at the meaning through the metaphor."[44]

The participatory nature of narratives means that they are always tremendously personal and elicit the self-involvement of the reader or hearer. To understand a narrative in the view of story theologians is not to gain more conceptual or "intellectual" knowledge but rather to be faced with viewing one's life in a new way as one encounters new metaphorical images. One's life, existence, or "vision" is thus shaped by the encounter with the metaphor. As McFague writes of parables: "the impact of the parables is directly tied to their qualities as aesthetic objects, their insistence that insight be embodied, incarnated...in human *lives*, not in the head alone but in and through the full scope and breadth of a human life." Human lives themselves as "stories" are examples of "lived out images."[45]

Thus one's own life can be seen as a "story" or a "coming to belief." From the Christian perspective, "Christian belief must always be a process of coming to belief—like a story—through the ordinary details of historical life (as it is in the parables, though in a highly compressed way)."[46] A "story theology" will use stories "to confront people with their own possibilities of coming to belief."[47] The examination of the lives of those who have sought to live according to their "visions" (including here the life of Jesus) will enable one to see the validity of the images they used and be led to further understanding of one's own "story."

As a narrative form, autobiographies are most helpful here to the story theologian. For

> autobiography is metaphoric story through and through. The story of the self can only be told indirectly and incarnationally since the mystery of the self only comes to appearance in and through concrete speech and action. When we write autobiographically, we move from the known to the unknown, through the details of our lives to the mystery of our selves. Each speech remembered and incident reported is a metaphoric unfolding of the "master form" of the teller's life–a form that is not only communicated through but constituted by the story told.[48]

As McFague put it: "In autobiographies, finally, intermediary theology has a source for understanding how language and belief move into a life, how a life can itself be a parable, a deformation of ordinary existence by its placement in an extraordinary context."[49]

The Functions of Scripture

For Christian story theologians, the Scriptures provide the central set of metaphors by which one's vision and life can be shaped.[50] The basic genre in Scripture is narrative. Forms of biblical expression such as creation, fall, prophecy, the Gospels, parables, and the theology of Paul are all dependent upon metaphor.[51] As such they involve participation and self-involvement. The "authority" of the Bible arises from its calls to new visions of life that provide new metaphors by which to live. The function of Scripture is what makes it a source of "metaphorical theology" that starts with the parables of Jesus and with Jesus as a parable of God:

> This starting place does not involve a belief in the Bible as authoritative in an absolute or closed sense; it does not involve acceptance of a canon or the Bible as "the Word of God"....For what we have in the New Testament are confessions of faith by people who, on the basis of their experience of the way their lives were changed by Jesus' Gospel and by Jesus, *gave* authority to him and to the writings about him. The New Testament writings are foundational; they are classics; they are a beginning. But if we take seriously the parables of Jesus and Jesus as a parable of God as our starting point and model, then we cannot say that the Bible is absolute or authoritative in any sense except the way that a "classic" text is authoritative: it continues to speak to us.[52]

For McFague, the Bible shares in the metaphorical mode itself in that

> one of the distinctive marks of metaphorical thinking is its refusal of identity: if all of our knowing is seeing one thing in terms of something else, those terms can never be collapsed. Whatever we know, we know only by indirection; hence, distance is forever between us and what we know. If we know God by the indirection of the Bible, then the Bible "is and is not" the word of God. The Bible is a metaphor of the word or ways of God, but as metaphor it is a relative, open-ended, secular, tensive judgment. It is...the premier metaphor, the classic model, of God's ways for Christians, but as a metaphor it cannot be absolute, "divinely inspired," or final.[53]

Due to the nature of Scriptural language, the task of interpreting Scripture is not to translate its stories into "concepts" or propositions. It is rather to be engaged and involved in the text from the total perspective of one's own life and "story." By drawing on the thought of contemporary hermeneutical theory, McFague claims these works show that in terms of the "authority" of Scripture

> there is no "canonical" or absolute text or interpretation: a text is never

"there," pristine and absolute, but exists only in relationship to its hearers *and* no interpretation can be final, for a text only has meaning in relationship to hearers, all of whom come with different interpretive contexts.[54]

For McFague and other story theologians, the Bible gains its "authority" in that "it epitomizes what a great text should be."[55] She goes on to explain that

> a great text is a poetic text in the broad sense of a particular fiction or recon-
> struction of reality as universally applicable across generations. It can be con-
> temporaneous or "timeless" in that it speaks a universal language through its
> own particularity, not because it says one thing, but because it can say many
> things. It is rich, open, diverse, for as a poetic text it is constituted by metaphors
> open to many interpretations. As such, it is also a classic text which lives beyond
> its own time as it meets and accommodates itself to the experiences and interpre-
> tations of diverse peoples. We shall argue that the authority of Scripture is the
> authority of a classic poetic text and that such a notion of authority is substan-
> tial and enduring, both because *its authority is intrinsic* (the world it presents,
> that is, the reality it redescribes, speaks with power to many people across the
> ages) and because *its interpretation is flexible* (the world it presents is open to
> different understandings).[56]

For the Christian, according to McFague, the Scripture is the "classic poetic text" which means that the Bible is

> an interpretive grid or screen by means of which many dimensions of Chris-
> tian experience of God are given shape. The Bible as classic model means not
> that the Bible is absolute, perfect, or final (no model is), but as Barr says, "The
> status of the Bible is one of sufficiency rather than perfection."[57]

As such, for McFague and other story theologians, the goal of interpreting Scripture will not be to find a set of "beliefs" but rather to find "the way
to belief."[58]

SCRIPTURE AS MEDIUM FOR METAPHORS

The emphasis of story theologians on narrative places "metaphor" in a
central position. For some, the Bible functions as a "poetic classic." It speaks
universally and "its particular metaphors and the world it describes meta-
phorically have proven themselves across the ages to many diverse peoples
when the Bible has been interpreted as other poetic texts are interpreted—
existentially, flexibly, openly."[59]

The emphasis of story theologians is more on the interpretation of Scripture than in formal questions about Scripture's "authority" or "inspiration."
The Bible is the medium for metaphors in that it invites a person into a new

vision of reality, to set one's life "story" in relation to its "story" and thus Scripture provides a new grid or set of images by which one may "come to belief" and interpret one's own life experiences.

The vision of life offered in Scripture receives its validation as it is lived out in the concrete lives of those who enter into its narrative and are affected by its metaphors. As a "poetic classic, the Bible cannot be irrelevant, or more accurately, the Bible has proven itself to *be* relevant time and time again-
.... The Bible as *poetic classic* underscores the enduring centrality which this book has for all who call themselves Christians."[60] When introduced to Scripture, one participates in a new life and may be set on a new life direction by appropriating these images as one's own.

XI

LIBERATION THEOLOGY
SCRIPTURE AS FOUNDATION FOR FREEDOM

There are various forms of "liberation theologies" today. Since 1965 the term "liberation" has begun to take on a more technical character when used to describe theological movements.[1] The focus of these movements has been to a large degree on nations that have not fully undergone the revolutions that have marked many other nations such as France, the United States, Russia, and China. But through the past decades, political and economic revolution have sought to take hold in many so-called "Third World" and "underdeveloped" nations.

A particular arena of ferment has been Latin America. There the desperate plight of the poor of the land, standing in stark contrast to the rich in the various modernized cities, has led to many revolutionary uprisings. From this context has come a theological movement with its watchwords: liberation and freedom. While it shares features with other forms of liberation theologies, Latin America liberation theology is forged out of its own particular history and struggles. Like Black theology, this theology

> arises out of a specific context of oppression. Like feminist theology, it contends that the reversal of these oppressive conditions will require a significant revision of Christian belief and practice. Like both, it promises liberation to all the bodily oppressed through deliverance from one particular form of oppression. In this case, however, *class* oppression is viewed as the underlying source and model of all other forms of human bondage.[2]

Since theologians in the Latin American context have been most active in defining the theological bases and program of liberation theology, attention will be given to them and their views of the nature and function of Scripture.[3]

127

BACKGROUNDS

In August, 1968, the Second General Episcopal Conference of Roman Catholic bishops (CELAM) was held at Medellin, Columbia. From that conference the theological meaning of "liberation" began to be shaped. For Medellin was "the first instance in which a significant portion of the Roman Catholic hierarchy has acknowledged the structural nature of evil and has analyzed violence as a component of the unjust structures."[4] While the conference was designed to examine the Latin American church in light of the Second Vatican Council, the sixteen documents that emerged often went far beyond what Vatican II had stated forthrightly.[5]

In the texts of these documents a number of social issues and problems were addressed. The underdevelopment of Latin America was described as "an unjust situation which promotes tensions that conspire against peace." Not only is there "a lamentable insensitivity of the privileged sectors to the misery of the marginated sectors" but also a calculated "use of force to repress drastically any attempt at opposition."[6] Also denounced were social inequality, unjust use of power by the powerful, the perpetration of economic dependency through distortion of trade, and "institutionalized violence" that takes shape through "a structural deficiency of industry and agriculture, or national and international economy, of culture and political life."[7] The task of peace is a "permanent task" and is "not the simple absence of violence and bloodshed. Oppression by the power groups may give the impression of maintaining peace and order, but in truth it is nothing but the 'continuous and inevitable seed of rebellion and war.' "[8]

In this situation, the oppressed must be able to determine their own lots and future and thus liberated from "cultural, social, economic, and political servitudes" that oppose "human development."[9] Yet liberation is set forth in a Christian context in that it is "an anticipation of the complete redemption of Christ"[10] and peace is "the fruit of love," since "love is the soul of justice."[11] The Medellin conference represents what has been called the "formulation of the 'Theology of Liberation' (1968-1972)."[12]

The path begun by Medellin as the first focused writing on the liberation theme was continued in a further Conference planned for April 1972 in Santiago, Chile. There the First Latin American Encounter of Christians for Socialism met.[13] After Medellin, the momentum built to the point that Roman Catholic priests who spent their lives living with the poor began to be convinced that mere "reformist" movements progressed too slowly to bring need social change. Additionally, these movements seemed ineffective. Priests discovered too that many of the people were influenced by the Marxist analysis of society. Thus it became important to relate Marxist social analysis to the Christian faith.

In 1971 a group of eighty Chilean priests (*Los Ochenta*) issued a statement calling for their bishops to relate their Christianity to political commitment in socialist terms. From this group came the plans for the April, 1972 meeting in Santiago. In comparison to the Medellin Conference, it can be said that

> if the distance between Vatican II and Medellin constitutes a step, the distance between the Medellin conference of bishops and the Santiago conference of Christians for Socialism resembles a leap. Medellin was in tune with Vatican II, even if beginning to move beyond it, whereas Santiago is more self-consciously "post-conciliar." Medellin usually leans toward a "third way" between capitalism and Marxism, whereas Santiago sees no "Christian solution" as such, denounces the collapse into a "third way," and insists that Christians be involved in the liberation process in socialist terms. With a few important exceptions...Medellin speaks of inequality between persons, whereas Santiago consistently links inequality to class struggle and the exploitation of the poor by the rich. Medellin presses strongly for basic reform, whereas Santiago sees no solution without revolution, not necessarily violent. Medellin hopes that love, working for justice, can provide solutions, while Santiago argues that love is not a historic force apart from engagement in class struggle. Medellin offers theoretical analyses of Marxism, while Santiago calls upon Christians to "form a strategic alliance with Marxists." At Medellin the theologians were summoned by the bishops, at Santiago they were summoned by the militant.[14]

The final document of the Santiago meetings captures the mood and thrust of the movement. After asserting that two-thirds of the human race was being oppressed while "a relatively small sector of humanity is making greater progress and growing richer every day" at the expense of the oppressed poor, it goes on to say that imperialist capitalism is the reason this is so. Imperialist capitalism has exploited the poor for centuries and uses de facto forms of violence to maintain its power. Reformism alone is not enough. For "the structures of our society must be transformed from the roots up."[15] Therefore delegates made a commitment to "the task of fashioning socialism [as] the only effective way to combat imperialism and to break away from our situation of dependence."[16] The basis for this action was to be theological in nature. Christianity's historic alliances with ruling classes had to be broken by siding with the exploited.

The section "Faith and Revolutionary Commitment" of this document urges Christians to realize that there is a "convergence between the radicality of their faith and the radicality of their political commitment." This means that "faith intensifies the demand that the class struggle move decisively towards the liberation of all men—in particular, of those who suffer the most acute forms of oppression." To be a Christian is to be committed in the midst of the struggle of the classes. To be neutral is not possible. For faith has a critical role to play in criticizing complicity between faith and the dominant culture. But faith's reality will not come by detached theorizing; it will come only "by joining parties and organizations that are authentic instruments of the struggle of the working class."[17]

In this context, as the Santiago document said, the attempt is made for "a new reading of the Bible and the Christian tradition."[18]

THE THEOLOGY OF LIBERATION

Latin American liberation theologians have focused attention on a number of particular themes rising from their experiences and social context. Among the prominent voices and works of these theologians are the following:

Camilio Torres (1929-66) who, though he did not directly participate in the emergence of Latin American Liberation theology, is recognized by contemporary Latin American liberation theologians as pointing the way by calling for changes in fundamental economic and social structures. Torres was deprived of his university post and left the priesthood in 1965 to join a guerilla group. On February 15, 1966 he was ambushed and killed, and he became a pioneer martyr of the liberation movement. Torres had said: "I am a revolutionary because I am a priest."[19] His statement that "in my view, the hierarchy of priorities should be reversed: love, the teaching of doctrine, and finally [formal] worship" foreshadowed emphasis on praxis as the starting point for theology.[20] For him, "revolutionary action is a Christian, a priestly struggle."[21] In terms of significance, Torres "incarnated for Latin America the significance of the slogan, *conscientization*."[22]

In 1969 Rubem Alves (b. 1933) published *A Theology of Human Hope*, which was his doctoral dissertation at Princeton Theological Seminary. This Brazilian has "produced the first systematic exploration of the theme of liberation."[23] In his analysis Alves turned to the philosophy of language rather than political science or sociology for his analytical tools. In this regard he also focused attention on biblical hermeneutics.

For Alves, language is "an expression of how a community has programmed a solution to its existential problems" so that behind language stands a community. For him (drawing on the Hebrew concept), truth is found not in the realm of pure ideas but takes shape as "action," as "the name given by a historical community to its historical deeds, which were, are, and will be efficacious in the liberation of man."[24] Alves sees in "messianic humanism" that the goal is the humanization of life which comes as God's gift of grace and opens a new future for God's people. The paradigm here is the event of the Exodus in the Old Testament, in which "God manifests himself as the power of liberation who rejects the objective and subjective impossibility of liberation of the 'given' condition of the Israelite tribes."[25] For Israel, "the future that was closed because of Egypt's oppressive power and Israel's own slave consciousness is broken open by a God who is free from the determinisms of history and is active in history."[26] Humans participate in the quest for freedom as they struggle in human communities.[27] This means that "liberation is not simply a history that breaks in from a future totally unconnected with the present: it is a project which springs from the protest born of the suffering of the present; a protest to which God grants a future in which man enters through his action."[28]

The emphasis on the concrete situation as the focus for theological work was struck also by the Brazilian priest Hugo Assmann. For Assmann, theology is done "beginning from concreteness," from "particular realities."[29] It is action which is the truth so that truth is found in history and not in speculative ideas. Thus, Assmann wrote:

> the criteria for a good theology are not any more strictly theological, just as the criteria for an effective love of God belong to the historical and human order of the neighbor, i.e., to the order of the nondivine. In fact, just as the *divine* dimension in the love of the neighbor is the God-reference in the neighbor, so the *theological* in the reflection on the historical praxis is present in the dimension of faith. If the divine, therefore, can only be found through the human, it is entirely logical that a Christian theology will find its ultimate theological character in the human references of history.[30]

The Peruvian priest Gustavo Gutiérrez (b. 1928) in his *A Theology of Liberation* (1971) has given fullest expression to the basics of liberation theology.[31] Many of his themes are captured in the concern he expressed when he wrote that

> in a continent like Latin America...the main challenge does not come from the nonbeliever but from the nonhuman—that, is the human being who is not recognized as such by the prevailing social order. These are the poor and exploited people, the ones who are systematically and legally despoiled of their being human, those who scarcely know what a human being might be. These nonhumans do not call into question our religious world so much as they call into question our *economic, social, political, and cultural world*. Their challenge impels us toward a revolutionary transformation of the very bases of what is now a dehumanizing society. The question, then, is no longer how we are to speak about God in a world come of age; it is rather how to proclaim him Father in a world that is not human and what the implications might be of telling nonhumans that they are children of God.[32]

Here social analysis shows the exploited and oppressed need to be humanized. The structures of society have deprived them of their basic dignity as children of God. A "revolutionary transformation" of societal structures is needed for a free humanity to begin to take shape. This is the process of liberation.

For Guitérrez, liberation takes shape on three levels. There is the political liberation. Here "liberation" expresses

> the aspirations of oppressed peoples and social classes, emphasizing the conflictual aspect of the economic, social, and political process which puts them at odds with wealthy nations and oppressive classes.[33]

Secondly, on the level of history "liberation" may refer to humans taking conscious responsibility for their own destiny. In the quest for true freedom a new humanity and a "qualitatively different society" may take shape.[34] Finally, theologically, "liberation" in the Bible is found in Jesus Christ who liberates humanity. Christ the Savior liberates humans from sin which is "the ultimate root of all disruption of friendship and of all injustice and oppression."[35] Christ makes people truly free and enables them to live in fellowship with him. This is the basis for all human community.

Guitérrez sees that while these three levels of liberation may be distinguished, they form a basic unity and one is not to be found without the others. As Guitérrez wrote:

> Without liberating historical events, there would be no growth of the Kingdom. But the very process of liberation will not have conquered the very roots of oppression and exploitation of man by man without the coming of the Kingdom which is above all a gift. Moreover, we can say that the historical, political liberating event *is* the growth of the Kingdom, and *is* salvific event, but it is not *the* coming of the Kingdom, not *all* of salvation.[36]

Thus, "political, historical, and spiritual liberation are inseparable parts of a single, all-encompassing salvific process."[37] For "in Christ the all-comprehensiveness of the liberating process reaches its fullest sense."[38]

It has been argued that the "originality" of Guitérrez's theology is "not to have discovered these three levels of meaning but to have started from their *unity* as the fundamental point of departure."[39] Guitérrez is repeatedly concerned with "the elimination of dualism"[40] in all realms which leads him to argue that "history is one" so that "there is only one human destiny, irreversibly assumed by Christ, the Lord of history. His redemptive work embraces all the dimensions of existence and brings them to their fullness. The history of salvation is the very heart of human history."[41] There is "only one history—a 'Christo-finalized' history."[42] In the one call to salvation there is given

> religious value in a completely new way to the action of man in history, Christian and non-Christian alike. The building of a just society has worth in terms of

the Kingdom, or in more current phraseology, to participate in the process of liberation is already, in a certain sense, a salvific work.[43]

The integration of the three levels of liberation for Guitérrez is possible because of his "new way of doing theology."[44] This is to do theology as "critical reflection on praxis."[45] For Guitérrez, the emphasis of the early church on "theology as wisdom" and of medieval scholasticism which stressed "theology as rational knowledge" are to be replaced now by a new vision. Guitérrez says that while "theology as a critical reflection on Christian praxis in the light of the Word does not replace the other functions of theology, such as wisdom and rational knowledge," it rather "presupposes and needs them."[46] thus the aim for theology is not "the discovery or refinement of doctrine as timeless truth but for the transformation of the world through reflection on praxis."[47] Praxis is not only "involvement in a situation" or "practice" but carries with it too the Marxist emphasis of "participation in a class struggle to bring about the creation of a new socialist society. Theology is totally internal to this praxis and deepens one's commitment within it."[48]

> Theology as critical reflection on historical praxis is a liberating theology, a theology of the liberating transformation of the history of mankind and also therefore that part of mankind—gathered into *ecclesia*—which openly confesses Christ. This is a theology which does not stop with reflecting on the world, but rather tries to be part of the process through which the world is transformed. It is a theology which is open—in the protest against trampled human dignity, in the struggle against the plunder of the vast majority of people, in liberating love, and in the building of a new, just, and fraternal society—to the gift of the Kingdom of God.[49]

Other significant Latin American liberation theologians have focused attention on biblical studies such as José Porfirio Miranda, an ex-Jesuit, who wrote *Marx and the Bible: A Critique of the Philosophy of Oppression* (Eng. 1974).[50] Hermeneutical considerations are developed by Juan Luis Segundo (b. 1925), a Uruguayan Jesuit, in his *The Liberation of Theology* (Eng. 1976). This was a development of initial ideas set forth in his earlier five-volume *A Theology for Artisans of a New Humanity* (orig. edition, 1968-72).[51] Segundo emphasizes among other things that the social sciences can be valuable tools for biblical interpretation. Major Christological studies have been produced by Jon Sobrino, a Spanish Jesuit, in his *Christology at the Crossroads: A Latin American Approach* (Eng. 1976)[52] and Leonardo Boff (b. 1938) in his *Jesus Christ Liberator: A Critical Christology for Our Time* (Eng. 1978).[53] Perhaps the best overview of how liberation theology has developed and its themes in general has been written by the Methodist scholar José Miguez-Bonino in his *Doing Theology in a Revolutionary Situation* (Eng. 1975).[54] His 1976 book *Christians and Marxists: The Mutual*

Challenge to Revolution analyzes the interrelationships between Christianity and Marxism.[55]

SCRIPTURE IN LIBERATION THEOLOGY

It is clear that the historical situations and contexts in which Latin American liberation theology developed significantly shapes its approach to the Bible. In the 1960s, attitudes of Latin Americans about their futures changed. The 1950s were "characterized by great optimism regarding the possibility of achieving self-sustained economic development."[56] For this to happen, however, the pattern of dependence upon foreign trade in which nations exported primary products and imported manufactured products had to end. Internal development and industrialization were needed. But in the 1960s, "a pessimistic diagnosis of economic, social, and political realities replaced the preceding optimism."[57] Development was not proceeding in many nations and the larger theory of development was questioned. In the emerging view it was argued that "the dynamics of the capitalist economy head to the establishment of a center and a periphery, simultaneously generating progress and growing wealth for the few and social imbalances, political tensions, and poverty for the many."[58] The imbalance between the developed and underdeveloped countries created further relationships of dependence so that "the poor, dominated nations keep falling behind; the gap continues to grow."[59]

In this context a new posture of "liberation" arose. This took political form in revolutionary political action in a variety of places.[60] As theologians became participants in these situations many of them joined with others in calling for the overthrow of the capitalistic system they found so oppressive. Liberation and the call for freedom became the focus towards which all energies were directed. As Guiterrez put it:

> the untenable circumstances of poverty, alienation, and exploitation in which the greater part of the people of Latin America live urgently demand that we find a path toward economic, social, and political liberation. This is the first step towards a new society.[61]

Theological Method

The themes of liberation theology show the basic starting point for theological inquiry must be with the poor of the world. The "marginalized," the poor who are the largest group in the human family "are not inconsequential. And it is with them that theology must start; not with theories, not with views from above, but with 'the view from below.' "[62] As Frederick Herzog put it, theology must start "where the pain is."[63]

This commitment to beginning with the poor is a theological commitment. Liberation theologians see that in the Bible it is in the lives and plight of the poor that God is to be discovered. For

> the God of the Old Testament is the God of the poor and the oppressed, a God who sides with them, taking their part and identifying with them. The God of the New Testament is the same God, a God who becomes incarnate not in one who possessed wealth or influence or a good name, but in one who belonged to the 'poor of the land' (the *am ha'aretz*), a lower class/working class Jew who cast his own lot with the poor to such a consistent degree that the rich and powerful found it necessary to destroy him.[64]

This means the "poor" have what Assmann has called an "epistemological privilege." The way the poor view the world is "closer to the reality of the world than the way the rich view it. Their 'epistemology,' i.e., their way of knowing, is accurate to a degree that is impossible for those who see the world only from the vantage point of privileges they want to retain."[65]

This starting point of the poor exemplifies the theological method of liberation theologians who stress the priority of praxis. It is the historical situation which is the context and where theological reflection must begin. Since theology is "critical reflection on praxis," there is a continuing dialogue between theology and life situations, between action and reflection (theory). It is action that causes one to look at theory and one's theory causes another look at one's action.

For liberation theologians, truth is found in action. Guitérrez wrote that "knowledge is not the conformity of the mind to the given, but an immersion in the process of transformation and construction of a new world."[66] Appealing to the Old Testament prophets and the New Testament Johannine writings, these theologians argue that true knowledge of God is not to be found in speculation and abstract theories of "truth." Rather it is in active obedience to God, in participation that truth is found. As Bonino put it: "Correct knowledge is contingent on right doing. Or rather, the knowledge is disclosed in the doing."[67] Theology is a "second act," in that it follows praxis as "critical reflection on praxis." The "first act" is the commitment of one's self to the transformation of society on behalf of the poor. In the "second act," theology, reflection on the first act is done and is the attempt to see this action in light of the resources of Christian faith. Clearly, "Christians can think their faith only as they practice it."[68]

The Functions of Scripture

From this context and theological method liberation theologians re-examined Scripture. What they found was that the "poor" who are the starting point for theological reflection and who are so prominent in the Bible itself have not been seen so in traditional classical theology or biblical exegesis.

This led to the suspicion that Western biblical interpretation was actually ideologically controlled. Since biblical commentaries were written by established scholars in positions of safety and power, the suspicion is that these have brought certain presuppositions and "ideologies" to Scripture and thus have been blind to any scriptural challenge of these ideologies. Biblical scholars did not hear what Scripture said about the importance of the poor because they were ideologically captive to the social status quo. As Brown wrote: "This bending of the evidence, in an effort to make reality conform to what one wants reality to be, is a prevailing tendency of ideological thought, and suggests the ideology will work on the side of conformity, of maintenance of things as they are, particularly as it is employed by those in power."[69] In "ideologization," the text of Scripture and tradition "is forced into the Procrustean bed of ideology, and the theologian who has fallen prey of this procedure is forever condemned to listen only to the echo of his own ideology. There is no redemption for this theology, because it has muzzled the Word of God in its transcendence and freedom."[70] Put simply, in Guitérrez's words, an ideology "rationalizes and justifies a given social and ecclesial order."[71]

With regard to reading Scripture, the pervasiveness of ideology leads to what the theologians called a "hermeneutics of suspicion." This is the suspicion that the usual interpretation of biblical texts do not take into account certain data that if considered would lead to a dramatically different interpretation. In light of the social analysis and "suspecting" taught by Freud and Marx, Bonino writes that "every interpretation of the text which is offered to us (whether as exegesis or as systematic or as ethical interpretation) must be investigated in relation to the praxis out of which it comes."[72] Thus, "very concretely, we cannot receive the theological interpretation coming from the rich world without suspecting it and, therefore, asking what kind of praxis it supports, reflects, or legitimizes."[73] The examples cited are the plainly political themes and implications of the life of Jesus which have remained "hidden" aspects of interpretation until recently. Or, as Brown asks, "Since the God of the Bible is on the side of the poor, why are we undisturbed by the fact that we are among the nonpoor?" His answer is that "We read what we can bear to read, we hear what is tolerable to hear, and we evade (or 'spiritualize') those parts which leave us uncomfortable, if not outraged."[74]

Liberation theologians use Scripture in a variety of ways. The chief appeal, however, is to the Exodus event in the Old Testament because, for liberation theology, "the Exodus experience is paradigmatic."[75] As Brown puts it, "if there is a single passage that encapsulates the liberation themes of the Bible, it is the exodus story, describing a God who takes sides, intervening to free the poor and oppressed."[76] This event is "the center of Scripture" in that "God's saving action is focused in the exodus, the liberation of a people from political, cultural, and religious bondage."[77]

A second area of appeal to Scripture by liberationists is to the ethical teachings of the prophets. Here the concern of the prophets for the oppressed is particularly prominent. This theme is capsulized in the phrase: "To know God is to do justice" (See Jer. 22:13-16).[78] According to the prophets, "where there is justice and righteousness, there is knowledge of Yahweh; when these are lacking, it is absent."[79] To love God is to establish just relationships among people and "to recognize the rights of the poor. The God of biblical revelation is known through interhuman justice. When justice does not exist, God is not known; he is absent."[80]

The doctrines of eschatology and the future coming Kingdom is another area of Scriptural appeal for liberation theologians. The Scriptures link the coming of Jesus with the Old Testament Exodus and also to the coming future *eschaton* which will embody the values and concerns that Jesus himself embraced: peace, justice, love, and freedom. For Guiterrez, eschatology is "the very key to understanding the Christian faith" as it looks to "that which is to come, towards a new action of God."[81] The establishment of the future Kingdom by God means that "peace, justice, love and freedom are not private realities; they are not only internal attitudes. They are social realities, implying a historical liberation."[82] In the struggle for liberation now, "the elimination of misery and exploitation is a sign of the coming of the Kingdom."[83]

SCRIPTURE AS FOUNDATION FOR FREEDOM

In liberation theology, traditional questions about revelation, inspiration, and the authority of the Scriptures are not as important as how the Bible functions in a Christian community. The Scriptures are validated continually as they are employed in the concrete action of liberation. The Scripture serves as a "foundation for freedom" in this theology because it provides the paradigms, the goals, and ultimately introduces humanity to the ultimate human liberator, Jesus Christ.

Liberation theologians appeal to various strands of Scripture, including narratives, ethical teachings, and eschatology. But central through it all is the contention that Scripture as liberating word is powerful because it is interpreted in the context of a praxis that involves one with the poor and oppressed who hunger for freedom. It is not theoretical evaluations that give validity to any scriptural interpretation. An interpretation is shown to be true or false only as it works itself out in action through the struggle for liberation. For "only by doing this truth will our faith be 'veri-fied,' in the etymological sense of the word."[84] The truth of any theological statement will be "confirmed in the *praxis* of the Christian community."[85]

XII

FEMINIST THEOLOGY
SCRIPTURE AS MOTHER OF MODELS

Most feminist theology, as it has emerged since the 1970s, is a form of liberation theology. It has centered on the struggle of women for liberation. Like other forms of liberation theology, feminist theology is a protest against traditional forms and methods of doing theology. It is concerned with the central theme of liberation, variously defined as "equality," "freedom," and "humanization." The voices of women theologians are being heard today in increasing numbers. The Women's Caucus of Religious Studies, a group affiliated with the American Academy of Religion, in 1980 listed 168 members. In 1984 the group listed 336 women theologians at professional or doctoral level theological work.[1]

Prominent women theologians have made significant impact in all the theological disciplines. Emerging forms of feminist theology are being developed that call into question traditional modes of theological thought and practice. While not all women who do theology today would wish to identify their theological work as "feminist theology," re-formulations of classic Christian understandings are developing from women who find themselves drawn to the wider, cultural feminist movement. Janet Kalven who has worked with women in an international Christian renewal movement for about forty years has said: "Feminist theology is not a matter of 'add women and stir.' Rather, feminist theology involves a profound rethinking of theology, its sources, methods and themes."[2]

Feminist theology is ecumenical in orientation. It has cut across traditional denominational lines and over barriers between Roman Catholics and Protestants. It has sought relations with people on many levels and in many contexts. As Beverly W. Harrison writes:

> To be a truly ecumenical person, is, from a feminist theological viewpoint, to live out a praxis that works to heal the brokenness of life in the world, however

139

differently feminists construe the meaning of that brokenness. Hypothetically, feminist 'ecumenism' requires address to all conflicts and differences that divide us from one another and from the full potential of creation and that prevent us from living into our power as bearers of God's image. But this is not yet clarified in the feminist theological process.[3]

Feminist theology thus has varied constituencies with many degrees of involvement apparent. There are varieties within the feminist theological process about precisely *what* tasks should be done and about *how* these tasks should be accomplished.

There are also diversities within feminist theology on the issue of Scripture. A basic recognition in feminist thought is that the Bible is a book composed in cultures that had patriarchal biases. Basic too is the contention that the Bible has been interpreted predominantly by males and that in many ways sexist interpretations have been dominant ones. In light of this, feminist theologians face the fundamental questions posed by Katharine Doob Sakenfeld: "How can feminists use the Bible, if at all? What approach to the Bible is appropriate for feminists who locate themselves within the Christian community? How does the Bible serve as a resource for Christian feminists?"[4] While feminists differ in their specific responses to these questions, almost all would agree with Letty M. Russell:

> Fresh insights are needed as the rising consciousness of women and people in the Third World or in other oppressed circumstances leads them to challenge accepted biblical interpretations that reinforce patriarchal domination. From this perspective the Bible needs to be liberated from its captivity to one-sided white, middle-class, male interpretation. It needs liberation from the privatized and spiritualized interpretations that avoid God's concern for justice, human wholeness, and ecological responsibility; it needs liberation from abstract, doctrinal interpretations that remove the biblical narrative from its concrete social and political context in order to change it into timeless truth.[5]

Thus Russell speaks of "the liberating Word," "liberating the Word," and "the liberated Word" to describe the process of emerging feminist hermeneutics.[6] This is the attempt of women searching today for "a feminist interpretation of the Bible that is rooted in the feminist critical consciousness that women and men are fully human and fully equal. This consciousness is opposed to teachings and actions that reinforce the social system that oppresses women and other groups in society."[7]

Backgrounds

Feminist Consciousness

The development of a "feminist consciousness" has taken place through the last few centuries.[8] In the western world, until the early nineteenth century, most

> intellectual and theological work was done out of a prefeminist perspective. There was no conscious awareness that women's experience *as* women's experience, was relevant to intellectual work. It was a man's world. Women were part of the male story. As women they remained invisible. This prefeminist consciousness acknowledged that women's lives did have some unique aspects, but the differences were unimportant.[9]

With the growing rise of the self-consciousness of women as women, issues related specifically to the Bible arose. For

> opponents of the women's rights movement used the Bible to argue that it was not legitimate for women to name or value their female experience. Women in the churches tried to reconcile their commitment to the authority of the Bible with emerging feminist activism. They also became interested in questions of biblical interpretation. How did the Bible affirm their lives? When a text was insensitive to women's experience, what was its authority?[10]

Questions about the use of the Bible in relation to the position of women in society were not new in America. In 1837 the noted antislavery lecturer and women's right author Sarah Grimke charged that part of a specific plot against women included a masculine bias in biblical interpretation and thus called for a new feminist scholarship. Antoinette Brown, the first ordained woman in Congregationalism, studied theology at Oberlin College and looked at the Pauline epistles with feminist questions. At her ordination, the Rev. Luther Lee who preached the sermon quoted Galatians 3:28–"There is neither Jew nor Greek, there is neither slave nor free, there is neither male nor female; for you are all one in Christ Jesus."[11]

Many feminist theologians today, however, trace the direct beginnings of a feminist consciousness about the Bible to the leadership of Elizabeth Cady Stanton. Stanton was active as a suffragist and thus had a political awareness of what certain actions could mean. She established a committee of twenty women who found all major biblical passages relating to women, discussed them and wrote extended commentaries on them from their own interpretive perspectives. Stanton said she undertook this task because she continued to hear so many "conflicting opinions about the Bible, some saying it taught woman's emancipation, and some her subjection."[12] The result was *The*

Woman's Bible published in two volumes in 1895 and 1898.[13]

Cady Stanton's work is "not a treatise in modern biblical criticism," but rather "a passionate feminist criticism of biblical religion which anticipates many of the themes of feminist theology."[14] But two crucial insights for a feminist theological hermeneutics arose. According to Elisabeth Schüssler Fiorenza these are: "(1) The Bible is not a 'neutral' book, but a political weapon against women's struggle for liberation. (2) This is so because the Bible bears the imprint of men who never saw or talked with God.[15] For Cady Stanton, a scholarly and feminist interpretation of the Bible was politically necessary because

i. Throughout history and especially today the Bible is used to keep women in subjection and to hinder their emancipation.

ii. Not only men but especially women are the most faithful believers in the Bible as the word of God. Not only for men but also for women the Bible has a numinous authority.

iii. No reform is possible in one area of society if it is not advanced also in all other areas. One cannot reform the law and other cultural institutions without also reforming biblical religion which claims the Bible as Holy Scripture. Since "all reforms are interdependent," a critical feminist interpretation is a necessary political endeavor, although it might not be opportune. If feminists think they can neglect the revision of the Bible because there are more pressing political issues, then they do not recognize the political impact of Scripture upon the churches and society, and also upon the lives of women.[16]

The Woman's Bible project was not popular among many. Female scholars who did not participate were in Cady Stanton's view "afraid that their high reputation and scholarly attainments might be compromised by taking part in an enterprise that for a time may prove very unpopular."[17] The National American Woman's Suffrage Association formally rejected the project as a political mistake.

It has also been argued that *The Woman's Bible* was opposed because of "its radical hermeneutic perspective which expanded and replaced the main apologetic argument of other suffragists that the true message of the Bible was obstructed by the translations and interpretations of men."[18] Instead, Cady Stanton maintained that the degrading ideas about women, which the churches said came from God, actually originated from the heads of men. For "over and against the doctrinal understanding of verbal inspiration of the Bible as the direct word of God, she stresses that the Bible is written by men and reflects the male interests of its authors. 'The only point in which I differ from all ecclesiastical teaching is that I do not believe that any man ever saw or talked with God.' "[19]

Cady Stanton was proposing the Bible be treated like any other book and that the cultural limits of its authors be recognized. The Bible was not to be accepted or rejected wholesale. There are varieties of teachings in Scripture. So every biblical passage on women must be analyzed and carefully evaluated. In this way its androcentric implications may become clear. For Cady Stanton, "men have put their stamp on biblical revelation. The Bible is not just interpreted from a male perspective, as some feminists argued. Rather, it is man-made because it is written by men and is the expression of a patriarchal culture."[20]

In the early twentieth century a new concern about the equality of the sexes began to surface. "Women's studies" were begun to show that while the sexes were different, there was a common humanity that men and women shared. Women and men are both the creatures of God. One did not have the proper perspective of human history if women's experiences were not noticed or appreciated. In that sense "history" was also "her story." In literature, psychology, sociology, economics, and politics dimensions of women's experiences were explored.

Women's studies continue and have greatly expanded knowledge in a variety of ways. In biblical studies

> the advent of women's studies expanded women's understandings of biblical authority. By helping everyone appreciate the place of women in the Bible and in the early church, it stretched orthodox assumptions about tradition. It offered alternative images of women. It suggested that more inclusive language could be important for the faith and the church.[21]

Women now may claim their equality in God's world and through the development of a feminist critical consciousness can develop "an authentic inclusive interpretive framework for all biblical, historical, and theological work."[22]

Further women's studies have led both to the critique of past assumptions and ways of perception about women as well as to the shaping of completely new interpretive methods for a feminist critical consciousness. Feminist studies developed in relationship with other liberation movements and began to ask questions about "every biblical text and every event in church history: What difference did it make that women were or were not included? If women were not taken into account, why? The answers to these questions challenged many sacred principles of doctrine and practice."[23]

Emerging feminist critical consciousness

> attacks majority positions and points out the injustices of history. Feminists are angry, iconoclastic, and revolutionary. A feminist critical consciousness does not always state positively what it stands for, but it knows and names its enemies. Feminism does not simply stretch the horizons of knowledge, it alters the landscape by tearing down many of the old patriarchal buildings.[24]

Put in a religious context this means that

> the religious feminist movement is about women's reclaim to freedom to relate
> to God in the church and wider outside world. They are coming out of their ex-
> periences and consciousness and are expressing themselves, at times, through
> their own definitions. They are acting out these new freedoms. What follows
> among Christian feminists is a critique of the institutional church—traditionally
> controlled and defined by men—which, these women say, has misunderstood,
> ignored, denigrated and blocked women's consciousness.[25]

Ultimately, the aim of a feminist consciousness is as one feminist writer
put it, "to make the experience and insights of women available to the entire
world, not simply to know more about women in and of themselves. Yet if
we are to include women in the total picture, we are called to rethink how we
interpret everything."[26] This comprehensive vision of the interpretation of reality shapes the feminist approach to theology and to the study of Scripture.

Feminist Critiques

An important early article in the area of feminist theology was published
in 1960 by Valerie Saiving. In "The Human Situation: A Feminine View,"
Saiving argued that a crucial dimension to how one perceives theology is
one's sexual identity.[27] She contended that

> there are significant differences between masculine and feminine experience
> and that feminine experience reveals in a more emphatic fashion certain aspects
> of the human situation which are present but less obvious in the experience of
> men. Contemporary theological doctrines of love have, I believe, been con-
> structed primarily upon the basis of masculine experience and thus view the hu-
> man condition from the male standpoint. Consequently, these doctrines do not
> provide an adequate interpretation of the situation of women—nor, for that
> matter, of men, especially in view of certain fundamental changes now taking
> place in our own society.[28]

A 1968 book by Mary Daly, *The Church and the Second Sex* claimed that
the church has encouraged the view that women are inferior to men and that
the church has been a leading instrument in the continuing oppression of
women.[29] Daly moved to the concept of "sisterhood" in 1971 to urge "the
bonding of those who have never been bonded before for the purpose of
overcoming sexism and its effects, both internal and external."[30] This signaled Daly's move outside the traditional boundaries and language of the
Roman Catholic church and her growing identification with the feminist and
women's liberation movements.

Daly's theological critique of the doctrine of God was stated in *Beyond
God the Father* (1973). In it she argued that the essential core of Christianity

is belief in the God of the Bible but that this is hopelessly patriarchal in nature.[31] The characteristic designation of God as "father" has the effect of legitimizing the image of a supreme heavenly patriarch who rules his people and thus sanctions a male-dominated order of society. The Church has equated the biblical Eve of the book of Genesis with evil and made her responsible for sin. Thus women become equated with sin. "God" must be recast, argued Daly, from noun to verb. God is the "Be-ing" in which we participate. In her 1975 revised edition of *The Church and the Second Sex* she wrote a "new feminist postchristian" introduction claiming that it was impossible to work with men who are the "oppressors" or with the church as the institution of oppression of women. Her goal was to sketch a new vision grounded fully in women's experience. The distinctiveness of women's experience will give insight into how women are related to the cosmos.[32]

The line begun by Daly is followed by others into what has been called the stream of "revolutionary feminism."[33] Revolutionary feminists look to women's *traditional* experiences as the norms and starting points for theology. These experiences including motherhood and marriage must be reappropriated by women from a feminist perspective. All sexist traditions must be rejected including the oppressive authority structures of Judaism and Christianity. New symbols and traditions are to be found rising from women's experience of ultimate reality.[34]

To indicate their stance, revolutionary feminists often claim the title "post-Christian" or "post-Jewish." Some see women's spirituality merging into the broad stream of pagan spirituality, including the practice of witchcraft.[35] The image of the "goddess" is invoked to return to a spirituality prior to the biblical traditions and among the most primitive known. For revolutionary feminists "the goddess symbol found in many traditions can aid modern women's liberation by providing an image of female power that can counteract the symbol of God as male."[36]

Among the new sources of "revelation" and "authority" for these feminists are dreams and fantasies, the present and future vision of sisterhood and Daly's androgynous future created by God the verb.[37] A metaphorical image for this stream of thought and practice is that feminists must "spook, spark and spin." This is in order that women's creative energies for survival may be used to break with male-dictated definitions of women's vocations so "sisters" may reach to the depths of themselves and let the creative powers of women flow in the midst of a world of death.[38] Among revolutionary feminists are Daly, Naomi Goldenberg, Judith Plaskow, Starhawk (Miriam Simos), Zsuzsanna Budapest, Carol Christ, and Penelope Washburn.[39]

A second stream of feminist theology may be labeled "reformist feminism." In these theologians appeal is made to women's *feminist* rather than traditional experience. Here the religious traditions of Christianity and Judaism are not to be forsaken but rather may be renewed, reformed, and reinterpreted to provide resources for freedom. Oppression can be recognized, sexist cultures and institutions confronted, and liberation occur when women's experience provides the source of critique and analysis.[40]

While these Christian feminists recognize the radical critique of Christianity from other feminists, they "continue to struggle with the symbols and their transformation. Yet they also realize that "both historically and in the present, the Christian symbols of God, Jesus, sin and salvation, the Church and the Holy Spirit have been life-giving and liberating for women."[41]

> The task is to search for resources within the biblical, theological, and intellectual traditions that enable Christian feminist theology to be understood as an intrinsic theological task,...i.e., applications of Christian themes to contemporary issues.[42]

This task, says Ann Carr, "implies not only a Christian critique of sexist or patriarchal culture but a feminist critique of Christianity."[43]

A metaphorical image for this group of feminist theologians is "reweaving the web of life."[44] Many see their central task to be the active pursuit of making and keeping peace which, they believe, women are better equipped to achieve than men. Nonviolence is a priority value. For the realizing of this vision, the resources of the Christian faith are considered to offer some help.

In order to appropriate the resources of the Christian tradition a re-examination of Christian roots is needed. This has led feminist theologians who have a basic allegiance to the biblical tradition but who reject the sexism that has accompanied it to be active in biblical studies, church history, theology, and ethics. Among the feminist theologians working in these areas are Phyllis Trible, Elizabeth Schüssler Fiorenza, Eleanor McLaughlin, Joan Morris, Letty Russell, Rosemary Radford Ruether, Patricia Wilson-Kastner, and Beverly Harrison.[45] Thus the diversities among feminist theologians are apparent. Their critiques of established traditions are similar; their positive prescriptions for constructive feminist theology vary. But in most general terms

> the religious feminists' critique is wide-ranging. Among other matters, it addresses religious authority and government and names as inauthentic the bases on which much of these rest. It puts the biblical writers and the early fathers into their historical context. It identifies systems of oppression—sexist, racist, classist—and makes the connections between them both in the church and in the world. It identifies with the poor and hurting. It insists that liberation in one area must lead to liberation in all. It denies the split between spirit and matter. It honors sexuality and women's bodies. It calls for reintegration with nature rather than its subjection.[46]

Further,

it insists that intuitive, subjective, creative, even 'emotional' ways of thinking are as necessary as the rational, abstract, linear, reputedly objective models of exploring reality. It demands that women's experiences, as interpreted by women themselves, be regarded as valid and redemptive. It recognizes new spiritualities and theologies that grow out of these experiences. It attempts new ways of speaking of God—rescuing God from the 'he' categories. It incorporates dance, song, visual arts and poetry into its worship and revelation. Its images and icons come out of women's historic and contemporary lives.[47]

SCRIPTURE IN FEMINIST THEOLOGY

Authority and Interpretation

The varieties among feminist theologians show themselves also on the issue of Scripture. The questions raised by Sakenfeld on how feminists can use the Bible are crucial. The problem feminists have with the Bible is clearly stated by Rosemary Ruether:

The feminist critique of sexism finds patriarchy not only in contemporary and historical Christian culture but in the Bible. The Bible was shaped by males in a patriarchal culture, so many of its revelatory experiences were interpreted by men from a patriarchal perspective. The ongoing interpretation of these revelatory experiences and their canonization further this patriarchal bias by eliminating traces of female experience or interpreting them in an androcentric way. The Bible, in turn, becomes the authoritative source for the justification of patriarchy in Jewish and Christian society.[48]

To speak of "the authority of the Bible" in a constructive or positive sense for feminist theologians means that substantial hermeneutical or interpretive problems must be overcome. As Russell puts it:

the authority of the Bible has to be understood in a way that accounts for the fact that, frequently, the texts are not only contradictory but also sexist, racist, and triumphalist. No interpretation of authority that reinforces patriarchal structures of domination would be acceptable for feminist interpretation.[49]

Thus authority and interpretation of the Bible are intimately bound up together for feminist theologians.

Implicit in Russell's statement is her recognition of what feminist theologians often call the "critical principle of feminist theology." Ruether defines this as the affirmation of and promotion of the full humanity of women. Whatever denies, diminishes, or distorts the full humanity of women is, therefore, to be appraised as not redemptive. Theologically speaking, this means that whatever diminishes or denies the full humanity of women must be presumed not to reflect the divine or authentic relation to the divine, or to reflect the authentic nature of things, or to be the message or work of an authentic redeemer or a community of redemption.[50]

This feminist critical principle means for Ruether the demand that "women stand outside of and in judgment upon this patriarchal bias of the scriptures."[51] Schüssler Fiorenza also applies this directly to the Bible when she writes that

feminist biblical interpretation must therefore challenge the scriptural authority of patriarchal texts and explore how the Bible is used as a weapon against women in our struggles for liberation. It must explore whether and how the Bible can become a resource in this struggle. A feminist biblical interpretation is thus first of all a political task. It remains mandatory because the Bible and its authority has been and is again today used as a weapon against women struggling for liberation.[52]

The relationship of the feminist critical principle to the Bible is a crucial one for feminist theologians.[53] If the Bible were *only* the "authoritative source for the justification of patriarchy in Jewish and Christian society," then, as Ruether points out, "the principle would also demand that feminism reject the scriptures altogether as normative for its own liberation. The Bible would reveal only a demonic falsification of woman's being; it would not provide touchstones for a liberating alternative."[54]

On the other hand, if a hermeneutic or practice of interpretation could be found that could meaningfully use the Bible as a source for understanding human life and persons, then a sense of the authority of Scripture could be acknowledged. For feminists to acknowledge the authority of Scripture in this sense *could* mean that

(1) at least scripture contains something more than a patriarchal view of human life, a support for sexism, and (2) the "more" that scripture embodies rings at least in harmony with the truth of women's reality as it is understood in feminist consciousness—touches it, perhaps unfolds it, makes it resonate with other truths, perhaps can help to test fidelity to it. For those for whom scripture has this authority, the interpretive task becomes imperative.[55]

Feminist Hermeneutics

There are several models to describe feminist biblical interpretation. "Feminist interpretation" can mean simply "the reading of a text (or the writing of an analysis, or the reconstructing of history) in light of the oppressive structures of patriarchal society."[56] Trible refers to it as "a critique of culture in light of misogyny."[57] This reading may be "negative" in that it seeks to expose patriarchal orientations or oppressive intentions in the text or it may be "positive" in that it tries to point out social, religious, and political power of women which has previously been neglected.[58] While all "reformist" feminist theologians acknowledge that "the Bible came into existence in a strongly patriarchal environment and is a product of its time," the question of "how strong that bias is and how it should be dealt with are points on which feminists differ."[59]

Three general approaches of feminist theologians to feminist interpretation may be distinguished.[60] These interpretive procedures carry with them hermeneutical theories which as feminist hermeneutics "attempts to ground its analyses in the experience of women's oppression."[61]

(1) *Reclaiming Texts*. In light of feminist perceptions of patriarchal biases and traditional sexist interpretations, some feminists seek to reclaim biblical texts. This may take the form either of reinterpreting well-known texts in light of feminist consciousness *or* focusing attention on texts that are "forgotten" or distorted by patriarchal hermeneutics. Examples of fresh interpretations that do not portray women in so negative a light as before would be Genesis 2-3, 1 Corinthians 14, and Ephesians 5. Texts formerly overlooked would include Galatians 3:28 and the stories of the relationship of Jesus with women in the Gospels as well as those which show women leaders such as Miriam, Deborah, the women at the tomb of Jesus, Priscilla, and others.[62]

An important practitioner of what might be called the "remnant" standpoint in trying to reclaim texts is Phyllis Trible. Trible seeks to uncover counter-cultural impulses within biblical texts about women and by the use of rhetorical criticism see interpretation as "participation in the movement of the text."[63]

(2) *Theological Perspectives*. A second approach to interpreting biblical texts from a feminist standpoint may be said to look not so much at specific biblical texts but from a theological perspective to see the message of Scripture as a whole. This view "approaches the Bible in the hope of recognizing what the gospel is really all about and then works from that recognition toward a specificity about women.[64]

One leading proponent of this approach is Rosemary Ruether. For Ruether

the Bible can be appropriated as a source of liberating paradigms only if it can be seen that there is a correlation between the feminist critical principle and that critical principle by which biblical thought critiques itself and renews its vision as the authentic Word of God over against corrupting and sinful deformations. It is my contention here that there is such a correlation between biblical and feminist critical principles. This biblical critical principle is that of the prophetic-messianic tradition.[65]

This "prophetic tradition" becomes for Ruether the "central tradition" of Scripture and functions as the norm by which biblical texts are judged. By this, aspects of the Bible are determined as to whether or not they are authoritative. This prophetic tradition has as its central theme the call for the liberation of the oppressed.[66]

The work of Letty Russell shows another approach to interpreting biblical texts from a specifically theological perspective. For Russell, "the Bible is 'scripture,' or sacred writing, because it functions as 'script,' or prompting for life."[67] Scripture's authority, says Russell,

> stems from its story of God's invitation to participation in the restoration of wholeness, peace, and justice in the world. Responding to this invitation has made it my own story, or script, through the power of the Spirit at work in communities of struggle and faith.[68]

Russell's approach distinguishes between scriptural *form* and *content*. The patriarchal language of the Bible is its form but not its content.[69] The theological message of Scripture is God's redemptive and liberating activity in Jesus Christ. This message is found in Scripture through

> God's intention for the mending of all creation. The Bible has authority in my life because it makes sense of my experience and speaks to me about the meaning and purpose of my humanity in Jesus Christ. In spite of its ancient and patriarchal worldviews, in spite of its inconsistencies and mixed messages, the story of God's love affair with the world leads me to a vision of New Creation that impels my life.[70]

The Bible also is the source of her "expectation of justice and liberation."[71]

From this, Russell urges a shift in paradigm to a new model of authority. She rejects the traditional picture of *authority as domination* in favor of *authority as partnership*. This means that people "participate in the common task of creating an interdependent community of humanity and nature."[72] According to Russell, this "shift in feminist interpretive framework means that we no longer need to divide feminist experience and biblical witness."[73]

(3) *Historical Reconstructions*. A third approach to feminist hermeneutics seeks to reconstruct biblical history. Practitioners of this approach attempt to show that "the actual situations of the Israelite and Christian religions allowed a greater role for women than the codified writings suggest."[74] In this view, the earliest phases of Christianity were egalitarian. Thus, "the patriar-

chalization process is not inherent in Christian revelation and community but progressed slowly and with difficulty. Therefore, a feminist biblical hermeneutics can reclaim early Christian theology and history as women's own theology and history."[75]

This emphasis has led Fiorenza to propose a "feminist-critical and a historical-concrete model of biblical interpretation" that is "multidimensional" in its approach. This model she says,

> should not search for a feminist formalized principle, a universal perspective, or a historical liberating dynamics but should carefully analyze how the Bible functions concretely in women's struggle for survival. Key elements in such a model, as far as I can see, are the following: (1) suspicion rather than acceptance of biblical authority, (2) critical evaluation rather than correlation, (3) interpretation through proclamation, (4) remembrance and historical reconstruction, and (5) interpretation through celebration and ritual.[76]

In these diversity of approaches to feminist biblical hermeneutics there is the development of issues and perspectives that will surely affect all biblical hermeneutics in the future.

SCRIPTURE AS MOTHER OF MODELS

Feminist theologians in the "reformist" stream wish to look to the Bible as "providing resources in the struggle for liberation from patriarchal oppression, as well as models for the transformation of the patriarchal church."[77] For this to occur, feminists reject the view of Scripture that sees the Bible as "some special canon of texts that can claim divine authority."[78] Rather, the Bible is viewed not as an "archetype"—as an ideal form that sets an unchanging, timeless pattern; but as a "prototype"—as critically open to the possibility of its own transformation."[79] The Bible is "an open-ended paradigm that sets experiences in motion and invites transformations."[80]

Scripture is a "mother of models." For the Bible is "an instrument by which God shows women their true condition as people who are oppressed and yet who are given a vision of a different heaven and earth and a variety of models for how to live toward that vision."[81] This understanding does not identify biblical revelation with "androcentric texts." It maintains rather that "such revelation is found in the life and ministry of Jesus as well as in the discipleship community of equals called forth by him."[82] Scripture provides a place where the feminist critical consciousness may find congruence with certain of the biblical witnesses.

In the feminist approach to Scripture, "many voices and many visions seek a biblical faith that brings wholeness and well-being."[83] Feminist theologians see their tasks of biblical interpretation as ongoing ones that to this point have only just begun. "What, then, comes next?" As Phyllis Trible has put it: "More work in exegesis and in the historical and social milieu of scripture; the expansion of the enterprise to welcome other women and men; and, perhaps, in God's good time, a biblical theology of womanhood."[84]

ENDNOTES

CHAPTER I

[1]The primary source for many Roman Catholic documents in their original languages is *Enchiridion Symbolorum, Definitionum, et Declarationum de Rebus Fidei et Morum*, eds. H. Denzinger and A. Schonmetzer, 32nd ed. (Freiburg: Herder, 1963); hereafter cited as DS. In English a most helpful collection is *Bible Interpretation*, ed. James J. Megivern, Official Catholic Teachings Series (Wilmington, North Carolina: Consortium Books, 1978). The documents of Vatican II are translated into English in *The Documents of Vatican II*, ed. and trans. W. M. Abbott and J. Gallagher (New York: America Press, 1966).

[2]See the relevant sections in Megivern.

[3]See Avery Dulles, "The Authority of Scripture: A Catholic Perspective," *Scripture in the Jewish and Christian Traditions: Authority, Interpretation, Relevance*, ed. Frederick E. Greenspahn (Nashville: Abingdon, 1982), p. 16.

[4]Dulles, "Authority," p. 17.

[5]Ibid., p.16.

[6]Cited in Jaroslav Pelikan, *The Emergence of the Catholic Tradition (100-600)*, The Christian Tradition: A History of the Development of Doctrine (Chicago: University of Chicago Press, 1971), p. 333. The Latin is *ubique, semper, ab omnibus*.

[7]Cited in Pelikan, *Emergence*, p. 333.

[8]Ibid., p. 334.

[9]See G. W. Bromiley, "Authority," *The International Standard Bible Encyclopedia*, ed. Geoffrey W. Bromiley, 4 vols. (Grand Rapids: Wm. B. Eerdmans Publishing Co., 1979), I, 366; hereafter cited as *ISBE*.

[10]On these see standard histories of the early church and early Christian doctrine. Of particular note are Pelikan, *Emergence*; J.N.D. Kelly, *Early Christian Doctrines*, rev. ed. (New York: Harper & Row, 1978) and the classic work by Adolf von Harnack, *History of Dogma*, trans. Neil Buchanan, 7 vols. (New York: Dover, 1961).

[11]*Paradosis*, the Greek work for "transmission" or "that which is transmitted" orally is used positively in the New Testament for Christian traditions in I Cor. 11:2 and II Thess. 2:15; 3:6. Cf. I Cor. 11:23 and 15:3. See *Teaching Authority & Infallibility in the Church; Lutherans and Catholics in Dialogue VI*, eds. Paul C. Empie, T. Austin Murphy, and Joseph A. Burgess (Minneapolis: Augsburg, 1978), p. 300 n. 24.

[12]See R.P.C. Hanson, *Tradition in the Early Church* (Philadelphia: Westminster Press, 1963), pp. 7ff.

[13]See J.C. Turro and R.E. Brown, "Canonicity," *The Jerome Biblical Commentary*, ed.

R.E. Brown, J.A. Fitzmyer, and R.E. Murphy (Englewood Cliffs, New Jersey: Prentice-Hall, 1968), no. 67 and F.F. Bruce, *Tradition: Old and New* (Grand Rapids: Zondervan, 1970).

[14]G.L. Robinson and R.K. Harrison, "Canon of the OT," in *ISBE*, I, 598. Cf. Kelly, *Doctrines*, p. 52.

[15]The interpretation of the Old Testament from a Christian perspective is a recurrent issue in the history of exegesis. Of particular interest as formative influences are the ways the Old Testament was interpreted by Jesus, Paul, and the New Testament writers. See Robert M. Grant, "Jesus and the Old Testament" and "Paul and the Old Testament" as well as C.K. Barrett, "The Interpretation of the Old Testament in the New" reprinted in *The Authoritative Word: Essays on the Nature of Scripture*, ed. Donald K. McKim (Grand Rapids: Wm. B. Eerdmans Publishing Co., 1983), chs. 2, 3, and 4.

[16]F.F. Bruce, "Tradition and the Canon of Scripture," from *Tradition: Old and New* reprinted in McKim, *Authoritative Word*, pp. 62-63.

[17]On the New Testament canon see R.P. Meye, "Canon of the NT" in *ISBE*, I, 601-606; Kelly, *Doctrines*, pp. 56-60; Werner Georg Kummel, *Introduction to the New Testament*, trans. Howard C. Kee, rev. English ed. (Nashville: Abingdon, 1975), Part II; Bruce, "Tradition" in McKim, *Authoritative Word*, pp. 68-76 and Hanson, ch. 5.

[18]See Hanson, Ch. 5 and Kümmel, pp. 484ff. for a full discussion.

[19]See Bruce, "Tradition," in McKim, *Authoritative Word*, p. 75. Cf. the discussion in Carl A. Volz, *Faith and Practice in the Early Church Foundations for Contemporary Theology* (Minneapolis: Augsburg, 1983), pp. 138-144.

[20]See C. H. Dodd, *The Apostolic Preaching and Its Development* (London: Hodder & Stoughton, 1936); J.N.D. Kelly, *Early Christian Creeds*, 3rd ed. (London: Longmans, Green & Co., 1972); Hanson, ch. 1.

[21]See Kelly, *Creeds* and A.S. Wood, "Creeds and Confessions" in *ISBE*, I, 805-812.

[22]Irenaeus, *Against Heresies*, I. 1. 20 cited in Hanson, p. 75. The Greek phrase is *kanon tes aletheias*.

[23]See Hanson, p. 77.

[24]Ibid., p. 128.

[25]The Creed came to its present form at the Council of Constantinople in 381. Thus the familiar creed is actually the Niceo-Constantinopolitan Creed. See Kelly, *Doctrines*, ch. IX.

[26]See Kelly, *Creeds* and Jack Rogers, *Presbyterian Creeds: A Guide to the Book of Confessions* (Philadelphia: Westminster Press, 1985), ch. 4.

[27]See "Common Statement" in *Teaching Authority*, p. 19 and Volz, pp. 160-170.

[28]"Common Statement" in *Teaching Authority*, p. 20.

[29]Ibid., p. 21.   [30]Ibid.

[31]Volz, p. 173. Stephen I (254-257) was seemingly the first bishop of Rome to assert that he held the see of Peter by succession. See *Teaching Authority*, p. 301 n. 37 and Geoffrey Barraclough, *The Medieval Papacy*, History of European Civilization Library, ed. Geoffrey Barraclough (Norwich, England: Harcourt, Brace & World, 1968), ch. 1 and Robert B. Eno, "Some Elements in the Pre-History of Papal Infallibility" in *Teaching Authority*, pp. 238-258.

[32]See Barraclough's "Bibliographical Notes," pp. 197-205 for reference works on the history of the papacy.

[33]Pelikan, *Emergence*, p. 352.

[34]Epistle *In requirendis* (Dss 217); E. Giles, *Documents Illustrating Papal Authority* (London: SPCK, 1952), p. 201 cited in "Common Statement" in *Teaching Authority*, p. 21.

[35]DS 363 cited in "Common Statement" in *Teaching Authority*, p. 21.

[36]Gregory the Great, *Epistles* 5.37 cited in Pelikan, *Emergence*, p. 352. Cf. Jaroslav Pelikan, *Reformation of Church and Dogma (1300-1700)* The Christian Tradition A History of the Development of Doctrine (Chicago: University of Chicago Press, 1984), pp. 114ff. for examples of later exegesis of the Matthew 16:18 passage.

[37]Cited in Jaroslav Pelikan, *The Growth of Medieval Theology (600-1300)* The Christian Tradition: A History of the Development of Doctrine (Chicago: University of Chicago Press, 1978), p. 47.

[38]Ibid., p. 48. Leo I (440-461) was the first to use the term *pontifex maximus* to refer to the Bishop of Rome.

[39]Ibid.

[40]On this period see Barraclough and Maurice Keen, *The Pelican History of Medieval Europe* (Middlesex, England: Penguin Books, 1969), Section One.

[41]See Barraclough, pp. 77ff.; Keen, pp. 77-80 n. 41; Jeffrey Burton Russell, *A History of Medieval Christianity Prophecy and Order* (New York: Thomas Y. Crowell Co., 1968), ch. X who speaks of "The Offensive of the Papacy" in the twelfth and thirteenth centuries; and Steven Ozment, *The Age of Reform 1250-1550: An Intellectual and Religious History of Late Medieval and Reformation Europe* (New Haven: Yale University Press, 1980), pp. 141-143.

[42]Barraclough, p. 113.

[43]Cited in Ozment, p. 143. Ozment notes that "in canon law 'plenitude of power' (*plenitudo potestatis*) was something the head of a corporation derived from the corporation members and exercised only in conjunction with them, not an all-embracing authority conferred on the pope directly by God." He cites Brian Tierney, *Foundations of the Conciliar Theory: The Contribution of the Medieval Canonists from Gratian to the Great Schism* (Cambridge: Cambridge University Press, 1955), pp. 141-153.

[44]On this history see the works of Barraclough, Keen, and Ozment.

[45]See Ozment, ch. 5: "On the Eve of the Reformation."

[46]Dulles, "Authority," p. 18.

[47]See Megivern, p. 48 for the Council of Hippo (393).

[48]See Megivern, p. 175 for the Council of Florence and p. 180 for the Council of Trent.

[49]Ibid., p. 191.

[50]Dulles, "Authority," p. 18.

[51]Ibid., p. 19.

[52]On this see R.H. Pfeiffer, "Canon of the OT" and F.W. Beare, "Canon of the NT" *The Interpreter's Dictionary of the Bible*, ed. G.A. Buttrick, 4 vols. (Nashville: Abingdon Press, 1962), I, 499-520 and 520-532.

[53]See Dulles, "Authority," pp. 21-22.

[54]Among other sources see Bruce Vawter, *Biblical Inspiration*, Theological Resources, eds. John P. Whalen and Jaroslav Pelikan (Philadelphia: Westminster Press, 1972); hereafter cited as *BI* and Luis Alonso Schökel, *The Inspired Word: Scripture in the Light of Language and Literature*, trans. Francis Martin (New York: Herder and Herder, 1972).

[55]Megivern, p. 175 (DS 1334). Vawter notes that it is here that "the term 'inspire' first entered into conciliar language," *BI*, p. 70. Cf. *Statuta Ecclesiae Antiqua* (DS 325).

[56]Megivern, p. 191 (DS 3006; cf. 3029).

[57]Ibid., p. 191, cf. p. 178. See Vawter's discussion, *BI*, pp. 70ff.

[58]On the various notions of the meaning of "author" for Vatican I see Schökel, pp. 77ff. and Vawter, *BI*, 70-71.

[59]Megivern, p. 216 (DS 3293).

[60]Ibid., p. 215.

[61]Vawter, *BI*, p. 74. Cf. p. 138. See the discussion by Raymond E. Brown, *The Critical Meaning of the Bible* (New York: Paulist Press, 1981), pp. 14ff. Vawter and Brown point out that in Brown's words, "Already in 1893 Pope Leo XIII in *Providentissimus Deus* (DBS 3288) excluded natural or scientific matters from biblical inerrancy, even if he did this through the expedient of insisting that statements made about nature according to ordinary appearances were not errors (p. 15). (An example might involve the sun going around the earth.) Vawter notes that formulation could be traced "all the way back to Aquinas and Augustine," p. 121 (citing Augustine, *Gen. ad. litt.* 2.9, *Patrologia Latina* 34: 270; Aquinas, *Summa Theologiae*, la 70.1 ad3). Leo had further stated that the same principles "will apply to cognate sciences, and especially to history" (Megivern, p. 214; DS 3290). Cf. Bruce Vawter, "The Bible in the Roman Catholic Church" in *Scripture in the Jewish and Christian Traditions*, p. 124.

Brown goes on to note that "thirty years later Pope Benedict XV attempted to close this door in *Spiritus Paraclitus* (1920) when he stated that one could not apply universally to the historical portions of the Scriptures the principles that Leo XIII had laid down for scientific matters, namely, that the authors were writing only according to appearances (DBS 3653)," p. 15.

[62]*Dei Veroum* 11 in Megivern, p. 409.

[63]Dulles, "Authority," p. 23.

[64]Ibid., p. 23.   [65]Ibid., p. 24.

[66]*Dei Verbum* 11 in Megivern, p. 409.

[67]Vawter, *BI*, p. 147 for a discussion of the various drafts of the Vatican II document on Scripture. Cf. Avery Dulles, "Scripture: Recent Protestant and Catholic Views," reprinted in *The Authoritative Word*, pp. 246-248.

[68]Vawter, *BI* p. 147. For interpretations of *Dei Verbum* on inerrancy see A. Grillmeier, "The Divine Inspiration and Interpretation of Sacred Scripture," *Commentary on the Documents of Vatican II*, ed. H. Vorgrimler, trans. W. Glen-Doepel, *et. al.* (New York: Herder and Herder, 1968), III, 199-246; N. Lohfink, "The Truth of the Bible and Historicity," *Theology Digest* (1967), pp. 26-29 and Brown, pp. 18-19.

[69]Brown, p. 19. further notes that "in the inerrancy question Vatican II assumes as *a priori* that God wants the salvation of His people. The extent to which truth in Scripture conforms to that purpose is an *a posteriori* issue." The question of the nature of "truth" is also important here. Vawter maintains that "the concept of biblical inerrancy is not to be confused with the venerable Jewish and Christian affirmation that the Bible is the true Word of God communicated without falsehood. *Falsehood*, not *error*, is the antinomy of the *truth* of the Bible that was sustained by the Fathers and the theologians of the medieval church." See "Bible," p. 128 and *BI*, pp. 132ff. where he writes while discussing Oswald Loretz, *The Truth of the Bible* (New York: Herder and Herder, 1968) that "the root idea of Biblical truth is thus reliability, permanency, steadfastness. Its opposite is not error, but deliberate *lying*, p. 150. Vawter states: "The fact is that in no council of the Universal Church, either before or after the Reformation, has the formula of inerrancy been applied to the Bible." See "Bible," p. 130.

[70]For discussions of Roman Catholic biblical studies see James T. Burtchaell, *Catholic Theories of Biblical Inspiration Since 1810* (Cambridge: Cambridge University Press, 1969); Vawter, *BI* ch. 5: "Inspiration and Contemporary Thinking"; Brown, chs. 1-4; and Megivern, "Introduction." Pope Pius XII's encyclical *Divino Afflante Spiritu* (September 30, 1943) on "The Most Opportune Way to Promote Biblical Studies" [Megivern, pp. 316-342] has been called *l'encyclique liberatrice* ("the encyclical of freedom") since it gave recognition to the literary forms of Scripture. See *BI*, p. 125. It marked "an undeniable about-face in attitude toward biblical criticism. The encyclical...instructed Catholic scholars to use the methods of a scientific approach to the Bible that had hitherto been forbidden to them," cited in Megivern, xxv from Raymond E. Brown, *Biblical Reflection on Crises Facing the Church* (New York: Paulist Press, 1975), p. 6f.

One of the major Roman Catholic theologians of the twentieth century whose views cannot be dealt with here was Karl Rahner (1904-1984). Among his numerous works see *Inspiration in the Bible*, trans, W.J. O'Hara (New York: Herder and Herder, 1964); and for his position after Vatican II: "Bible. I.B. Theology," *Encyclopedia of Theology: The Concise "Sacramentum Mundi"* (New York: Herder and Herder, 1975), pp. 99-108. On Rahner see Dulles, "Scripture," pp. 243-245.

[71]Heiko Augustinus Oberman, *The Harvest of Medieval Theology: Gabriel Biel and Late Medieval Nominalism*, rev. ed. (Grand Rapids: Wm. B. Eerdmans Publishing Co., 1967), p. 6. Oberman calls these "Tradition I" and "Tradition II." See p. 371.

[72]Oberman, p. 372.

[73]Ibid., p. 372. This is the stream in which John Wycliffe (1330?-1384) stands.

[74]Pelikan, *Reformation*, p. 119.

[75]From Occam, *Dialogue* 1.2.2 cited in Pelikan, *Reformation*, p. 120.

[76]Oberman, p. 380. Cf. p. 381. Occam's nominalist philosophy shows here. See Jack B. Rogers and Donald K. McKim, *The Authority and Interpretation of the Bible: An Historical Approach* (San Francisco: Harper & Row, 1979), pp. 48ff. on Occam.

[77]In this stream, Oberman names Occam, Pierre d'Ailly (d. 1420), and Jean Charlier de Gerson (d. 1429).

[78]Pelikan, *Reformation*, pp. 120-121.

[79]Ibid., p. 122.

[80]Augustine, *Against the Epistle of Manicheus Called Fundamental*, 5 (*Corpus scriptorum ecclesiasticorum latinorum* [Vienna, 1866–], 25, 197); Biel, *In Defense of Apostolic Obedience*, 1 cited in Pelikan, *Reformation*, p. 125.

[81]In Vawter, "Scripture," p. 119 (DS 1501). On the proceedings of Trent on this topic see George H. Tavard, *Holy Writ or Holy Church: The Crisis of the Protestant Reformation* (New York: Harper and Brothers, 1959), ch. XII. The standard history of the Council of Trent is Hubert Jedin, *A History of the Council of Trent*, trans. Ernest Graf (London: Nelson, 1961). Cf. *The Canons and Decrees of The Council of Trent*, trans. H.J. Schroeder, 2 vols. (St. Louis: Herder, 1941).

[82]Tavard, p. 208. Cf. Vawter, *BI*, p. 154 who writes that "Catholic belief has consistently maintained that the biblical word must be read and heard within the context of tradition, whose truth is safeguarded by the Church's teaching authority. That authority, in turn, functions within the tradition and is constantly informed by the hearing of the word, for the Church is essentially the pupil of the Holy Spirit (*Dei Verbum*, art. 23)." The Vatican II document states that the Church "has always regarded, and continues to regard the Scriptures, taken together with sacred Tradition, as the supreme rule of her faith." See *Dei Verbum*, art. 21 in Megivern, p. 414. Cf. art. 24 in Megivern, p. 415.

[83]See Brian Tierney, *The Origins of Papal Infallibility, 1150-1350* (Leiden, The Netherlands: E.J. Brill, 1972) and his "Origins of Papal Infallibility," *Journal of Ecumenical Studies*, Vol. 8 (Fall 1971), 841-864.

[84]Guido Terrena, *Question on the Infallible Magisterium of the Roman Pontiff* cited in Pelikan, *Reformation*, p. 107.

[85]See "Common Statement" in *Teaching Authority*, p. 23.

[86](DS 3073, 3074). This translation is in Peter Chirico, *Infallibility: The Crossroads of Doctrine*, Theology and Life Series 1 (Wilmington, Delaware: Michael Galzier, 1983), p. xxxix.

[87]See the extensive treatment by Chirico, *Infallibility*. The following points are taken from p. 143ff.

[88]See Avery Dulles, "Infallibility: the Terminology," in *Teaching Authority*, p. 78.

[89]See Chirico, p. 146 and Dulles, "Infallibility," p. 80.

[90]See Dulles, "Infallibility," p. 90.

[91]Ibid., p.90.

[92]See "Roman Catholic Reflections" on "Common Statement" in *Teaching Authority*, p. 49. The documents are in DS 2803, 3903.

[93]See Hans Küng, *Infallible? An Inquiry*, trans. Edward Quinn (New York: Doubleday, 1971) and Carl J. Peter, "A Rahner-Küng Debate and Ecumenical Possibilities," in *Teaching Authority*, pp. 159-168.

[94]See Megivern, p. 407. Cf. article 10 which states that "Sacred tradition and sacred Scripture make up a single sacred deposit of the Word of God, which is entrusted to the Church," Megivern, p. 408.

[95]See Dulles, "Authority," p. 35.

CHAPTER II

[1]There are numerous fine treatments of the history of the Protestant Reformation. See among the many: Roland Bainton, *The Reformation of the Sixteenth Century* (Boston: Beacon, 1952); Harold J. Grimm, *The Reformation Era 1500-1650* (London: Macmillan, 1965); John M. Todd, *Reformation* (New York: Doubleday, 1971) and Hans J. Hillerbrand, *Christendom Divided: The Protestant Reformation*, Theological Resources, eds. John P. Whalen and Jaroslav Pelikan (Philadelphia: Westminster, 1971).

The larger context of the Reformation is explored in works such as: A.G. Dickens, *Reformation and Society in Sixteenth-Century Europe*, ed. Geoffrey Barraclough, Library of European Civilization (London: Thames and Hudson, 1977); Peter J. Klassen, *Europe in the*

Reformation (Englewood Cliffs, New Jersey: Prentice-Hall, 1979) and S. Harrison Thomson, *Europe in Renaissance and Reformation* (New York: Harcourt, Brace & World, 1963). A very excellent source for numerous aspects of the Reformation is *Reformation Europe: A Guide to Research*, ed. Steven Ozment (St. Louis: Center for Reformation Research, 1982).

[2]The literature on Luther is enormous. Among the biographies, Roland Bainton, *Here I Stand! A Life of Martin Luther* (Nashville and New York: Abingdon, 1950) is most notable. There is scholarly debate as to whether or not Luther actually posted his 95 Theses. Erwin Iserloh, *Luthers Thesenanschlag, Tatsache oder Legend?* (Wiesbaden, 1962) argued that he did not. Other Luther scholars do not agree, however. But the formal scholarly debate Luther sought through his Theses was never held.

[3]*Luther's Works.* American edition, eds. Jaroslav Pelikan and Helmut Lehmann (Philadelphia and St. Louis: Fortress Press and Concordia Publishing House, 1955).

[4]See Heiko Oberman, *Forerunners of the Reformation: The Shape of Late Medieval Thought* (Philadelphia: Fortress, 1981, rpt. 1966), pp. Cf. Luther's teachings as described in Paul Althaus, *The Theology of Martin Luther*, trans. Robert C. Schultz (Philadelphia: Fortress, 1966), pp. 234ff.

[5]Renaissance humanism originated in Italy as a philosophical and literary movement in the second half of the fourteenth century and spread throughout Europe. It looked back to antiquity to seek a revival and development of the human capacities of the ancients. This meant the full education of humans and the cultivation of the "humanities"–the study of poetry, rhetoric, history, ethics and politics. Leading humanists included Gianozzo Manette (1396-1459), Marsilio Ficino (1433-1499), and Pico della Mirandola (1463-1494). Christian humanists applied methods of historical and linguistic scholarship to the Bible. Among the leading Christian humanists were Desiderius Erasmus (1469-1536) and John Colet (1466?-1519). See Paul Oskar Kristeller, *Renaissance Thought: The Classic, Scholastic, and Humanist Strains* (New York: Harper & Row, 1961), ch. 1; Nicola Abbagnano, "Humanism," trans. Nino Languilli, *The Encyclopedia of Philosophy*, ed. Paul Edwards, 8 vols. (New York: Collier Macmillan, 1972), IV, 69-72; hereafter cited as *EP*. Cf. James D. Tracy, "Humanism and the Reformation" in *Reformation Europe*, pp. 33-57 for a valuable discussion and review of the literature. Humanism with its emphasis on history and rhetoric stood as a markedly different approach to learning than was taken by the reigning methods of medieval scholasticism in the Aristotelian tradition, which emphasized philosophy and logic. See Kristeller, chs. 2 and 5.

[6]See Eric W. Gritsch, *Martin–God's Court Jester Luther in Retrospect* (Philadelphia: Fortress, 1983), ch. 9 and Althaus, ch. 18 among other treatments of Luther's theology for Luther's view of justification by faith.

[7]Zwingli became aware of humanism when studying at the University of Vienna. The 320 books and 28 manuscripts in his library also reveal his knowledge of German humanists. See Robert C. Walton, *Zwingli's Theocracy* (Toronto: University of Toronto Press, 1967), p. 22. Cf. G.R. Potter, *Zwingli* (Cambridge: Cambridge University Press, 1976), and *Zwingli and Bullinger*, ed. G.W. Bromiley, Library of Christian Classics (Philadelphia: Westminster, 1973) and Gottfried Locher, *Zwingli's Thought: New Perspectives, Studies in the History of Christian Thought*, ed. Heiko A. Oberman (Leiden, The Netherlands: E.J. Brill, 1981). Cf. Robert C. Walton, "Zwingli: Founding Father of the Reformed Churches," *Leaders of the Reformation*, ed. Richard L. DeMolen (Sellingrove, Pa.: Susquehanna University Press, 1984).

[8]On Erasmus' text of the New Testament see Roland Bainton, *Erasmus of Christendom* (London: Wm. Collins Sons & Co., 1969), ch. 6.

[9]See Walton, "Zwingli," pp. 82ff. for details.

[10]See John T. McNeill, *The History and Character of Calvanism* (New York: Oxford University Press, 1954) and John H. Leith, *Introduction to the Reformed Tradition* (Atlanta: John Knox Press, 1977), ch. 2.

[11]See *Calvin's Commentary on Seneca's 'De Clementia'*, ed. and trans. Ford Lewis Battles and André Malan Hugo (Leiden: E.J. Brill, 1969), particularly the first nine chapters of essays by Battles and Hugo. For a discussion of the importance of Calvin's training as a Christian humanist for his understanding and interpretation of Scripture see Jack B. Rogers and Donald K. McKim, *The Authority and Interpretation of the Bible: An Historical Approach*

(San Francisco: Harper & Row, 1979), pp. 89ff.; hereafter cited as *AIB*.

¹²See *Institution of the Christian Religion* (1536), trans. Ford Lewis Battles (Atlanta: John Knox, 1975) and *Institutes of the Christian Religion*, ed. John T. McNeill, trans. Ford Lewis Battles, 2 vols. Library of Christian Classics (Philadelphia: Westminster, 1960) for the English texts of the 1536 and 1559 editions.

¹³See T.H.L. Parker, *John Calvin: A Biography* (Philadelphia: Westminster, 1975) and Franfois Wendel, *Calvin: The Origins and Development of His Religious Thought*, trans. Philip Mairet (London: William Collins, Sons & Co. Ltd., 1965) and Williston Walker, *John Calvin: The Organiser of Reformed Protestantism*, rep. 1906 (New York: Schocken, 1969) for several of the best studies of Calvin's life and work.

¹⁴See *The Book of Concord: The Confessions of the Evangelical Lutheran Church*, ed. and trans. Theodore G. Tappert (Philadelphia: Fortress, 1959) for the standard English translation.

¹⁵Notable collections of Reformed Confessions may be found in Arthur C. Cochrane, ed., *Reformed Confessions of the 16th Century* (Philadelphia: Westminster, 1966); Philip Schaff, *Creeds of Christendom*, 6th ed. 3 vols., rep. 1919 (Grand Rapids: Baker, 1977); and John H. Leith, ed. *Creeds of the Churches* (New York: Doubleday, 1963) as well as in *The Constitution of the Presbyterian Church (U.S.A.): Part I The Book of Confessions* (New York and Atlanta: The Office of the General Assembly, 1983); hereafter cited as *The Book of Confessions*.

¹⁶See *The Book of Confessions*, *9 and 10. Cf. Edward A. Dowey, Jr., *A Commentary on the Confession of 1967 and an Introduction to "The Book of Confessions"* (Philadelphia: Westminster, 1968) and Jack Rogers, *Presbyterian Creeds: A Guide to The Book of Confessions* (Philadelphia: Westminster, 1985).

¹⁷This approach is adopted rather than focusing specifically on the teachings of Luther and Calvin. For these see *AIB*, pp. 75-116.

¹⁸It is thus sometimes said that the Reformed Confessions are built on the "formal principle" of the Reformation—the authority of canonical Scripture while the Lutheran Symbols are built on its "material principle"—the doctrine of justification by grace through faith. See Edward A. Dowey, Jr., "Revelation and Faith in the Protestant Confessions," *Pittsburgh Perspective* (March 1961), p. 9. This was noted earlier by Karl Barth. See *Church Dogmatics*, trans. G.T. Thomson and Harold Knight (Edinburgh: T.&T. Clark, 1956), I/2, 547.

¹⁹Edmund Schlink, *Theology of the Lutheran Confessions* (Philadelphia: Fortress, 1961), p. 24.

²⁰Schlink, p. 24. Schlink also writes: "This intense concern with the Gospel suggests that the Gospel is the norm in Scripture and Scripture is the norm for the sake of the Gospel. From this point of view we can understand why none of the Confessions before the Formula of Concord contain a section on Holy Scripture, because not only do individual articles specifically treat the Gospel, but in the final analysis all articles in the Confessions are concerned with the Gospel."

²¹Cochrane, *Reformed Confessions*, p. 146. Cf. Brian A. Gerrish, ed. *The Faith of Christendom: A Sourcebook of Creeds and Confessions* (Cleveland: World, 1963), pp. 126ff. for an introduction to this Confession and the English text.

²²Cochrane, *Reformed Confessions*, p. 165. The original language of the Confession is in Schaff, *Creeds of Christendom*, III, 437ff.

²³*The Book of Concord*, p. 464. Lutheran dogmaticians later affirmed this clearly. Abraham Calov (1612-1686) wrote that the first requirement for a Symbol was that it "must agree with Scripture and contain nothing which is not in Scripture either literally or virtually"; cited in Robert D. Preus, *The Inspiration of Scripture* (Mankato, Minnesota: Lutheran Synod Book Company, 1955), p. 132 from Calov's, *Exegema Augustanae Confessionis* (1665). The Lutherans often made the distinction between Scripture and the Confessions by designating Scripture as "the *norma normans* of theology" ("the standard which rules all") and the Confessions as "the *norma normata*" ("that ruled by the standard"). Thus, "in controversy the appeal must be made from the Symbols to the higher authority of Scripture." See Robert D. Preus, *The Theology of Post-Reformation Lutheranism* (St. Louis: Concordia, 1970), p. 38.

²⁴See Barth, *CD* I/2, 475-476.

[25]See Calvin, *Institutes* I. vii. 2. As Calvin writes: "If the teaching of the prophets and apostles is the foundation, this must have had an authority before the church began to exist."

[26]Cochrane, *Reformed Confessions*, p. 120.

[27]*The Book of Concord*, p. 464.

[28]Ibid., p. 25, sec. 8.   [29]Ibid., p. 48.

[30]Ibid., p. 95, sec. 5.   [31]Ibid., p. 99, sec. 9.

[32]Ibid., p. 295, sec. 15.   [33]Ibid., p. 465, sec. 7.

[34]Schaff, *Creeds of Christendom*, I, 313.

[35]*Book of Concord*, 503-504, sec. 3.

[36]No attempt is made here to be exhaustive of either the Reformed Confessions or the complete teachings on Scripture in the ones cited. For a fuller treatment of sixteenth-century Reformed Confessions on Scripture see *AIB*, pp. 116-125.

[37]For the text of Zwingli's Sixty-seven Articles see Cochrane, *Reformed Confessions*, pp. 33-44.

[39]For the text of the French Confession see Cochrane, *Reformed Confessions*, pp. 137-158.

[40]For the text of the Scots Confession see *The Book of Confessions*, 3.01-3.251 and Cochrane, *Reformed Confessions*, pp. 159-184. Cf. Rogers, *Presbyterian Creeds*, pp. 79-95.

[41]For the text of the Second Helvetic Confession see *The Book of Confessions* which is reprinted from Cochrane, *Reformed Confessions*, pp. 220-301. On the Second Helvetic Confession see Rogers, *Presbyterian Creeds*, pp. 116-139.

[42]See *AIB*, p. 125.

[43]For the text of the Westminster Confession see the section reprinted in *AIB*, pp. 468-470 from *The Confession of Faith of the Assembly of Divines at Westminster: From the Original Manuscript Written by Cornelius Burges in 1646*, ed. S.W. Carruthers and published by the Presbyterian Church of England in 1946. Cf. *The Book of Confessions*, 6.001-6.178. On the Westminster Confession see Rogers, *Creeds*, pp. 140-171.

[44]For a detailed exposition of the Westminster Confession's views on Scripture see Jack B. Rogers, *Scripture in the Westminster Confession* (Grand Rapids: Wm. B. Eerdmans Publishing Co., 1967); cf. *AIB*, pp. 200-218 and Rogers, *Presbyterian Creeds*, pp. 161-165.

[45]For the text of The Theological Declaration of Barmen see Arthur C. Cochrane, *The Church's Confession Under Hitler* (Philadelphia: Westminster Press, 1962), pp. 237-242; reprinted in *The Book of Confessions*, 8.01-8.28 and Cochrane, *Reformed Confessions*, pp. 332-336.

[46]See Cochrane, *Church's Confession*; Rogers, *Presbyterian Creeds*, pp. 175-201 and Donald K. McKim, "The Declaration of Barmen After 50 Years," *The Presbyterian Outlook* Vol. 166, no. 2 (June 4, 1984), pp. 6-8.

[47]For the text of The Confession of 1967 see *The Book of Confessions*, 9.01-9.56.

[48]On the Confession of 1967 see *AIB*, pp. 437-440 and Rogers, *Presbyterian Creeds*, pp. 202-230. Of further interest are two studies on Scripture received in 1982 and 1983 by the current Presbyterian Church (USA). These are *Biblical Authority and Interpretation*, Advisory Council on Discipleship and Worship (475 Riverside Drive, Room 1020, New York, N.Y. 10115) and *Presbyterian Understanding and Use of Holy Scripture*, Presbyterian Church (USA), Office of the General Assembly (341 Ponce de Leon Ave. NE, Atlanta, Ga 30365).

[49]The term "left wing" was coined by Roland Bainton in "The Left Wing of the Reformation," *The Journal of Religion*, Vol. 21 (1941), pp. 124-134 and then revised in *Studies on the Reformation* (1966). For "radical Reformation" see George H. Williams, *The Radical Reformation* (Philadelphia: Westminster Press, 1962).

[50]Ernst Troeltsch, *The Social Teaching of the Christian Churches*, trans. Olive Wyon, 2 vols. (Chicago: University of Chicago Press, 1981), II, 69lff. Cf. 742.

[51]See *Spiritualist and Anabaptist Writers*, eds. George H. Williams and Angel M. Mergal, Library of Christian Classics (Philadelphia: Westminster Press, 1957), p. 20ff.

[52]See Henning Graf Reventlow, *The Authority of the Bible and the Rise of the Modern World*, trans. John Bowden (Philadelphia: Fortress Press, 1985), p. 49 who cites H. Fast,

ed., *Der linke Flugel der Reformations* (1962) for this delineation.

[53]Reventlow, p. 50 and the extensive notes he cites.

[54]Jaroslav Pelikan, *Reformation of Church and Dogma (1300-1700), The Christian Tradition: A History of the Development of Doctrine* (Chicago: University of Chicago Press, 1984), p. 314.

[55]Harold J. Grimm, *The Reformation Era 1500-1650* (New York: The Macmillan Co., 1965), p. 265.

[56]Among sources on Anabaptism see W.R. Estep, *The Anabaptist Story* (Grand Rapids: Wm. B. Eerdmans Publishing Co., 1975); Hans J. Hillerbrand, *A Fellowship of Discontent* (New York: Harper & Row, 1967); William Keeney, *The Development of Dutch Anabaptist Thought and Practice 1539-1564* (Nieuwkoop: de Graaf, 1968); William Klassen, *Covenant and Community* (Grand Rapids: Wm. B. Eerdmans Publishing Co., 1968). Cf. the bibliography in Grimm, pp. 645ff.

[57]See Grimm, p. 266.

[58]Cited in Hans J. Hillerbrand, *Christendom Divided*, Theological Resources, eds. John P. Whalen and Jaroslav Pelikan (Philadelphia: Westminster Press, 1971), p. 73.

[59]Hillerbrand, *Christendom Divided*, p. 73.

[60]On these see among others the works of Grimm, Hillerbrand, *Christendom Divided* and Peter J. Klassen, *Europe in the Reformation* (Englewood Cliffs, New Jersey: Prentice-Hall, 1979), pp. 116ff.

[61]Williams, ed., *Spiritual and Anabaptist Writers*, p. 31.

[62]For the Schleitheim Confession see the translation by John H. Yoder in *The Legacy of Michael Sattler* (Scottdale, Pa.: Herald Press, 1973), pp. 34-43 and also J.C. Wenger, "The Schleitheim Confession of Faith," *Mennonite Quarterly Review*, 19 (1945), pp. 243-253. Cf. the "Introduction" in John Calvin, *Treatises Against the Anabaptists and Against the Libertines*, ed. and trans. Benjamin Wirt Farley (Grand Rapids: Baker Book House, 1982). This work was Calvin's response to the Schleitheim Confession. Cf. Willem Balke, *Calvin and the Anabaptist Radicals*, trans. William Heynen (Grand Rapids: Wm. B. Eerdmans Publishing Co., 1981).

[63]Pelikan, *Reformation*, p. 317.

[64]Reventlow, p. 52 citing H. Bender, *Das tauferische Leitbild*, p. 44.

[65]See particularly Franklin Littell, *The Anabaptist View of the Church*, 2nd ed., rev. (Boston: Starr King, 1957), p. 11ff.

[66]Cited in Pelikan, *Reformation*, p. 319.

[67]Grimm, p. 267.

[68]Reventlow, p. 53.

[69]Reventlow, p. 53. Cf. John H. Yoder, "The Hermeneutics of the Anabaptists," in *Essays on Biblical Interpretation: Anabaptist-Mennonite Perspectives*, ed. Willard Swartley, Text–Reader Series No. 1 (Elkhart, Indiana: Institute of Mennonite Studies, 1984), p. 18. This is a most helpful volume with an extensive Bibliography.

[70]Reventlow, p. 53. Cf. William Klassen, "Anabaptist Hermeneutics: The Letter and the Spirit" in Swartley, ed., pp. 77-90.

[71]Yoder, "Hermeneutics," p. 18.

[72]Ibid.

[73]These points are summarized from Ben C. Ollenburger, "The Hermeneutics of Obedience Reflections on Anabaptist Hermeneutics" in Swartley, ed., pp. 47-48.

[74]These points are summarized from Ollenburger, pp. 48-50. Cf. the similar emphases in Yoder, "Hermeneutics."

[75]See Farley's "Introduction" to Calvin, *Treatises Against the Anabaptists and Against the Libertines*, p. 28. Cf. Reventlow, pp. 57-59. Zwingli had also written against the Anabaptists in his *Refutation of the Tricks of the Baptists* in *Ulrich Zwingli: Selected Works*, ed. Samuel Macauley Jackson (Philadelphia: University of Pennsylvania, 1972), pp. 123-258.

[76]Henry Poettcker, "Menno Simons' Encounter with the Bible" in Swartley, ed., p. 65.

[77]Walter Klaassen, "Anabaptist Hermeneutics: Presuppositions, Principles and Practice," in Swartley, ed., p. 10.

[78]Ibid., p. 10. [79]Ibid., p. 6.

[80]Cited in Reventlow, p. 53.

[81]Reventlow links the Anabaptists' use of Scripture to Erasmus when he writes: "Following the insights gained by Erasmus, this theology of scripture culminates in an ethic of discipleship modelled on the example and the teaching of Jesus," p. 54. Numerous essays in Swartley's book bear out this stress on obedience and discipleship. See for example C.J. Dyck, "Hermeneutics and Discipleship," pp. 29-44.

[82]Melchior Hofmann, "Ordinance of God" from *Spiritual and Anabaptist Writers*, p. 203.

CHAPTER III

[1]Quoted in Karl Barth, *Protestant Theology in the Nineteenth Century: Its Background & History* (Valley Forge: Judson Press, 1973), p. 425.

[2]Barth, *Protestant Theology*, p. 425.

[3]On Schleiermacher, see Barth, *Protestant Theology*, pp. 425-473 and his 1923/24 Göttingen lectures published as *The Theology of Schleiermacher*, ed. Dietrich Ritschl, trans. Geoffrey W. Bromiley (Grand Rapids: Eerdmans, 1982). Among the other vast literature see Martin Redeker, *Schleiermacher: Life and Thought*, trans. John Wallhausser (Philadelphia: Fortress Press, 1973); Robert R. Williams, *Schleiermacher the Theologian: The Construction of the Doctrine of God* (Philadelphia: Fortress, 1978) and Brian A. Gerrish, *A Prince of the Church* (Philadelphia: Fortress, 1984).

[4]This would be true of theologians such as Karl Barth and Paul Tillich.

[5]For this story see among other sources William E. Hordern, *A Layman's Guide to Protestant Theology* (New York: Macmillan, 1968), p. 73ff.; Robert Clyde Johnson, *Authority in Protestant Theology* (Philadelphia: Westminster Press, 1959), Parts II and III.

[6]Kenneth Cauthen, *The Impact of American Religious Liberalism* (New York: Harper & Row, 1962), p. 3.

[7]Ibid., p. 5.

[8]*Liberal Protestantism*, ed. Bernard M.G. Reardon, A Library of Modern Religious thought, ed. Henry Chadwick (Stanford California: Stanford University Press, 1968), p. 11.

[9]Hordern, p. 74.

[10]See Barth, *Protestant Theology*, p. 459, Hordern, pp. 44-47 and Lloyd J. Averill, *American Theology in the Liberal Tradition* (Philadelphia: Westminster Press, 1967), pp. 34-39.

[11]Williams, p. 2. Barth deals with Kant in *Protestant Theology*, ch. 7.

[12]Friedrich Schleiermacher, *On Religion: Speeches to Its Cultured Despisers*, intro. Rudolf Otto (New York: Harper & Brothers, 1958), p. 31. Cf. Averill, p. 37.

[13]Schleiermacher wrote: "The sum total of religion is to feel that, in its highest unity, all that moves us in feeling is one; to feel that aught single and particular is only possible by means of this unity; to feel, that is to say, that our being and living is a being and living in and through God," *On Religion*, pp. 49-50.

[14]Ibid., p. 39.   [15]Ibid., p. 36.

[16]See Barth, *Protestant Thought*, p. 467.

[17]Averill, pp. 36-37.

[18]Hordern, p. 46.

[19]On Ritschl see Barth, *Protestant Thought*, ch. 29; Hordern, pp. 46-49; David Müller, *An Introduction to the Theology of Albrecht Ritschl* (Philadelphia: Westminster, 1969); Reardon, pp. 20-34 and Averill, pp. 39-43.

[20]Albrecht Ritschl, *The Christian Doctrine of Justification and Reconciliation* (Edinburgh: T.&T. Clark, 1902), III, 10. Cf. William R. Hutchison, *The Modernist Impulse in American Protestantism* (Cambridge, Massachusetts: Harvard University Press, 1976), pp. 122-129 on "Ritschlianism and the Uniqueness of Christianity."

[21]Hordern, p. 47.

[22]On Harnack see Reardon, pp. 44-48; Averill, pp. 45-47; Philip Hefner, *Faith and the Vitalities of History* (New York: Harper & Row, 1966); G. Wayne Glick, *The Reality of Christianity: A Study of Adolf von Harnack as Historian and Theologian*, Makers of Mod-

ern Theology, ed. Jaroslav Pelikan (New York: Harper & Row, 1967), and Hutchison who points out that Harnack influenced more American liberals than had Ritschl, pp. 129-130.

[23]Adolf von Harnack, *What is Christianity?*, trans. T.B. Saunders (New York: Harper & Brothers, 1957), p. 8. Harnack's 1899-1900 lectures were entitled "Das Wesen des Christentums."

[24]Ibid., p. 51.

[25]The following discussion is drawn from Cauthen's excellent study, ch. 1. Also of value is Averill, ch. 3: "A Profile of American Theological Liberalism 1879-1917."

[26]Cauthen, p. 6.

[27]Ibid., p. 9.

[28]Ibid.   [29]Ibid., p. 12.

[30]Cauthen, p. 16. Cauthen points out that this reaction is seen in various philosophies such as the distinctions between the pure and practical reason (Kant), understanding and reason (Coleridge), the natural and the supernatural (Bushnell), and nature and moral personality (Ritschl).

[31]On the period generally see *AIB*, p. 407 and H.G. Reventlow, *Biblical Authority and the Rise of the Modern World*, trans. John Bowden (Philadelphia: Fortress, 1985).

[32]John Herman Randall, Jr., *The Making of the Modern Mind* (Boston: Houghton Mifflin Co., 1926), p. 391.

[33]Cauthen, p. 22.

[34]Cauthen, p. 23. Cauthen points out that "this application of evolutionary ideas to the study of the Hebrew religion by the Wellhausen school of thought came to dominate biblical studies in the latter part of the nineteenth century."

[35]Harry Emerson Fosdick, *The Living of These Days* (New York: Harper & Brothers, 1956), p. vii.

[36]Cauthen, p. 27.

[37]Harry Emerson Fosdick, *The Modern Use of the Bible* (New York: Macmillan, 1961), Lecture IV. Cauthen cites Henry P. Van Dusen, *The Vitality of the Christian Tradition*, ed. George F. Thomas (New York: Harper & Brothers, 1944), pp. 168-169 as the source of the distinctions among liberals. Also helpful is Averill's ch. 4, "The Varieties of Liberalism: Three Significant Variables" where he makes methodological, ethical, and institutional distinctions.

[38]Cauthen, p. 30. Cauthen's work analyzes the thought of representatives of both varieties of liberal theology. Cf. the selections in *American Protestant Thought: The Liberal Era*, ed. William R. Hutchison (New York: Harper & Row, 1968).

[39]Cauthen, p. 45. Cf. Avery Dulles, *Models of Revelation* (New York: Doubleday, 1983), ch. 5.

[40]Cauthen, p. 45, who makes this comment in his study of William Adams Brown.

[41]L. Harold DeWolf, *The Case for Theology in Liberal Perspective* (Philadelphia: Westminster Press, 1959), p. 17. Walter Rauschenbusch wrote that for a Christian "the only sure guide in speaking of God is the mind of Christ. That is our logic and metaphysic," *A Theology for the Social Gospel* (New York: The Macmillan Company, 1917), p. 264.

[42]DeWolf, *Case*, p. 18.

[43]Ibid., p. 18.

[44]C.H. Dodd, *The Authority of the Bible*, rev. ed. (London: Collins, 1967), p. 27. Dodd's whole approach exemplifies the emphases of liberalism. In this early writing (originally published in 1929), he sees the writers of Scripture as "religious geniuses."

[45]DeWolf, *Case*, p. 17.

[46]Ibid., p. 46.   [47]Ibid., p. 47.

[48]Paul J. Achtemeier, *The Inspiration of Scripture Problems and Proposals* (Philadelphia: Westminster, 1980), p. 42 cites examples of some of these drawn from liberal theologians. Cf. DeWolf, *Case*, pp. 47-48.

[49]DeWolf, *Case*, p. 48.

[50]See Achtemeier, p. 43.

[51]L. Harold DeWolf, *A Theology of the Living Church*, rev. ed. (New York: Harper & Brothers, 1960), p. 75.

[52]DeWolf, *Case*, p. 48.

[53]DeWolf, *A Theology*, p. 76.

[54]See Achtemeier, p. 44.

[55]See Bruce Vawter, *Biblical Inspiration* (Philadelphia: Westminster, 1972), pp. 89, 126.

[56]Donald E. Miller, *The Case for Liberal Christianity* (San Francisco: Harper & Row, 1981), p. 36.

[57]Ibid., p. 74.   [58]Ibid., p. 75.

[59]*Spectrum of Protestant Beliefs*, ed. Robert Campbell (Milwaukee: Bruce Publishing Co., 1968), p. 34.

[60]Miller, p. 75.

[61]DeWolf, *Case*, pp. 56, 57.

[62]Fosdick, *The Modern Use of the Bible*, pp. 97-130.

[63]Campbell, ed., *Spectrum*, p.34. Cf. Leland Harder, "Zwingli's Reaction to the Schleitheim confession of Faith of the Anabaptists," *The Sixteenth Century Journal*, (1980), pp. 51-66.

[64]Cauthen, p. 66. Cf. pp. 217-218. Rauschenbusch said: "Theology needs periodic rejuvenation. Its greatest danger is not mutilation but senility," *A Theology for the Social Gospel*, p. 12.

CHAPTER IV

[1]*The Fundamentalist Phenomenon*, ed. Jerry Falwell with Ed Dobson and Ed Hinson (New York: Doubleday, 1981), p. 1. The statement was written by Dobson and Hindson, Falwell's pastoral associates at the Liberty Baptist Church in Lynchburg, Virginia.

[2]George M. Marsden, *Fundamentalism and American Culture: The Shaping of Twentieth-Century Evangelicalism 1870-1925* (New York: Oxford University Press, 1980), p. 6.

[3]*The Fundamentalist Phenomenon*, p. 1.

[4]Martin E. Marty, "Fundamentalism as a Social Phenomenon," in *Evangelicalism and Modern America*, ed. George Marsden (Grand Rapids: Eerdmans, 1984), p. 56.

[5]Martin E. Marty, "Fundamentalism Reborn," *Saturday Review* (May 1980), p. 38 as cited in *The Fundamentalist Phenomenon*, p. 1.

[6]Richard N. Ostling, "Evangelical Publishing and Broadcasting," in *Evangelicalism and Modern America*, p. 48.

[7]*The Fundamentalist Phenomenon*, pp. 1-2.

[8]Stewart G. Cole, *The History of Fundamentalism* (New York: Richard R. Smith, Inc., 1931), p. xi.

[9]H. Richard Niebuhr, "Fundamentalism," *Encyclopedia of Social Sciences*, VI (New York, 1937), pp. 526-527. Marsden notes that Niebuhr originally came to this interpretation in his *The Social Sources of Denominationalism* (New York, 1929) but that "later in life he repudiated such exclusively sociological explanations," p. 283.

[10]Norman F. Furniss, *The Fundamentalist Controversy, 1918-1931* (New Haven: Yale University Press, 1954); Ray Ginger, *Six Days or Forever? Tennessee v. John Thomas Scopes* (Boston: Beacon Press, 1958). See also Timothy P. Weber "The Two-Edged Sword: The Fundamentalist Use of the Bible," in *The Bible in America*, eds. Nathan O. Hatch and Mark A. Noll (New York: Oxford University Press, 1982), p. 101ff.

[11]Richard Hofstadter, *Anti-Intellectualism in American Life* (New York: Random House, 1962), p. 121. Cf. Marsden, ch. XXIII: "Fundamentalism as a Social Phenomenon."

[12]Paul Carter, "The Fundamentalist Defense of the Faith," *Change and Continuity in Twentieth-Century America: The 1920s*, eds. John Braeman, Robert Bremner, David Brody (Columbus: Ohio State University Press, 1968), pp. 179-214.

[13]Ernest R. Sandeen, *The Roots of Fundamentalism* (Chicago: University of Chicago Press, 1970).

[14]Marsden, p. 4.

[15]Weber, p. 102.

[16]Marsden, p. 6.

[17]On Darwinism see Marsden, pp. 18-21 and John D. Woodbridge, Mark A. Noll, and Nathan O. Hatch, *The Gospel in America: Themes in the Story of America's Evangelicals* (Grand Rapids: Zondervan, 1979), pp. 49ff.; hereafter cited as *Gospel*.

[18]See George M. Marsden, *The Evangelical Mind and the New School Presbyterian Experience* (New Haven: Yale University Press, 1970).

[19]*Gospel*, pp. 50-51.

[20]Marsden, pp. 21-22.

[21]On Liberal theology see ch. IV of the present work.

[22]*Gospel*, p. 52.

[23]Ibid., p. 54.

[24]*The Fundamentals: A Testimony to the Truth*, ed. R.A. Torrey and others (rpt. Grand Rapids: Baker Book House, 1980).

[25]See William R. Hutchison, *The Modernist Impulse in American Protestantism* (Cambridge, Mass.: Harvard University Press, 1976), p. 198 and *Gospel*, p. 58.

[26]On Dispensationalism see Marsden, *Evangelical Mind* and *Gospel*, pp. 70-73.

[27]See Marsden, pp. 119-120.

[28]Ibid., ch. XVI.

[29]On the variations of these points see Marsden, p. 262 n. 30 and Sandeen, *Roots*, xiv-xv. In 1919 the General Assembly of the Presbyterian Church adopted five points that all ordination candidates had to affirm as "essential and necessary doctrines." These were the inerrancy of Scripture, the virgin birth of Christ, Christ's death as a sacrifice to satisfy divine justice and reconcile humankind to God, and Christ's mighty miracles. See Lefferts A. Loetscher, *The Broadening Church: A Study of Theological Issues in the Presbyterian Church since 1869* (Philadelphia: University of Pennsylvania Press, 1954), p. 98. Cf. *The Fundamentalist Phenomenon*, p. 7.

[30]See J. Gresham Machen, *Christianity and Liberalism* (New York: Macmillan, 1923). On Machen see C. Allyn Russell, *Voices of American Fundamentalism: Seven Biographical Studies* (Philadelphia: Westminster Press, 1976), ch. 6: "J. Gresham Machen: Scholarly Fundamentalist."

[31]On this controversy see Marsden, ch. XIX and Russell, ch. 8: "Clarence E. Macartney: Preacher–Fundamentalist."

[32]See Marsden, ch. XXI.

[33]Ibid., p. 191.

[34]On the history see Louis Gasper, *The Fundamentalist Movement 1930-1956* (rpt. Grand Rapids: Baker Book House, 1981). Cf. *The Fundamentalist Phenomenon*, chs. 5-6.

[35]Marsden, p. 195.

[36]See Donald G. Bloesch, *The Future of Evangelical Christianity: A Call for Unity Amid Diversity* (New York: Doubleday, 1983), pp. 28-29 for a most helpful listing of fundamentalist organizations, institutions and leaders.

[37]On this see chapter 5 of the present work.

[38]A.A. Hodge and B.B. Warfield, "Inspiration," *Presbyterian Review* (1881), 245. Cf. *AIB*, ch. 6.

[39]A.A. Hodge and B.B. Warfield, "Inspiration," p. 234. Cf. p. 243.

[40]Harold Lindsell, *The Battle for the Bible* (Grand Rapids: Zondervan, 1976), p. 210. Lindsell's sequel along the same line is *The Bible in the Balance* (Grand Rapids: Zondervan, 1978). Harold J. Ockenga writes: "By 1942, evangelical was equated with orthodox, as was evidenced by the naming of the interdenominational cooperative movement 'The National Association of Evangelicals.' Evangelicalism became a synonym for fundamentalism." See "From Fundamentalism, Through New Evangelicalism, to Evangelicalism" in *Common Roots*, ed. Kenneth Kantzer (Nashville: Thomas Nelson, 1978), p. 38.

[41]On Neo-Evangelicalism see chapter 7 of this work.

[42]See Bloesch, p. 25. The authors of *The Fundamentalist Phenomenon* write that "the predominant characteristic of Fundamentalism in the last thirty years has been its strong commitment to separatism," p. 145.

[43]George M. Marsden, "From Fundamentalism to Evangelicalism: A Historical Analysis," in *The Evangelicals*, eds. David F. Wells and John D. Woodbridge (Nashville: Abingdon,

1975), p. 128. George W. Dollar, *A History of Fundamentalism in America* (Greenville, South Carolina: Bob Jones University Press, 1973) distinguishes "militant" from "moderate" fundamentalists, pp. 283-284. Richard Quebedeaux, *The Young Evangelicals: Revolution in Orthodoxy* (New York: Harper & Row, 1974) distinguishes "separatist" and "open" Fundamentalists. See pp. 18-28.

[44]See Bloesch, *Future*, p. 25.

[45]Ibid., pp. 26-27.

[46]Bloesch cites the Philadelphia Conference on Reformed Theology as an heir to the scholastic stream though "the sponsors of the conference have moved from a rigid fundamentalist posture and are better classified as neo-fundamentalist or neoevangelical," *Future*, p. 27. Cf. Kenneth S. Kantzer, "Unity and Diversity in Evangelical Faith," in *The Evangelicals*, pp. 38-67 for a description of varieties of "evangelicalism" in the Fundamentalist tradition.

[47]Dispensationalism was spread through American Fundamentalism by the *Schofield Reference Bible*. See James Barr, *Fundamentalism* (Philadelphia: Westminster, 1977), pp. 191-207.

[48]See Chapter 5 of the present work.

[49]Charles C. Ryrie, *What You Should Know About Inerrancy* (Chicago: Moody Press, 1981), p. 17.

[50]Ryrie, p. 15.

[51]Ibid., p. 15.

[52]"The Chicago Statement" is found in *Inerrancy*, ed. Norman L. Geisler (Grand Rapids: Zondervan, 1979) and in *Evangelicals and Inerrancy*, ed. Ronald Youngblood (Nashville: Thomas Nelson, 1984), pp. 230-239; hereafter cited as *EI*. The quotation is from Article VI in *EI*, p. 232. The emphasis on the original, autographic text is furthered in Article X which reads: "We affirm that inspiration, strictly speaking, applies only to the autographic text of Scripture, which in the providence of God can be ascertained from available manuscripts with great accuracy. We further affirm that copies and translations of Scripture are the Word of God to the extent that they faithfully represent the original," *EI*, p. 233.

[53]Ryrie, p. 16.

[54]"Chicago Statement," Article VI in *EI*, p. 232.

[55]Ryrie, p. 16.

[56]"Chicago Statement," Article XI in *EI*,. p. 233.

[57]Ibid., in *EI*, p. 237.

[58]Ibid., Article VII in *EI*, p. 232.

[59]John R. Rice, *The Sword of the Lord* (January 10, 1975), p. 14 cited in Ryrie, p. 35. Another contemporary fundamentalist Bob Jones, Jr. writes that "God Himself chose the very word that should be put down to convey exactly what He meant to convey. This precludes any possibility of human personality intruding upon and interfering with what God had to say." But he goes on to say: "We do not mean to imply by this that God merely dictated the Word to those who wrote It—that He made out of them a typewriter upon which His fingers played. God does not intrude upon human personality in that way." See *Spectrum of Protestant Beliefs*, ed. Robert Campbell (Milwaukee: Bruce Publishing Co., 1968), p. 30.

[60]John R. Rice, *Our God-Breathed Book—The Bible* (Murfreesboro, Tennessee: Sword of the Lord, 1969), p. 286 as cited in Norman L. Geisler, *Decide for Yourself* (Grand Rapids: Zondervan, 1982), p. 72.

[61]Rice, p. 287 cited in Geisler, p. 72. Lindsell affirms that he does not know "any scholar who believes in biblical inerrancy who holds that the Scriptures were received by dictation," *Battle*, p. 33.

[62]Ryrie, p. 16.

[63]Ibid., p. 30.

[64]"Chicago Statement," in *EI*, p. 237.

[65]Ibid., p. 233. This latter statement concerning the teaching of Scripture on creation and the flood represents a continuation of fundamentalism's fight against evolutionism. See above note 32.

[66]"Chicago Statement," Article XI in *EI*, p. 233.

[67]Clark H. Pinnock, *Biblical Revelation—The Foundation of Christian Theology* (Chicago: Moody, 1971), p. 78.

[68]Carl F.H. Henry in *Spectrum of Protestant Beliefs*, p. 32.

[69]Lindsell, *Battle*, pp. 30-31. In the "Summary Statement" of the "Chicago Statement" one point is that Scripture is "of infallible divine authority in all matters upon which it touches: It is to be believed, as God's instruction, in all that it affirms," in *EI*, p. 231.

Article XIII elaborates the relation of inerrancy to the phenomena of Scripture: "We further deny that inerrancy is negated by Biblical phenomena such as a lack of modern technical precision, irregularities of grammar or spelling, observational descriptions of nature, the reporting of falsehoods, the use of hyperbole and round numbers, the topical arrangement of material, variant selections of material in parallel accounts, or the use of free citations," in *EI*, p. 234.

[70]Weber, "Fundamentalist Use of the Bible," p. 106.

[71]Ryrie, p. 82. Cf. "Chicago Statement," Article XIV where it is denied that "errors and discrepancies that have not yet been resolved vitiate the truth claims of the Bible," in *EI*, p. 234.

[72]Cited in the Presidential Address of Stanley N. Gundry to the Evangelical Theological Society in *EI*, p. 244.

[73]Ronald Youngblood, "Preface" in *EI*, p. xi.

[74]Avery Dulles, *Models of Revelation* (New York: Doubleday, 1983), p. 39.

[75]Carl F.H. Henry, *God, Revelation and Authority*, Vol. II (Waco, Texas: Word, 1976), 87.

[76]Henry, *God, Revelation, and Authority*, II, 12; cf. III, 455. Dulles also cites Gordon Clark: "Aside from imperative sentences and a few exclamations in the Psalms, the Bible is composed of propositions. These give information about God and his dealings with men," *Karl Barth's Theological Method* (Nutley, New Jersey: Presbyterian and Reformed Publishing Co.), p. 150; Francis Schaeffer: "God has spoken in a linguistic propositional form, truth concerning himself and truth concerning man, history, and the universe," *The God Who Is There* (Chicago: Inter-Varsity Press, 1968), p. 93 and Pinnock: "Revelation is enshrined in written records and is essentially propositional in nature," *Biblical Revelation*, p. 66.

[77]J.I. Packer, *"Fundamentalism" and the Word of God* (Grand Rapids: Eerdmans, 1958), pp. 91-92.

[78]Ryrie, p. 40.

[79]Ibid., p. 41.

CHAPTER V

[1]See Sydney E. Ahlstrom, *A Religious History of the American People* (New Haven: Yale University Press, 1972), p. 813.

[2]See Ahlstrom, pp. 813ff. and more extensively Ernest R. Sandeen, *The Roots of Fundamentalism: British and American Millenarianism, 1800-1930* (Chicago: University of Chicago Press, 1970), ch. 5 and George M. Marsden, *Fundamentalism and American Culture: The Shaping of Twentieth-Century Evangelicalism 1870-1925* (New York: Oxford University Press, 1980), chs. XIII and XIV.

[3]See particularly, *AIB*, chs. 5 and 6; John C. Vander Stelt, *Philosophy and Scripture: A Study in Old Princeton and Westminster Theology* (Marleton, New Jersey: Mack Publishing Co., 1978) and the significant unpublished paper by John W. Stewart, "The Princeton Theologians: The Tethered Theology" (1975). For a variant viewpoint see John D. Woodbridge, *Biblical Authority: A Critique of the Rogers/McKim Proposal* (Grand Rapids: Zondervan, 1982), ch. VII; John D. Woodbridge and Randall H. Balmer, "The Princetonians and Biblical Authority: An Assessment of the Ernest Sandeen Proposal" in D.A. Carson and John D. Woodbridge, eds., *Scripture and Truth* (Grand Rapids: Zondervan, 1983), pp. 251-279; D. Clair Davis, "Princeton and Inerrancy: The Nineteenth-Century Philosophical Background of Contemporary Concerns" in John D. Hannah, ed., *Inerrancy and the Church* (Chicago: Moody Press, 1984), pp. 359-378 and Mark A. Noll, ed. and compiler, *The Princeton Theology 1812-1851* (Grand Rapids: Baker, 1983).

[4]See *AIB* and the earlier essay by Jack Rogers, "The Church Doctrine of Biblical Authority," in Jack Rogers, ed., *Biblical Authority* (Waco, Texas: Word, 1977), pp. 17-46 reprinted in Donald K. McKim, ed., *The Authoritative Word: Essays on the Nature of Scripture* (Grand Rapids: Eerdmans, 1983), pp. 197-224. The Rogers/McKim view is questioned by Woodbridge and Balmer.

[5]On Alexander see Lefferta A. Loetscher, *The Broadening Church: A Study of Theological Issues in the Presbyterian Church since 1869* (Philadelphia: University of Pennsylvania Press, 1954) and Loetscher's, *Facing the Enlightenment and Pietism: Archibald Alexander and the Founding of Princeton Theological Seminary* (Westport, Connecticut: Greenwood Press, 1983); hereafter cited as *Alexander*. Cf. the biography by James W. Alexander, *The Life of Archibald Alexander* (New York: Charles Scribner, 1854).

[6]See Noll, p. 13 and his selections from Alexander's writings; *AIB*, pp. 265-274 and Loetscher, *Alexander*.

[7]See Loetscher, *Alexander*, chs. 1-7.

[8]See *AIB*, p. 267 and Loetscher, *Alexander*, ch. 3: "Educational Background."

[9]Loetscher, *Broadening Church*, p. 23.

[10]See Noll, pp. 25ff.

[11]On Charles Hodge see Archibald Alexander Hodge, *The Life of Charles Hodge* (New York: Charles Scribner's Sons, 1880). The anthology by Noll contains an excellent Selective Bibliography of writings by and about the Old Princeton theologians.

[12]Noll, p. 19 provides the statistics of those who received their primary theological training under these four Princeton professors. The 3000 figure for Charles Hodge includes those who studied under him when he was a Professor of Oriental and Biblical Literature. The list is:

Alexander	1815-1840	1114
C. Hodge	1841-1878	2082
A.A. Hodge	1879-1886	440
B.B. Warfield	1887-1920	2750

[13]Noll, p. 14. See *AIB*, p. 275.

[14]Rogers and McKim maintain that the fact Turretin's work was the primary textbook from 1812-72 is "one of the most important and least known facts of American church history," *AIB*, xvii.

[15]See Noll, p. 14. On the spiritual dimensions of the work of the Princeton theologians see W. Andrew Hoffecker, *Piety and the Princeton Theologians* (Phillipsburg, New Jersey: Presbyterian and Reformed Publishing Co., 1981). Ch. 2 is on Charles Hodge.

[16]Noll describes A.A. Hodge as having "the greatest capacity for precise and concise expression among the major Princetonians," p. 14.

[17]On McCosh see J. David Hoeveler, Jr., *James McCosh and the Scottish Intellectual Tradition: From Glasgow to Princeton* (Princeton: Princeton University Press, 1981). On the Scottish philosophy see Sydney E. Ahlstrom, "The Scottish Philosophy and American Theology," *Church History* 24 (1955), pp. 257-272; Theodore Dwight Bozeman, *Protestants in an Age of Science: The Baconian Ideal and Antebellum American Religious Thought* (Chapel Hill: University of North Carolina Press, 1977), pp. 3-31 and S.A. Grave, *The Scottish Philosophy of Common Sense* (Oxford: Clarendon Press, 1960) among other literature cited in Noll, pp. 30ff. For the influence of this philosophy on the Princeton view of Scripture see *AIB*, *passim*.

The Scottish Common Sense Philosophy is associated with the works of Thomas Reid (1710-96), a Scots philosopher who sought to answer the skepticism of David Hume (1711-1776). Reid assumed that objects in the external world were real and that the mind could encounter them directly. This assumption was based on Reid's own intuitive judgment.

[18]On Warfield, see the piece by his brother Ethelbert D. Warfield, "Biographical Sketch of Benjamin Breckinridge Warfield" in Benjamin Breckinridge Warfield, *Revelation and Inspiration* (New York: Oxford University Press, 1927), p. vff. and Samuel G. Craig, "Benjamin B. Warfield" in Benjamin Breckinridge Warfield, *Biblical and Theological Studies* (Philadelphia: Presbyterian and Reformed Publishing Co., 1952), pp. xi-xlviii as well as Noll, p. 15ff. and *AIB*, pp. 323-348.

[19]On the controversy with Briggs see Loetscher, *Broadening Church*, ch. 6 and *AIB*, pp. 348-361.

[20]On Machen see Ned B. Stonehouse, *J. Gresham Machen: A Biographical Memoir* (Grand Rapids: Eerdmans, 1954), C. Allyn Russell, "J. Gresham Machen: Scholarly Fundamentalist" in his *Voices of American Fundamentalism* (Philadelphia: Westminster, 1976), ch. 6 and Paul Wooley, *The Significance of J. Gresham Machen Today* (Nutley, New Jersey: Presbyterian and Reformed Publishing Co., 1977).

[21]For more details see *AIB* pp. 366ff.

[22]Edwin H. Rian, *The Presbyterian Conflict* (Grand Rapids: Eerdmans, 1940) presents an account of the conflicts from the view of those who founded Westminster Seminary.

[23]Noll mentions Professor Roger Nicole of Gordon-Conwell Theological Seminary and Professor John H. Gerstner, retired from Pittsburgh Theological Seminary, p. 18.

[24]See *AIB*, p. 279. This was prescribed in the "Plan" of the Seminary.

[25]See the description by Noll in his section "The Princetonians and Modern Controversy," pp. 41ff.

[26]This is the position developed by Rogers and McKim in *AIB*. It also represents the basic issue in the Warfield/Briggs controversy. See *AIB*, pp. 348-61.

[27]Contemporary evangelical and Calvinist theologians who criticized the Princeton theology on these points were Thomas M. Lindsay, "The Doctrine of Scripture: The Reformers and the Princeton School," *The Expositor*, ed. W. Robertson Nicoll, Fifth series, I (London: Hodder & Stoughton, 1895), 278-293 and James Orr, *Revelation and Inspiration* (New York: Charles Scribner's Sons, 1910). For an exposition of these critiques see *AIB*, pp. 380-405.

[28]See the works of John Woodbridge and Randall Balmer.

[29]Noll, p. 30.

[30]See the treatments of each figure in *AIB*, chs. 5 and 6.

[31]Ibid., p. 269.

[32]Archibald Alexander, *Evidences of the Authenticity, Inspiration and Canonical Authority of the Holy Scriptures* (Philadelphia: Presbyterian Board of Publication, 1836), p. 10.

[33]Ibid., p. 12.

[34]Since this was so, B.B. Warfield particularly emphasized the role of apologetics or the defense of the faith since everyone should be able to be convinced of the existence of God. From there the next step was to "prove" that the Bible was God's Word. See *AIB*, p. 325ff.

[35]B.B. Warfield, *The Inspiration and Authority of the Bible* (Philadelphia: Presbyterian and Reformed Publishing Co., 1970; rpt. 1948), p. 75.

[36]For Charles Hodge's treatment of the work of the Holy Spirit see his *Systematic Theology*, 3 vols. (New York: Charles Scribner's Sons, 1871), III, 68; hereafter cited as *ST*.

[37]*ST*, III, 42.

[38]Ibid., 62.

[39]B.B. Warfield, *Studies in Theology* (New York: Oxford University Press, 1932), p. 15.

[40]See *AIB*, p. 333.

[41]Warfield claimed that Calvin believed that "when the soul is renewed by the Holy Spirit to a sense for the divinity of Scripture, it is through the *indicia* of that divinity that it is brought into its proper confidence in the divinity of Scripture," *Calvin and Augustine*, ed. Samuel G. Craig (Nutley, New Jersey, Presbyterian and Reformed Publishing Co., 1974; rpt. 1956), p. 89.

[42]Charles Hodge, *The Way of Life* (Philadelphia: American Sunday School Union, 1941), ch. I: "The Scriptures Are the Word of God," in Noll, p. 134.

[43]*Selected Shorter Writings of Benjamin B. Warfield–II*, ed. John E. Meeter (Nutley, New Jersey: Presbyterian and Reformed Publishing Co., 1973), p. 537; hereafter cited as *SWW-II*.

[44]See *AIB*, p. 335.

[45]Alexander, *Evidences*, p. 225.

[46]Selections from "Inspiration," *Princeton Review* (October 1857), pp. 660-698 are found in Noll, pp. 135-141. The section in Hodge's *Systematic Theology* is I, 153-182. A letter to Marcus Dods, Free Presbytery of Glasgow (November 2, 1877) on this subject was printed

in *The Presbyterian* 48 (January 12, 1878), p. 9.

[47]*ST*, I, 154.

[48]Hodge, "Inspiration," p. 685.

[49]Warfield, *IAB*, p. 420.

[50]B.B. Warfield, "The Real Problem of Inspiration." This piece is reprinted in *IAB*, pp. 169-226.

[51]*SWW-II*, 546. Warfield wrote: "The fundamental principle of this conception is that the whole of Scripture is the product of divine activities which enter it, however, not by superseding the activities of the human authors, but confluently with them; so that the Scriptures are the joint product of divine and human activities, both of which penetrate them at every point, working harmoniously together to the production of a writing which is not divine here and human there, but at once divine and human in every part, every word and every particular," p. 547. Cf. p. 629.

[52]Hodge, "Inspiration," p. 682.

[53]Ibid., pp. 682-683.

[54]*ST*, I, 170.

[55]Hodge, "Inspiration," p. 669.

[56]*ST*, I, 163.

[57]Hodge, "Inspiration," p. 683.

[58]A.A. Hodge, *Outlines of Theology* (New York: Robert Carter and Brothers, 1879), p. 301ff. For a fuller treatment, see *AIB*, p. 298ff.

[59]A.A. Hodge, *Outlines* (1879), pp. 75-76. Hodge included in his volume (pp. 656-663) a translation of the Helvetic Consensus Formula (1675) which asserted among other things that the inspiration of the "Hebrew Original of the Old Testament" was found "not only in its consonants, but in its vowels—either the vowel points themselves, or at least the power of the points." What was unknown in 1675 was that the original Hebrew Scriptures were written without vowel points. But the strong emphasis on the inspiration of the autographs of Scripture was appealing to Hodge and the Princeton theologians.

[60]This significant essay has been reprinted with an Introduction by Roger Nicole. See Archibald Alexander Hodge and B. B. Warfield, *Inspiration* (Grand Rapids: Baker, 1979). The piece was originally published as "Inspiration," *The Presbyterian Review* 2 (April 1881), pp. 225-260.

[61]*Presbyterian and Reformed Review* 4 (1893), p. 499. While A.A. Hodge and Warfield did not use the term "inerrancy" in their 1881 joint article, their commitment to the term and concept is clear as for example in Warfield's, "The Inerrancy of the Original Autographs," *The Independent* 45 (March 23, 1893), p. 382f., reprinted in *SWW—II*, pp. 580-·587; "The Westminster Confession and the Original Autographs," *The Presbyterian Messenger* 1, no. 50 (September 13, 1894), 118f., reprinted in *SWW-II*, pp. 588-594. Warfield believed that the inerrancy of the original autographs was taught by the Westminster Confession.

[62]*IAB*, p. 150. In the 1881 article, A.A. Hodge contended that "the historical faith of the Church has always been, that all the affirmations of Scripture of all kinds, whether of spiritual doctrine or duty, or of physical or historical fact, or of psychological or philosophical principle, are without any error, when the *ipsissima verba* of the original autographs are ascertained and interpreted in their natural and intended sense," p. 238.

[63]*SWW—II*, p. 584.

[64]A.A. Hodge and B.B. Warfield, "Inspiration," p. 242.

[65]Hodge and Warfield, "Inspiration," p. 245. Warfield's further works on Scripture can be seen from John E. Meeter and Roger Nicole, *A Bibliography of Benjamin Breckinridge Warfield 1851-1921* (Philadelphia: Presbyterian and Reformed Publishing Co., 1974).

[66]For further discussions of the Old Princeton view see also Daniel P. Fuller, "Benjamin B. Warfield's View of Faith and History," *Journal of the Evangelical Theological Society*, Vol. 11 no. 2 (Spring 1968), 75-83; George M. Marsden, "Everyone One's Own Interpreter?: The Bible, Science and Authority in Mid-Nineteenth-Century America" *The Bible in America: Essays in Cultural History*, eds. Nathan O. Hatch and Mark A. Noll (New York: Oxford, 1982), pp. 79-100; Randall H. Balmer, "The Princetonians and Scripture: A

Reconsideration," *Westminster Theological Journal* 44 (1982), pp. 352-365; John H. Gerstner, "Warfield's Case for Biblical Inerrancy," in *God's Inerrant Word*, ed. John Warwick Montgomery (Minneapolis: Bethany Fellowship, 1974), pp. 115-142 and other works cited in *AIB* and Noll, "Selective Bibliography."

[67]While scholars differ in the exact extent to which Protestant scholasticism of the seventeenth century (*e.g* Francis Turretin) determined the "scope and sweep" of the Princeton theology, it is undeniable that the Old Princeton theologians saw themselves as inheritors and perpetrators of the Protestant scholastic tradition which was marked in its most general way by a concern for a structured theology as a logical system of belief, most heavily relying on Aristotelian syllogistic reasoning. The emphasis was on a rational defense of a settled deposit of doctrines. This approach can be spelled out further with specific regard to the doctrine of Scripture. See *AIB*, pp. 185-187 for a description of the characteristics of Protestant scholasticism. On the influence of Turretin on Old Princeton see *AIB*, pp. 279-281 and *passim* as well as Noll, pp. 28-30. Noll also reprints a selection from Charles Hodge on "The Virtues of Seventeenth-Century Theologians," pp. 114-116.

[68]Richard J. Mouw, "The Bible in Twentieth-Century Protestantism: A Preliminary Taxonomy" in Hatch and Noll, *The Bible in America*, p. 143.

[69]Mouw, p. 143 quoting Charles Hodge, "The Theology of the Intellect and That of Feelings," *Essays and Reviews* (New York: Robert Carter & Bros., 1857), p. 610.

[70]David H. Kelsey, *The Uses of Scripture in Recent Theology* (Philadelphia: Fortress, 1975), p. 24.

[71]Mouw, p. 143.

[72]See the opening pages of Charles Hodge's *Systematic Theology*, Vol. I. It has been noted that the word "fact" or "truth" which is synonymous for Charles Hodge occurs twenty-seven times in *ST*, I, 1-3. See Theodore Dwight Bozeman, *Protestants in an Age of Science* (Durham, North Carolina: University of North Carolina Press, 1977), p. 147.

[73]Warfield, *IAB*, p. 208.

[74]"The Real Problem of Inspiration," *Presbyterian and Reformed Review* 4 (1893), p. 173.

[75]In 1978 "The International Council on Biblical Inerrancy" was formed by some three hundred persons committed to the doctrine of inerrancy. A four thousand-word "Chicago Statement on Biblical Inerrancy" was signed by most of the participants. The group committed itself to a ten-year attempt to bring the doctrine of inerrancy into renewed prominence in Christian churches.

CHAPTER VI

[1]On this see among other sources: *Revolutionary Theology in the Making: Barth-Thurneysen Correspondence 1914-1925*, trans. James D. Smart (Richmond: John Knox Press, 1964); *The Beginnings of Dialectic Theology*, ed. James M. Robinson, trans. Keith R. Crim and Lous De Grazia (Richmond: John Knox Press, 1968); and Thomas F. Torrance, *Karl Barth: An Introduction to His Early Theology 1910-1931* (London: SCM Press, 1962) as well as the accounts in the splendid biography by Eberhard Busch, *Karl Barth: His Life from Letters and Autobiographical Texts*, trans. John Bowden (Philadelphia: Fortress Press, 1976).

[2]On these figures see Busch, and Alasdair I.C. Heron, *A Century of Protestant Theology* (Philadelphia: Westminster Press, 1980).

[3]See Donald G. Bloesch, *The Future of Evangelical Christianity* (New York: Doubleday, 1984), p. 43ff. for his discussion of neo-orthodoxy. Cf. William E. Hordern, *A Layman's Guide to Protestant Theology*, rev. ed. (New York: Macmillan, 1968), chs. 5-7.

[4]On Niebuhr see among other sources Theodore Minnema, "Reinhold Niebuhr" in *Creative Minds in Contemporary Theology*, ed. Philip Edgcumbe Hughes, 2nd ed. (Grand Rapids: Wm. B. Eerdmans Publishing Co., 1969), ch. 12.

[5]See Robinson, ed., p. 24 from the second edition of Barth's commentary. The Forewords to the successive editions are in Karl Barth, *The Epistle to the Romans*, trans. Edwyn C. Hoskyns (London: Oxford University Press, 1968; rpt. of 1933 edition).

[6]See T.H.L. Parker, *Karl Barth* (Grand Rapids: Wm. B. Eerdmans Publishing Co., 1970), pp. 47-48.

[7]Heron, p. 76.

[8]For this emphasis of liberal theology see the chapter above on "Liberal Theology" as well as Busch, ch. 3.

[9]Cited from Busch, p. 81.

[10]Cited in Busch, p. 85. Cf. Robinson, ed., p. 41.

[11]The phrase "the strange new world in the Bible" is from the address of that name in Barth's, *The Word of God and the Word of Man*, trans. Douglas Horton (New York: Harper & Row, 1957), p. 45.

[12]See Barth, *Romans*, p. 1. This is also given in Robinson, ed., p. 61.

[13]See Parker, p. 36ff.; Robinson, ed., ch. 2; Busch, pp. 92-109.

[14]See Karl Barth, *Church Dogmatics*, trans. G.W. Bromiley, I/2 (Edinburgh: T.&T. Clark, 1956), 494; hereafter cited as *CD*. See the debate on the historical-critical method between Barth and Harnack in 1923 recorded in Martin Rumscheidt, *Revelation and Theology: An Analysis of the Barth-Harnack Correspondence of 1923* (Cambridge: Cambridge University Press, 1972).

[15]*CD*, I/2, 494. Cf. *AIB*, p. 425.

[16]See *CD*, I/2, 481ff.; cf. pp. 103, 72, 119.

[17]On this second edition see *AIB*, pp. 410-411; Robinson, ed., p. 24ff.; Busch, pp. 117-125 and Parker, p. 38ff.

[18]Heron, pp. 76-77.

[19]This is from Barth's commentary on Rom. 8:3 in *Romans*, p. 278.

[20]See Heron, p. 78.

[21]See Barth, *Romans*, p. 422. The concept of "witness" is crucial for Barth who often referred to John the Baptist as a "witness" to Jesus Christ. The painting that stood above the desk on which Barth wrote his *Church Dogmatics* (now housed in Barbour Library at Pittsburgh Theological Seminary in Pittsburgh, Pennsylvania) was the painting of the crucifixion by Matthias Grünewald. In this painting, John the Baptist is seen standing off to the right and pointing with what Barth called his "prodigious index finger" at the crucified Christ. See *CD*, I/1 (trans. Bromiley), 112, 262; I/2, 125.

[22]Barth, *Romans*, p. 93.

[23]See Heron, p. 79. Cf. Busch, pp. 138-153.

[24]See Busch, pp. 126-134. Barth's lectures on Schleiermacher from the winter semester of 1923/24 are available as Karl Barth, *The Theology of Schleiermacher*, ed. Dietrich Ritschl, trans. Geoffrey W. Bromiley (Grand Rapids: Wm. B. Eerdmans Publishing Co., 1982). His further assessment of Schleiermacher is found in Karl Barth, *Protestant Theology in the Nineteenth Century: Its Background & History* (Valley Forge, Pennsylvania: Judson Press, 1973), ch. 11.

[25]On this see Parker, p. 69 and *AIB*, pp. 413-414; cf. Busch, pp. 153-164.

[26]See Busch, pp. 205-209; Parker, ch. 5. Barth's *Fides quaerens intellectum: Anselm's Beweis der Existenz Gottes* translated as *Anselm: Fides quaerens intellectum: Anselm's Proof of the Existence of God in the Context of his Theological Scheme* is reprinted in the Pittsburgh Reprint Series No. 2, ed. Dikran Y. Hadidian (Pittsburgh: Pickwick Press, 1975) as the translation of Ian W. Robertson (London: SCM Press, 1960). Arthur C. Cochrane has provided a preface for the reprint edition.

[27]More fully see *AIB*, pp. 414-416.

[28]Cited in Busch, p. 210. Barth's commitment to theology as a science of the church is seen in the switch of names from *Christian Dogmatics* to *Church Dogmatics*.

[29]*CD* I/1. 295, 117ff.

[30]*CD* I/1, 132. Cf. I/1, 136. 141. 150 and Karl Barth, *Evangelical Theology: An Introduction*, trans. Grover Foley (London: Collins, 1969; rpt. 1963), pp. 22-23.

[31]*CD* I/1, 119ff; cf. 137, 157. On Barth's doctrine of reconciliation see Donald G. Bloesch, *Jesus Is Victor! Karl Barth's Doctrine of Salvation* (Nashville: Abingdon, 1976).

[32]*CD* I/1, 88-124.

[33]*CD* I/1, 120-21. The interrelationships among the three forms constitute the unity of God. For Barth this threefold form is the singular analogy to the triunity of God. As he

wrote: "In the fact that we can substitute for revelation, Scripture and proclamation the names of the divine persons Father, Son and Holy Spirit and *vice versa*," I/1, 121.

[34]*CD* I/1, 101. "Canon" means "rod," "ruler" or "standard." For the first three-hundred years of the church it represented "that which stands fast as normative." After the fourth century, it particularly meant the list of books of Holy Scripture the church recognized as normative for its faith and practice.

[35]*CD* I/1. 107-108ff.

[36]Ibid., 109.   [37]Ibid. 110.

[38]*CD* I/1, 110. Barth contrasted his view with that of seventeenth-century scholastic theologians who viewed the Bible as having its own divine power without regard to any effect on a reader. Thus the theologian David Hollaz (1648-1713) could write that the Bible is God's Word "in the same way as the sun gives warmth even behind clouds, or as a seed of grain has force even in the unfruitful earth, or as the hand of a sleeping man is a living hand."

[39]*CD* I/1, 111.

[40]Ibid. Here in reference to Grünewald's crucifixion painting Barth calls John the Baptist "the model of the biblical witness" since he "stands so notably at midpoint between the Old Testament and the New, between the prophets and the apostles," p. 112.

[41]*CD* I/1, 112.

[42]Ibid., 113.   [43]Ibid., 113-114.

[44]Ibid., 115.   [45]Ibid., 115, 116.

[46]Ibid., 117.   [47]Ibid., 118.

[48]*CD* I/2, 537.

[49]Ibid., 457.   [50]Ibid., 485.

[51]*Evangelical Theology*, p. 29. Barth deals with the unity of the Old and New Testament witness on p. 30ff.

[52]*CD* I/2, 490ff.

[53]A most helpful treatment of Barth's doctrine of inspiration is Howard John Loewen, "Karl Barth and the Church Doctrine of Inspiration (An Appraisal for Evangelical Theology)," 2 vols., Diss. Fuller Theological Seminary, 1976. See p. 562.

[54]*CD* I/2, 504ff. Loewen examines these passages extensively, pp. 124-182.

[55]*CD* I/2, 505.

[56]Ibid.   [57]Ibid., 517.

[58]Ibid., 517, 518.   [59]Ibid., 520.

[60]Ibid., 522-523   [61]Ibid., 523.

[62]Ibid., 523. Cf. 524.   [63]Ibid., 525.

[64]See the Preface to the second edition of the *Commentary on Romans.*

[65]*CD* I/2, 521.

[66]*CD* I/2, 49; cf. I/1, 165, 166.

[67]*CD* I/2, 501. Cf. I/2, 530 where Barth writes that the Bible is "an instrument in the hand of God, i.e., it speaks to and is heard by us as the authentic witness to divine revelation and is therefore present as the Word of God." Yet, "Holy Scripture cannot stand alone as the Word of God in the Church," I/2, 501.

[68]*CD* I/2, 501. Scripture is the Word of God in that "it too can and must—not as though it were Jesus Christ. but in the same serious sense as Jesus Christ—be called the Word of God: the Word of God in the sign of the word of man, if we are going to put it accurately," I/2, 500. See Loewen, pp. 570-571. Barth warned against trying to extract from the Bible "truths" or propositions to be propounded as "the truths of faith, salvation, and revelation." He asked if when Scripture "tries to be more than witness, to be direct impartation, will it not keep from us the best, the one real thing, which God intends to tell and give us and which we ourselves need?" I/2, 507.

[69]*CD* I/1. Cf. I/2, 457.

[70]*CD* I/2, 530.

[71]Ibid., 529. Cf. I/2, 532.

[72]Ibid., 533.   [73]Ibid., 508.

[74]Ibid., 509. Cf. I/2, 525, 508.

[75]Ibid., 509-510.   [76]Ibid., 531.

CHAPTER VII

[1]See *Christianity Today* 29 (March 15, 1985), pp. 34-36 on the life and contributions of Ockenga. On Schaeffer's life and contributions see *Christianity Today* 28 (June 15, 1984), pp. 60-63. Among numerous assessments of Schaeffer see Jack Rogers, "Francis Schaeffer: The Promise and the Problem" *The Reformed Journal* 27/5 (1977), pp. 12-15 and 27/6 (1977), pp. 15-19.

[2]*Christianity Today* 29 (March 15, 1985), p. 34. Cf. Ockenga's account of the need for this term in his essay, "From Fundamentalism, Through New Evangelicalism, to Evangelicalism" in *Evangelical Roots*, ed. Kenneth Kantzer (Nashville: Thomas Nelson, 1978), pp. 35-46.

[3]On these leaders see among other sources Louis Gasper, *The Fundamentalist Movement 1930-1956* (rpt. Grand Rapids: Baker Book House, 1981); Richard Quebedeaux, *The Young Evangelicals* (New York: Harper & Row, 1974); and John D. Woodbridge, Mark A. Noll, and Nathan O. Hatch, *The Gospel in America: Themes in the Story of America's Evangelicals* (Grand Rapids: Zondervan, 1979); hereafter cited as *Gospel*.

[4]See the fine treatment by Donald G. Bloesch, *The Future of Evangelical Christianity: A Call for Unity Amid Diversity* (New York: Doubleday, 1983), ch. 2 and his *Essentials of Evangelical Theology*, 2 vols. (San Francisco: Harper & Row, 1982), I, ch. 1.

[5]A most helpful treatment of the controversies over Scripture within evangelicalism is found in Robert K. Johnson, *Evangelicals at an Impasse: Biblical Authority in Practice* (Atlanta: John Knox Press, 1979), ch. II.

[6]See "Half of U.S. Protestants are 'Born Again' Christians," *The Gallup Poll* (September 26, 1976), pp. 1-7 cited in Richard Quebedeaux, *The Worldly Evangelicals* (San Francisco: Harper & Row, 1980), p. 4.

[7]See Donald G. Bloesch, *The Evangelical Renaissance* (Grand Rapids: Wm. B. Eerdmans Publishing Co., 1973); Bloesch, *Future*, p. 9; and Quebedeaux, *Worldly*, ch. 1.

[8]Quebedeaux, *Worldly*, p. 3.

[9]See Deane William Ferm, *Contemporary American Theologies: A Critical Survey* (New York: Seabury, 1981), p. 96 citing *Christianity Today* of January 27, 1978.

[10]See James Davison Hunter, *American Evangelicalism: Conservative Religion and the Quandry of Modernity* (New Brunswick, New Jersey: Rutgers University Press, 1983), p. 49. Cf. Appendix 1.

[11]Hunter, p. 7.

[12]Sydney E. Ahlstrom, "From Puritanism to Evangelicalism: A Critical Perspective," *The Evangelicals*, eds. David F. Wells and John D. Woodbridge (Nashville: Abingdon, 1975), p. 271.

[13]Bloesch, *Future*, p. 15.

[14]For "the legacy of Pietism" for Evangelicalism see Bloesch, *Renaissance*, ch. V.

[15]On these see *Gospel*, ch. 5; W.G. McLoughlin, *The American Evangelicals, 1800-1900* (New York: Harper & Row, 1968); W.G. McLoughlin, *Modern Revivalism: Charles G. Finney to Billy Graham* (New York: Ronald, 1959) and Timothy L. Smith, *Revivalism and Social Reform in Mid-Nineteenth Century America* (Nashville: Abingdon, 1957).

[16]For this emphasis see Bernard L. Ramm, *The Evangelical Heritage* (Waco, Texas: Word Publishing Co., 1973), ch. 2: "Evangelical Theology Belongs to Reformation Theology." This emphasis is also struck in John H. Gerstner, "The Theological Boundaries of Evangelical Faith," in *The Evangelicals*, ch. 1.

[17]Bloesch, *Future*, p. 17. Cf. *Renaissance*, ch. III: "The Hallmarks of Evangelicalism" and *Essentials of Evangelical Theology*.

[18]See Harold Lindsell, *The Battle for the Bible* (Grand Rapids: Zondervan, 1976) and his *The Bible in the Balance: A Further Look at the Battle for the Bible* (Grand Rapids: Zondervan, 1979). On the Old Princeton theology see ch. V of the present work.

[19]Bloesch, *Future*, p. 11. Cf. Johnston's discussion of the varying positions on biblical authority within evangelicalism. Bloesch rejects the attempt to define "evangelical" on the basis of an affirmation of the divine authority and inspiration of Scripture since "this could include sacramentalist Roman Catholics, Moonies, Mormons, the Local Church of Witness Lee, the more tradition-bound Eastern Orthodox, and many others who would find it difficult if not impossible to accept the basic message of the Protestant Reformation," *Future*, p. 13.

[20]See Mark A. Noll, "Evangelicals and the Study of the Bible" in *Evangelicalism and Modern America*, ed. George Marsden (Grand Rapids: Wm. B. Eerdmans Publishing Co., 1984), n. 39, pp. 198-199 gives a list of twenty-seven books, most published since 1979 on the controversies over Scripture. Noll calls this a "partial list."

[21]Johnston, p. 3.

[22]See Quebedeaux, *The Young Evangelicals* and *Worldly*, p. 7. Sydney Ahlstrom also uses the term "inerrancy" as a defining mark of an "evangelical" when among his six criteria he lists: "insist upon verbal inerrancy of the received biblical text, tend to interpret revelation in strict propositional terms, and question the value of historico-critical studies of biblical religion," *The Evangelicals*, p. 270.

[23]On this see Ch. 4 of the present work.

[24]See George M. Marsden, *Fundamentalism and American Culture* (New York: Oxford University Press, 1980), p. 178.

[25]Joel A. Carpenter, "From Fundamentalism to the New Evangelical Coalition," in *Evangelicalism and Modern America*, p. 4.

[26]Carpenter, p. 4.

[27]Ibid., p. 5.

[28]Carpenter, p. 5. See his discussion of these three motifs, p. 5ff. Cf. Hunter, p. 39.

[29]Carpenter, p. 12.

[30]Quoted in Gasper, p. 23. Cf. Martin E. Marty, "Tensions Within Contemporary Evangelicalism: A Critical Appraisal," in *The Evangelicals*, p. 172.

[31]Carpenter, p. 12.

[32]Quoted in Gasper, p. 25.

[33]Hunter, p. 41.

[34]Carpenter, p. 13.

[35]Quebedeaux, p. 43. See his discussion of the NAE, pp. 42-44.

[36]Ockenga, *Evangelical Roots*, p. 38.

[37]Quoted in Lowell D. Streiker and Gerald S. Strober, *Religion and the New Majority: Billy Graham, Middle America, and the Politics of the 70s* (New York: Association Press, 1972), p. 112 cited in Marty, p. 182. Ockenga later wrote: "Doctrinally, the fundamentalists are right, and I wish to be always classified as one. In ecclesiology, I believe they are wrong and I cannot follow them." See Ockenga, p. 40.

[38]Quebedeaux, *Worldly*, p. 22 and *passim* for his discussion of these "symbols." Quebedeaux says that "in the 60s and 70s, the term *neo-evangelical* has generally been replaced by the more historic and inclusive designation, evangelical," *Worldly*, p. 9.

[39]See James Barr, *Fundamentalism* (Philadelphia: Westminster Press, 1977).

[40]Hunter, p. 7.

[41]See Quebedeaux, *Young*, pp. 18-28.

[42]See Quebedeaux, *Worldly*, pp. 8-9.

[43]Bloesch, *Future*, p. 22.

[44]Ibid., p. 24.

[45]Ibid., ch. III.

[46]Bloesch, *Future*, p. 52. Bloesch identifies his own position as "catholic evangelical" (p. 51) but notes also that "it can be shown that I stand partly in both neoevangelicalism and neo-orthodoxy, even though I belong mostly to catholic evangelicalism," p. 165 n. 67. His position on the doctrine of Scripture accords well with the approach of other "neo-evangelicals."

[47]Bloesch, *Future*, p. 30.

[48]Bloesch, *Future*, p. 30. Part II of Quebedeaux's *Worldly Evangelicals* is devoted to "The

Evangelical Right and Center." Part III considers "The Young Evangelical Left."

[49]Bloesch categorizes those within the wings of evangelicalism on the Scripture issue: "Evangelical theologians who still move within the thought patterns of fundamentalism but try to engage in dialogue with the modern world include Francis Schaeffer, R.C. Sproul, James Boice, James Packer, Harold O.J. Brown, John Gerstner, John Warwick Montgomery and Harold Lindsell. Scholars noted for their ecumenical openness and innovative spirit but who generally remain within the framework of the Hodge-Warfield position on biblical authority and inerrancy are Carl Henry, Roger Nicole, John R.W. Stott, Morris Inch, Vernon Grounds, Ronald Nash and Kenneth Kantzer. Other scholars have questioned the emphasis on inerrancy but still see the Bible as the infallible standard for faith and practice. Among these are Clark Pinnock, F.F. Bruce, Bernard Ramm, H.M. Kuitert, Ray S. Anderson, Stephen Davis, Bruce Metzger, George Eldon Ladd, Kenneth Grider, Robert Johnston, Richard Colemen, Jack Rogers, Richard Mouw, James Daane, Ward Gasque, Paul Jewett, Lewis Smedes, M. Eugene Osterhaven and Timothy L. Smith. Not all these theologians would jettison the term "inerrancy," but they would reinterpret it in order to do justice to the true humanity of Scripture. [See in particular Clark H. Pinnock, *The Scripture Principle* (San Francisco: Harper & Row, 1984)]. The Lausanne Covenant, which declares that the Bible is 'without error in all that it affirms,' reflects the viewpoint of the dominant stream in neoevangelicalism today," *Future*, p. 33.

[50]Lindsell's contention that inerrancy should be the mark of the evangelical was countered by the essays in *Biblical Authority*, ed. Jack Rogers (Waco, Texas: Word Publishing, 1977).

[51]Johnston's four positions for evangelicals on Scripture are: (1) Detailed Inerrancy, (2) Partial Infallibility, (3) Irenic Inerrancy and (4) Complete Infallibility. See his ch. II.

[52]On these scholars see *AIB*, ch. 7.

[53]See particularly Berkouwer's, *Holy Scripture*, ed. and trans. Jack B. Rogers (Grand Rapids: Wm. B. Eerdmans Publishing Co., 1975). Berkouwer's esteem in the eyes of some evangelicals changed after the publication of this work. For "authors who had for years praised Berkouwer's evangelical theology felt obligated to dismiss his doctrine of Scripture because it critiqued the old Princeton slogan of 'inerrancy.' " See *AIB*, p. 428 citing reviews by J.I. Packer and Charles C. Ryrie.

[54]See particularly Bloesch's *Essentials*, *Future*, pp. 117-121, *Renaissance*, pp. 55-59. *The Ground of Certainty* (Grand Rapids: Wm. B. Eerdmans Publishing Co., 1971); Rogers' *Confessions of a Conservative Evangelical* (Philadelphia: Westminster Press, 1974), *Scripture in the Westminster Confession* (Grand Rapids: Wm. B. Eerdmans Publishing Co., 1967), [with Donald K. McKim], *AIB*; and Ramm's, *The Christian View of Science and Scripture* (Grand Rapids: Wm. B. Eerdmans Publishing Co., 1954), *Special Revelation and the Word of God* (Grand Rapids: Wm. B. Eerdmans Publishing Co., 1961), *After Fundamentalism: The Future of Evangelical Theology* (San Francisco: Harper & Row, 1983).

[55]See *AIB*, pp. 23-25.

[56]G.C. Berkouwer, *Man: The Image of God*, trans. Dirk W. Jellema (Grand Rapids: Wm. B. Eerdmans Publishing Co., 1962), p. 135.

[57]G.C. Berkouwer, *General Revelation* (Grand Rapids: Wm. B. Eerdmans Publishing Co., 1955), p. 67. On Berkouwer's rejection of reason as the basis for the certainty of faith see Gary D. Watts, "G.C. Berkouwer's Theological Method," Diss. (Fuller Theological Seminary 1980), p. 139ff.

[58]Bloesch, *Essentials*, I, 102.

[59]G.C. Berkouwer, *The Providence of God*, trans. Lewis B. Smedes (Grand Rapids: Wm. B. Eerdmans Publishing Co., 1952), p. 253. Of help here has been Gary Watts and Jack Rogers, "Six Theological Models of the Early 1980s: Their Theological Methods with Special Reference to Their Use of Scripture," Unpublished paper, Fuller Theological Seminary (August 1980), "Neo-Evangelical Theology."

[60]See *AIB*, pp. 209-211. Cf. Rogers, *Scripture in the Westminster Confession*.

[61]Bloesch, *The Ground of Certainty*, p. 190.

[62]Berkouwer, *Holy Scripture*, p. 184. Cf. p. 272 where Berkouwer writes that "in their controversy with Rome, the Reformers repeatedly emphasized that the message of salvation really came through; this was the purpose of Scripture."

[63]Berkouwer, *Holy Scripture*, p. 184.

⁶⁴Berkouwer, *Holy Scripture*, p. 125. He quotes Bavinck on the "theological purpose of Scripture" to be "that we might know God unto salvation," p. 126.

⁶⁵Herman Bavinck, *Gereformeerde Dogmatiek*, Vol. 1, p. 414 (hereafter cited as *GD*) cited in *AIB*, p. 389.

⁶⁶Bloesch, *Renaissance*, p. 56.

⁶⁷John Calvin, *Institutes of the Christian Religion*, ed. John T. McNeill, trans. Ford Lewis Battles, Library of Christian Classics, 2 vols. (Philadelphia: Westminster Press, 1960), I. vii. 1. On Calvin see *AIB*, pp. 89-116 and Donald K. McKim, "Calvin's View of Scripture" in *Readings in Calvin's Theology*, ed. Donald K. McKim (Grand Rapids: Baker Book House, 1984), pp. 43-68.

⁶⁸Berkouwer, *Holy Scripture*, pp. 148-149.

⁶⁹Ibid., p. 149.

⁷⁰Bloesch, *Essentials*, I, 76.

⁷¹Berkouwer, *Holy Scripture*, pp. 54-55. This chapter on "The Testimony of the Spirit" is reprinted in *The Authoritative Word: Essays on the Nature of Scripture*, ed. Donald K. McKim (Grand Rapids: Wm. B. Eerdmans Publishing Co., 1983), pp. 155-181.

⁷²Berkouwer, *Holy Scripture*, p. 41. Berkouwer's language is reminiscent of Calvin's who said: "We ought to seek our conviction in a higher place than human reasons, judgments, or conjectures, that is, in the secret testimony of the Spirit" and "the testimony of the Spirit is more excellent than all reason" (*Institutes*, I. vii. 4). For Berkouwer, "the *testimonium* does not supply an *a priori* certainty regarding Scripture, which afterwards is supplemented with and through its message," *Holy Scripture*, p. 44.

⁷³Bavinck, *GD*, I, 564-565 cited in *AIB*, p. 389.

⁷⁴Bavinck, *GD*, I, 569 cited in *Holy Scripture*, p. 241.

⁷⁵See *AIB*, pp. 106-109, 114-116.

⁷⁶Bavinck, *GD*, I, 409-410 cited in *AIB*, p. 391. Cf. Berkouwer, *Holy Scripture*, pp. 151-157.

⁷⁷Bavinck, *GD*, I, 410 cited in *AIB*, p. 402.

⁷⁸Of major significance in understanding the nature of Scripture and inspiration is the concept of "accommodation." This is an insight adapted from the classical rhetoricians and shared by such theologians as Origen, Chrysostom, Augustine, and Calvin which stressed that in Scripture God condescended to the limits of human capacities in order to communicate with humanity. See the development of this theme throughout *AIB*. A most important article on accommodation in Calvin's thought is Ford Lewis Battles, "God Was Accommodating Himself to Human Capacity," *Interpretation* 31 (1977), pp. 19-38.

⁷⁹Berkouwer, *Holy Scripture*, p. 181. It is argued by neo-evangelicals that this "moral" understanding of error in terms of purposeful deceit was the understanding of the central tradition of the Christian church including Augustine and Calvin. See *AIB*.

⁸⁰See chapter 5 of the present work and Johnston, p. 36 who contrasts "inerrancy" and "infallibility." Bloesch writes: "Many latter day evangelical Christians have felt the need to extend the meaning of inerrancy to cover purely historical and scientific matters, even where the treatment of these in the Bible does not bear upon the message of faith....A view of error is entertained that demands literal, exact, mathematical precision, something the Bible cannot provide," *Essentials*, I, 66. Earlier he had written that "when evangelical theology affirms that Scripture does not err, it means that whatever Christ teaches in Scripture is completely true." In a note he added: "And we must hasten to add that this includes not only its testimony concerning God and salvation, but also its interpretation of man, life and history. But this does not imply perfect factual accuracy in all details as the extreme literalist holds," *Renaissance*, p. 56.

⁸¹Berkouwer, *Holy Scripture*, p. 183.

⁸²Berkouwer, *Holy Scripture*, p. 180. Berkouwer writes: "We may add the awareness that the purpose of Scripture is not to orient us concerning the composition of the cosmos in its created parts, nor to inform us scientifically about the 'composition of man.'...the purpose of Scripture is directly aimed at the revelation of God *in* this world and *to* man," p. 245.

⁸³Berkouwer, *Holy Scripture*, pp. 145, 147.

⁸⁴Ibid., p. 333.   ⁸⁵Ibid.

Chapter VIII

[1]See Wilhelm and Marion Pauck, *Paul Tillich: His Life and Thought* (New York: Harper & Row, 1976), pp. 127-130 and Ronald H. Stone, *Paul Tillich's Radical Social Thought* (Atlanta: John Knox Press, 1980), p. 65.

[2]Tillich's theological stature is attested to by Reinhold Niebuhr who described him as "the Origen of our period, seeking to relate the Gospel message to the disciplines of our culture and whole history of culture." See "Biblical Thought and Ontological Speculation in Tillich's Theology," in *The Theology of Paul Tillich*, ed. Charles W. Kegly and Robert W. Bretall (New York: Macmillan, 1952), p. 217. John Herman Randall, Jr. described him as "the ablest Protestant theologian of the present day." See "The Ontology of Paul Tillich," in Kegly and Bretall, p. 161. In 1977 a survey of 554 theologians in North America revealed that Tillich ranked first as the major influence on their thought and that his three-volume *Systematic Theology* was the most widely used textbook among the theologians. See John P. Newport, *Paul Tillich*, Makers of the Modern Theological Mind, ed. Bob E. Patterson (Waco, Texas: Word, 1984), p. 16.

[3]On Tillich's life see Newport; Pauck and Pauck and the books of Tillich's widow Hannah Tillich, *From Place to Place* (New York: Stein and Day, 1976) and *From Time to Time* (New York: Stein and Day, 1973).

[4]This is seen in the varieties of topics of interest to Tillich and on which he wrote. These included beside theology, philosophy, and the history of Christian thought in such areas as culture, art, politics, and social concerns.

[5]See Paul Tillich, *Systematic Theology*, 3 vols. (Chicago: University of Chicago Press, 1951, 1957, 1963); hereafter cited as *ST* and his *A History of Christian Thought: From Its Judaic and Hellenistic Origins to Existentialism*, ed. Carl E. Braaten (New York: Simon and Schuster, 1967).

[6]Paul Tillich, *On the Boundary: An Autobiographical Sketch* (London: Collins, 1967), p. 13.

[7]Paul Tillich, *Religiose Verwirklichung* (Berlin: Furche, 1929), p. 1 cited in *On the Boundary*, p. 13.

[8]Tillich's *On the Boundary* was initially published as the first chapter in his *The Interpretation of History*, trans. N.A. Rasetski and Elsa L. Talmey (New York: Charles Scribner's Sons, 1936).

[9]*ST*, II, 90.

[10]See Stone, p. 36.

[11]See Newport, p. 27 and p. 78ff. for his description of the theological and philosophical influences on Tillich's thought. Cf. Arthur C. Cochrane, *The Existentialists and God* (Philadelphia: Westminster, 1966), ch. IV and George F. McLean, "Paul Tillich's Existential Philosophy of Protestantism," *Paul Tillich in Catholic Thought*, eds. Thomas A. O'Meara and Celestin D. Weisser (Dubuque, Iowa: The Priory Press, 1964), pp. 42-84.

[12]Tillich, *On the Boundary*, p. 83.

[13]Newport, p. 27.

[14]Tillich, *On the Boundary*, p. 56.

[15]Ibid., p. 57.

[16]*ST*, I, 23. [17]*ST*, I, 3.

[18]*ST*, I, 4-8. [19]*ST*, I, 12-15.

[20]*ST*, I, 15. [21]*ST*, I, 15-18.

[22]*ST*, I, 18-24. [23]*ST*, I, 27.

[24]*ST*, I, 28. [25]*ST*, I, 28-34.

[26]*ST*, I, 34-40.

[27]*ST*, I, 40. Cf. George Tavard, "Christology as Symbol" in O'Meara and Weisser, pp. 219-223.

[28]*ST*, I, 43.   [29]*ST*, I, 46.

[30]*ST*, I, 47.   [31]*ST*, I, 50.

[32]*ST*, I, 50. Gustave Weigel wrote that the "New Being" is "the pure essence of Tillich's theology." See his "Tillich's Theological Significance" in O'Meara and Weisser, p. 12.

[33]*ST*, I, 51-52.   [34]*ST*, I, 53-54.

[35]*ST*, I, 57.   [36]*ST*, I, 58.

[37]*ST*, I, 61.   [38]*ST*, I, 60.

[39]*ST*, I, 61.   [40]*ST*, I, 62.

[41]*ST*, I, 63.   [42]*ST*, I, 64.

[43]*ST*, I, 66-68.

[44]See Kenan B. Osborne, *New Being: A Study of the Relationship Between Conditioned and Unconditioned Being According to Paul Tillich* (The Hague: Martinus Nijhoff, 1969), pp. 87-89.

[45]See *ST*, I, 71ff.   [46]*ST*, I, 75.

[47]*ST*, I, 79-81.   [48]*ST*, I, 80.

[49]*ST*, I, 242.

[50]Newport, p. 95.

[51]*ST*, I, 178. Cf. III, 406-410.

[52]*ST*, I, 83. Newport writes that "Tillich's whole theological or onto-theological system derives its structure and form from his understanding that ultimate reality is involved in a movement of unactualized essence into existence and then in a return to fulfilled essentialization," p. 66. "Essentialization" is "a return to fulfilled essence," p. 69. Cf. pp. 95-96.

[53]*ST*, I, 110.   [54]*ST*, I, 110.

[55]Avery R. Dulles, "Paul Tillich and the Bible" in O'Meara and Weisser, p. 110.

[56]*ST*, I, 110.   [57]*ST*, I, 110.

[58]*ST*, I, 112. Cf. pp. 111-118. For Tillich a miracle is "an unusual event—extraordinary either in its regularity or its irregularity—which somehow points to the ultimate source of reality and meaning," Dulles, "Paul Tillich and the Bible," p. 111.

[59]Newport, p. 99.

[60]*ST*, I, 127.   [61]*ST*, I, 127.

[62]David H. Kelsey, *The Uses of Scripture in Recent Theology* (Philadelphia: Fortress Press, 1975), p. 66.

[63]*ST*, I, 133, 135. Cf. II, 97-138.

[64]*ST*, I, 134. Tillich defines a final revelation as one that "has the power of negating itself without losing itself," I, 133. This is found in the biblical picture of "Jesus as the Christ."

[65]*ST*, I, 137.   [66]*ST*, I, 146.

[67]*ST*, I, 146.

[68]*ST*, I, 147. For Tillich, "the religious word for what is called the ground of being is God," I, 156.

[69]*ST*, I, 147.   [70]*ST*, I, 157.

[71]*ST*, I, 157-159.   [72]*ST*, I, 159.

[73]*ST*, I, 35.   [74]*ST*, I, 35.

[75]*ST*, I, 124.   [76]*ST*, I, 124.

[77]*ST*, I, 129.   [78]*ST*, I, 145.

[79]Kelsey, p. 66.

[80]Kelsey points out that with regard to the "personal life" of Jesus: " 'personal life' we know is always marked by the conditions of 'existence,' that is to say, by alienation from self, neighbor, and God [Tillich's description of 'sin'], while 'New Being' designates unbroken unity between God and man. Yet Jesus managed to overcome the conditions of 'existence' and preserve unbroken unity with God while nonetheless truly and fully participating in our common human life," p. 66. Cf. *ST*, II, 148, 126, 136.

[81]See Kelsey, p. 130. Cf. *ST*, II, 121ff.

[82]Kelsey, p. 72. For Tillich, Jesus as the Christ is "the ultimate criterion of every healing and saving process," *ST*, II, 168.

CHAPTER IX

[1]See Jack B. Rogers, "The Search for System: Theology in the 1980's," *The Journal of Religious Thought* 37 (1980), 5-14.

[2]Jack Rogers, "Bibliography: Process Theology," TSF Research (Theological Student's Fellowship, 233 Langdon Street, Madison, Wisconsin).

[3]On Whitehead's life see Jack B. Rogers and Forrest Baird, "The Case of Whitehead" in their *Introduction to Philosophy: A Case Study Approach* (San Francisco: Harper & Row, 1981), ch. 11.

[4]Alfred North Whitehead, *Process and Reality* (New York: Macmillan, 1929). This work is quite technical in both its language and concepts.

[5]Alfred North Whitehead, *Science and the Modern World* (New York: Macmillan, 1925).

[6]See Alfred North Whitehead, *Religion in the Making* (New York: Macmillan, 1926). Other works on Whitehead include: *A Key to Whitehead's Process and Reality*, ed. Donald W. Sherburne (New York: Macmillan 1966); *The Philosophy of Alfred North Whitehead*, ed. Paul Arthur Schilpp, The Library of Living Philosophers, 2nd ed. (New York: Tudor Publishing Co., 1951); Norman Pittenger, *Alfred North Whitehead*, Makers of Contemporary Theology (Richmond: John Knox Press, 1969); Victor Lowe, *Understanding Whitehead* (Baltimore: Johns Hopkins University Press, 1962); and W. Mays, *The Philosophy of Whitehead* (New York: Crowell-Collier, 1962).

[7]Alasdair I.C. Heron, *A Century of Protestant Theology* (Philadelphia: Westminster, 1980), p. 145.

[8]John B. Cobb, Jr. and David Ray Griffin, *Process Theology: An Introductory Exposition* (Philadelphia: Westminster, 1976). Cobb and Griffin are two of the leading American process theologians of today.

[9]Cobb and Griffin, p. 19. A very lucid and helpful exposition of process thought on this theme is Marjorie Hewitt Suchocki, *God Christ Church* (New York: Crossroad, 1982), ch. 2.

[10]Cobb and Griffin, p. 20.

[11]Ibid.   [12]Ibid., p. 21.

[13]Whitehead, *Science and the Modern World*, p. 88.

[14]Whitehead, *Process and Reality*, p. 33.

[15]Whitehead, *Process and Reality*, pp. 34, 35. Whitehead wrote: "That 'all things flow' is the first vague generalization which the unsystematized, barely analyzed, intuition of men has produced...it appears as one of the first generalizations of Greek philosophy in the form of the saying of Heraclitus....Without doubt, if we are to go back to that ultimate, integral experience, unwarped by the sophistications of theory, that experience whose elucidations is the final aim of philosophy, the flux of things is one ultimate generalization around which we must weave our philosophical system," *Process and Reality*, pp. 43, 53, 317. See Norman L. Geisler, "Process Theology" in *Tensions in Contemporary Theology*, eds. Stanley N. Gundry and Alan F. Johnson, 2nd ed. (Grand Rapids: Baker Book House, 1983), ch. 6.

[16]Hartshorne's significant work is *The Divine Relativity: A Social Conception of God* (New Haven: Yale University Press, 1948). In it he argues that process theology and biblical thought are compatible. The Divinity School of the University of Chicago is "the major center of theological receptivity to Whitehead's influence." See Cobb and Griffin, p. 176 who provide a guide to the literature on process theology including the Chicago school.

[17]See Cobb and Griffin, pp. 47-48.

[18]Suchocki, p. 226. Cf. p. 38.

[19]Suchocki, p. 225. Cobb and Griffin state that Whitehead's consequent nature of God is "largely identical with what Hartshorne has called God's concrete actuality," p. 48. On the differences between Whitehead and Hartshorne see David R. Griffin, "Hartshorne's Differences from Whitehead," *Two Process Philosophers: Hartshorne's Encounter with Whitehead*, AAR Studies in Religion No. 15 (Tallahassee: AAR, 1973), pp. 35-57 and Lewis S. Ford, "Whitehead's Differences from Hartshorne," pp. 58-83.

[20]Rogers and Baird, p. 189.
[21]Cobb and Griffin, p. 48.
[22]Ibid.   [23]Ibid., p. 30.
[24]Ibid., pp. 35, 36.   [25]Ibid., p. 36.
[26]Ibid.
[27]Whitehead, *Religion in the Making*, p. 128.
[28]Ibid., p. 132.
[29]Cobb and Griffin, p. 161. "Since we believe that the prereflective content of faith refers to God and the world as well as to human existence, we prize Whitehead's for its ability to render explicit this prethematized vision of reality."
[30]For a thorough listing of the literature and persons associated with process thought see Cobb and Griffin, Appendix B. Among the contemporary major figures are Cobb and Griffin, Schubert M. Ogden, Norman Pittenger, Daniel Day Williams, Leslie Dewart, Bernard Meland, and Marjorie Suchocki.
[31]Suchocki, p. 93.
[32]Ibid., pp. 93-94.   [33]Ibid.
[34]Ibid., p. 95.   [35]Ibid.
[36]Ibid., p. 96.   [37]Ibid., p. 101.
[38]Ibid.
[39]Whitehead wrote that "Religion collapses unless its main positions command immediacy of assent." See *Science and the Modern World*, p. 274.
[40]As David Tracy writes of Cobb: "First, Cobb insists that an integral contemporary Christian theology must assume responsibility for a critical investigation of both the Christian tradition and the modern world vision.... There, is, then, no substitute via any 'authorities' for careful historical investigation of either the 'vision of reality,' structure of existence,' or 'cognitive beliefs' of Christianity." See David Tracy, "John Cobb's Theological Method: Interpretation and Reflections," in *John Cobb's Theology in Process*, ed. David Ray Griffin and Thomas J.J. Altizer (Philadelphia: Westminster, 1977), p. 26. Cobb had earlier written: "Where then can the theologian find data for a doctrine of God such that it will overcome all rational obstacles to belief? Clearly he cannot merely point to authoritative pronouncements in Bible and creed, for it is precisely in connection with such claims to authority that much serious doubt arises. Either such claims to authority that much serious doubt arises. Either such claims must themselves be substantiated in terms of less doubtful criteria or else more primitive data must be found." John Cobb, "Theological Data and Method," *Journal of Religion* 33 (July 1953), p. 215. Particularly helpful in delineating aspects of the process view of Scripture has been Gary Watts and Jack Rogers, "Six Theological Models of the Early 1980s: Their Theological Methods with Special Reference to Their Use of Scripture," Unpublished paper (Fuller Theological Seminary, 1980).
[41]Cobb and Griffin, p. 37.
[42]Suchocki, p. 104.
[43]Ibid.
[44]Cobb and Griffin, p. 40.

CHAPTER X

[1]James William McClendon, Jr., *Biography as Theology: How Life Stories Can Remake Today's Theology* (Nashville: Abingdon, 1974), p. 7.
[2]Lonnie D. Kliever, *The Shattered Spectrum: A Survey of Contemporary Theology* (Atlanta: John Knox Press, 1981), p. 160.
[3]Gabriel Fackre, "Narrative Theology: An Overview," *Interpretation* 37 (1983), p. 343.
[4]Kliever, p. 153. He cites Joseph Campbell, *Myths to Live By* (New York: Viking Press, 1972), pp. 214-215 and *The Masks of God: Creative Mythology* (New York: Viking Press, 1970), pp. 608-624 for discussion of the interlocking functions of myth in primitive cultures.

[5]Kliever, p. 155.

[6]See Kliever, p. 155 who cites Robert Scholes and Robert Kellog, *The Nature of Narrative* (London: Oxford University Press, 1966) as a source for the historical development of the narrative tradition in terms of both formal and functional analyses of story.

[7]Kliever, p. 155.

[8]Fackre, "Narrative Theology," p. 341.

[9]Kliever, p. 156.

[10]Ibid.

[11]Kliever, p. 157. He cites here Frank Kermode, *The Sense of an Ending* (London: Oxford University Press, 1977).

[12]Kliever, p. 157.

[13]Kliever, p. 157. Cf. John S. Dunne, *Time and Myth* (Garden City, New York: Doubleday, 1973), p. 113.

[14]See George W. Stroup, "A Bibliographical Critique," *Theology Today* 32 (1975), pp. 133-143 and Stroup's, *The Promise of Narrative Theology: Recovering the Gospel in the Church* (Atlanta: John Knox Press, 1981), ch. III. Cf. Fackre, "Narrative Theology" and Kliever, ch. 7.

[15]Sam Keen, *To a Dancing God* (New York: Harper & Row, 1970); Harvey Cox, *The Seduction of the Spirit* (New York: Simon and Schuster, 1973); Michael Novak, *Ascent of the Mountain, Flight of the Dove* (New York: Harper & Row, 1971); Robert P. Roth, *Story and Reality* (Grand Rapids: Wm. B. Eerdmans Publishing Co., 1973); Gabriel Fackre, *The Christian Story* (Grand Rapids: Wm. B. Eerdmans Publishing Co., 1978); and John Shea, *Stories of God* (Chicago: Thomas More Press, 1978). On Novak, Cox, and Keen see also Stanley T. Sutphin, *Options in Contemporary Theology* (Lanham, Maryland: University Press of America, 1977), ch. 1.

[16]Stroup, *Promise*, p. 72.

[17]Stephen Crites, "The Narrative Quality of Experience," *Journal of the American Academy of Religion* 39 (1971), p. 291.

[18]Crites, p. 305.

[19]John S. Dunne, *A Search for God in Time and Memory* (New York: Macmillan, 1969), p. 170.

[20]Stroup, *Promise*, p. 77. For an extended treatment of Dunne see Kliever, pp. 160-168.

[21]Dunne, *Search*, xi.

[22]Dunne, *Search*, xi. Stroup offers his critique of Dunne in *Promise*, p. 78.

[23]McClendon, p. 37.

[24]A fuller treatment of McClendon is found in Kliever, pp. 168-175.

[25]Stroup cites the works of Gerhard von Rad, *Old Testament Theology*, trans. James Stalker, 2 vols. (New York: Harper & Row, 1962, 1965); Oscar Cullmann, *Christ and Time* (Philadelphia: Westminster Press, 1964); and G. Ernest Wright, *God Who Acts: Biblical Theology as Recital*, Studies in Biblical Theology No. 8 (London: SCM Press, 1952) as significant representatives of this approach. See *Promise*, p. 79, n. 25.

[26]Amos Wilder, *The Language of the Gospel: Early Christian Rhetoric* (New York: Harper & Row, 1964), pp. 64, 67.

[27]Eric Auerbach, *Mimesis: The Representation of Reality in Western Literature*, trans. Willard R. Trash (Princeton: Princeton University Press, 1965), pp. 14-15.

[28]Stroup, *Promise*, p. 81. This is the point made by Hans Frei in Hans W. Frei, *The Eclipse of Biblical Narrative* (New Haven: Yale University Press, 1974).

[29]See James A. Sanders, *Torah and Canon* (Philadelphia: Fortress, 1972). Cf. Sander's "Torah and Christ," *Interpretation* 29 (1975), pp. 372-390.

[30]Brevard S. Childs, *Introduction to the Old Testament as Scripture* (Philadelphia: Fortress Press, 1979), p. 72. Cf. Child's, "The Old Testament as Scripture of the Church," *Concordia Theological Monthly* 43 (1972), pp. 709-722.

[31]See James Barr, *Holy Scripture Canon, Authority, Criticism* (Philadelphia: Westminster Press, 1983) and Child's review of it: *Interpretation* 38 (1984), pp. 66-70. Cf. Donald K. McKim's review in *Journal of the American Academy of Religion* 52 (1984), p. 375.

[32]See Sallie McFague, *Speaking in Parables* (Philadelphia: Fortress Press, 1975) and her se-

quel, Sallie McFague, *Metaphorical Theology: Models of God in Religious Language* (Philadelphia: Fortress Press, 1982). A detailed discussion of her work on parables is found in Kliever, pp. 175-181.

[33]McFague, *Metaphorical Theology*, p. 15. Cf. 32ff.

[34]McFague, *Metaphorical Theology*, p. 15. Cf. *Parables*, p. 39 where she writes: "As we have seen, metaphor is the poet's way to try and define something for which there is not dictionary meaning; it is his or her attempt to be precise and clear about something for which ordinary language has no way of talking."

[35]McFague, *Metaphorical Theology*, p. 17.

[36]McFague, *Metaphorical Theology*, p. 18. Jesus as a "parable of God" means Jesus both "is and is not God," writes McFague, p. 19. She sees value in this approach in that a metaphorical theology guards against literalistic realism and idolatry. McFague writes: "In such a theology *no* finite thought, product, or creature can be identified with God and this includes Jesus of Nazareth, who as parable of God both 'is and is not' God."

[37]This is the "tensive quality" of metaphors. McFague identifies the leading contemporary theorists on metaphor as I.A. Richards, Max Black, Douglas Berggren, Walter Ong, Nelson Goodman, and Paul Ricoeur. Ricoeur's work in particular has been significant for many story theologians.

[38]See McFague, *Parables*, p. 22.

[39]Dunne, *Search*, p. 218.

[40]McFague, *Metaphorical Theology*, p. 40.

[41]See Kliever, p. 164. Of particular help here also has been Gary Watts and Jack Rogers, "Six Theological Models of the Early 1980s: Their Theological Methods with Special Reference to Their Use of Scripture," Unpublished paper (Fuller Theological Seminary, August, 1980), "Story Theology."

[42]McClendon, p. 152.

[43]McFague, *Parables*, p. 58.

[44]Ibid., p. 16.   [45]Ibid., p. 79.

[46]McFague, *Parables*, p. 3. Dunne's whole point is that life should be viewed as "story."

[47]Kliever, p. 180.

[48]Ibid.

[49]McFague, *Parables*, p. 94.

[50]See McClendon, p. 95; Fackre, *The Christian Story*, p. 20 and McFague who writes: "The various forms of metaphorical language operative in biblical literature an in the Christian literary tradition ought to be looked at carefully as resources for theological reflection," *Parables*, p. 64.

[51]See McFague, *Parables*, pp. 35-36, 158-162 and Fackre, *The Christian Story*, pp. 15, 42.

[52]McFague, *Metaphorical Theology*, p. 19. The concept of the "classic" text is dealt with substantially in David Tracy, *The Analogical Imagination: Christian Theology and the Culture of Pluralism* (New York: Crossroad, 1981).

[53]McFague, *Metaphorical Theology*, p. 54. She goes on to criticize "conservatives" who "absolutize Scripture, refusing to admit its metaphorical quality while liberation theologies, especially radical feminist theology, relativize Scripture to the point of undercutting the relevance of its basic images."

[54]McFague, *Metaphorical Theology*, p. 57.

[55]Ibid., p. 59.   [56]Ibid.

[57]Ibid., p. 61.

[58]McFague writes: "To see belief not as a set of beliefs but as a story, an experience of coming to belief, means that theological reflection ought itself to be shaped by the story, take to itself, both in form and content, the story....From the novelist as well as from the stories in Scripture the theologian should take courage to concentrate on the experience of coming to belief, not on the 'beliefs' themselves (the sedimentation of experiences of coming to belief)," *Parables*, p. 139. Cf. p. 72.

[59]McFague, *Metaphorical Theology*, p. 62.

[60]Ibid.

CHAPTER XI

[1]Harvie M. Conn, "Theologies of Liberation: An Overview" in *Tensions in Contemporary Theology*, eds. Stanley N. Gundry and Alan F. Johnson, 2nd ed. (Grand Rapids: Baker Book House, 1983), p. 327. Cf. Conn's following essay, "Theologies of Liberation: Toward a Common View," pp. 395-434 for a fine discussion of various liberation theologies.

[2]Lonnie D. Kliever, *The Shattered Spectrum: A Survey of Contemporary Theology* (Atlanta: John Knox Press, 1981), p. 86.

[3]Other forms of liberation theology are dealt with by Conn and on a smaller scale in Stanley T. Sutphin, *Options in Contemporary Theology* (Lanham, Maryland: University Press of America, 1977), ch. 2. Cf. Kliever, ch. 4.

[4]Robert McAfee Brown, *Theology in a New Key: Responding to Liberation Themes* (Philadelphia: Westminster Press, 1978), p. 52.

[5]The English texts of the Medellin Conference are in *The Church in the Present-Day Transformation of Latin America in the Light of the Council Volume II. Conclusions* (Washington, D.C.: U.S. Catholic Conference, 1973). The historical backgrounds of Latin American developments are found in Enrique Dussel, *History and the Theology of Liberation* (Maryknoll, New York: Orbis, 1976). Cf. *Theology in the Americas*, eds. Sergio Torres and John Eagleson (Maryknoll, New York: Orbis, 1976) and Francis P. Fiorenza, "Latin American Liberation Theology," *Interpretation* (1974), pp. 441-457 for additional backgrounds.

[6]Cited in Brown, p. 53.

[7]See Conn, p. 344.

[8]Cited in Brown, p. 54.

[9]Conn, p. 344.

[10]Ibid.

[11]Brown, p. 54.

[12]*The Emergent Gospel Theology from the Underside of History*, eds. Sergio Torres and Virginia Fabella (Maryknoll, New York: Orbis, 1978), p. 182.

[13]See the account of this group and documents of this conference in *Christians and Socialism*, ed. John Eagleson (Maryknoll, New York: Orbis, 1975).

[14]Brown, pp. 55-56.

[15]Cited in Brown, p. 57.

[16]Ibid., p. 57.   [17]Ibid., p. 59.

[18]Ibid., p. 59.

[19]Cited in José Miguez Bonino, *Doing Theology in a Revolutionary Situation*, ed. William H. Lazareth (Philadelphia: Fortress Press, 1975), p. 43. Cf. Gustavo Gutiérrez, *A Theology of Liberation History, Politics and Salvation*, trans. and ed. Sister Caridad Inda and John Eagleson (Maryknoll, New York: Orbis, 1973), p. 105; hereafter cited as *TL*.

[20]Cited in Bonino, pp. 43-44.

[21]Bonino, p. 44.

[22]Conn, p. 359.

[23]Bonino, p. 74. See Rubem Alves, *A Theology of Human Hope* (Washington, D.C.: Corpus Books, 1969).

[24]Cited in Bonino, p. 74.

[25]Ibid., p. 76.

[26]Conn, p. 360.

[27]Alves was critical of the view of Júrgen Moltmann, *Theology of Hope* (New York: Harper & Row, 1967) that hope is mediated only through biblical promises. This Alves calls "a new form of docetism, in which God loses his present-day dimension." See Alves, pp. 55-68.

[28]Bonino, p. 76.

[29]Cited in Bonino, p. 72 from Assmann's *Opresion-Liberacion*. The English translation of this book is found in Assmann's, *Practical Theology of Liberation* (London: Search, 1975), ch. 2. Cf. his *Theology for a Nomad Church* (Maryknoll, New York: Orbis, 1976).

[30]Cited in Bonino, p. 73.

ENDNOTES

[31]A shorter discussion of Gutiérrez's views is in his "Freedom and Salvation: A Political Problem," in *Liberation and Change*, ed. Ronald H. Stone (Atlanta: John Knox Press, 1977), pp. 3-94.
[32]From *Frontiers of Theology in Latin America*, ed. Rosini Gibellini (Maryknoll, New York: Orbis, 1979), p. x.
[33]Gutiérrez, *TL*, p. 36.
[34]Ibid., pp. 36-37.
[35]Ibid., p. 37. Cf. p. 175.   [36]Ibid., p. 177.
[37]Kliever, p. 87.
[38]Gutiérrez, *TL*, p. 178.
[39]Bonino, p. 70.
[40]Gutiérrez, *TL*, p. 70.
[41]Ibid., p. 153.   [42]Ibid.
[43]Ibid., p. 72. Bonino comments that "all the chapters in Guiterrez's presentation take this fundamental unity to different areas of theological thought. The couples liberation/salvation, love of the neighbor/Christology, politics/eschatology, humanity/Church, human solidarity/sacraments, cover the classical *loci* of theology indissolubly relating them to the search for socio-political liberation and the building of a new humanity," p. 71.
[44]Gutiérrez, *TL*, p. 15.
[45]Ibid., p. 6.   [46]Ibid., p. 13.
[47]Conn, p. 362.
[48]Stephen C. Knapp, "A Preliminary Dialogue with Gutierrez' 'A Theology of Liberation,'" in *Evangelicals and Liberation*, ed. Carl E. Armerding (Nutley, New Jersey: Presbyterian and Reformed Publishing Company, 1977), p. 17.
[49]Gutiérrez, *TL*, p. 15. The implications of this for the Eucharist and human community are also explicated by Gutiérrez. See pp. 262-279.
[50]José Porfirio Miranda, *Marx and the Bible: A Critique of the Philosophy of Oppression*, trans. John Eagleson (Maryknoll, New York: Orbis, 1974). Cf. J. Emmette Weir, "The Bible and Marx: A Discussion of the Hermeneutics of Liberation Theology," *Scottish Journal of Theology* 35 (1982), pp. 337-350.
[51]Juan Luis Segundo, *The Liberation of Theology*, trans. John Drury (Maryknoll, New York: Orbis, 1976). Cf. Deane William Ferm, *Contemporary American Theologies: A Critical Survey* (New York: Seabury, 1981), p. 68; Conn, pp. 366-368 and Alfred T. Hennelly, "The Challenge of Juan Luis Segundo," *Theological Studies* (1977), pp. 125ff.
[52]Jon Sobrino, *Christology at the Crossroads: A Latin American Approach*, trans. John Drury (Maryknoll, New York: Orbis, 1978). Cf. Alfred T. Hennelly, "Theological Method: The Southern Exposure," *Theological Studies* 38 (1977), p. 722.
[53]Leonardo Boff, *Jesus Christ Liberator: A Critical Christology for Our Time*, trans. Patrick Hughes (Maryknoll, New York: Orbis, 1978).
[54]Bonino is "considered by many to be the dean of Latin American Protestant theologians." See Conn, p. 371. He is an Argentinian and teaches at the Higher Institute of Theological Studies in Buenos Aires.
[55]Jose Miguez Bonino, *Christians and Marxists: The Mutual Challenge of Revolution* (Grand Rapids: Wm. B. Eerdmans Publishing Co., 1976). Cf. Conn, pp. 372-373.
[56]See Gutiérrez, *TL*, pp. 81-88 and Bonino, *Theology*, pp. 21-37 for historical analyses.
[57]Gutiérrez, *TL*, p. 83.
[58]Ibid., p. 84.   [59]Ibid., p. 86.
[60]See Conn, p. 348.
[61]Gutiérrez, *TL*, p. 87.
[62]Brown, pp. 60-61.
[63]Frederick Herzog, *Liberation Theology* (New York: Seabury, 1972), p. 258.
[64]Brown, p. 61.
[65]Ibid.
[66]Cited in Brown, p. 71. Bonino says similarly: "There is, therefore, no knowledge except in action itself, in the process of transforming the world through participation in history," *Theology*, p. 88.

[67]Bonino, p. 90.

[68]Conn, p. 400. Cf. Brown, pp. 72-74. Brown's characteristics of liberation theology and its differences from classical theology are:
1. a different starting point: the poor
2. a different interlocutor: the nonperson
3. a different set of tools: the social sciences
4. a different analysis: the reality of conflict
5. a different mode of engagement: praxis
6. a different theology: the "second act"
See Brown, p. 60. Cf. the analysis by C. René Padilla, "Liberation Theology (I)," *The Reformed Journal* 33 (1983), pp. 21-23 and his "Liberation Theology (II) An Evaluation," *The Reformed Journal* 33 (1983), pp. 14-18.

[69]Brown, p. 79. He cites instances where the "poor" in the New Testament are "spiritualized" by biblical commentators.

[70]Bonino, *Theology*, p. 87.

[71]Gutiérrez, *TL*, p. 12.

[72]Bonino, *Theology*, p. 91. Cf. his whole ch. 5: "Hermeneutics, Truth, and Praxis." For a discussion of Segundo's "hermeneutical circle" in this regard see Padilla, "Liberation Theology (I)," p. 23 and Conn, p. 367.

[73]Bonino, *Theology*, p. 91.

[74]Brown, p. 81. Cf. Bonino, *Theology*, pp. 101-102.

[75]Gutiérrez, *TL*. Of help in seeing these uses of Scripture in liberation theology have been Gary Watts and Jack Rogers, "Six Theological Models of the Early 1980s: Their Theological Methods with Special Reference to Their Use of Scripture," Unpublished paper (Fuller Theological Seminary, 1980), "Liberation Theology."

[76]Brown, p. 88. Cf. John Goldingay, "The Hermeneutics of Liberation Theology," *Horizons in Biblical Theology* 4-5 (1982-1983), pp. 139ff.

[77]Daniel L. Migliore, *Called to Freedom: Liberation Theology and the Future of Christian Doctrine* (Philadelphia: Westminster, 1980), p. 31.

[78]See Gutiérrez, *TL*, p. 194 and Brown, p. 90ff.

[79]Gutiérrez, *TL*, p. 195.

[80]Ibid., p. 195.   [81]Ibid., pp. 162, 163.
[82]Ibid., p. 167.   [83]Ibid..
[84]Ibid., p. 10.   [85]Ibid., p. 135.

Chapter XII

[1]Joan Turner Beifuss, "Feminist Theologians Organize, Make Gains," *National Catholic Reporter* 20 (April 13, 1984), p. 3. The whole issue is devoted to "Women Doing Theology."

[2]Beifuss, p. 3. As Letty Russell writes: "strictly speaking feminist theology is *not* about women. It is about God. It is not a form of 'ego-logy' in which women just think about themselves. When women do it, they speak of feminist theology in order to express the fact that the experience from which they speak and the world out of which they perceive God's words and actions and join in those actions is that of women seeking human equality. Another way of expressing this is to say that the ecology of their theology is that of a woman living in a particular time and place," *Human Liberation in a Feminist Perspective–A Theology* (Philadelphia: Westminster Press, 1974), p. 53.

[3]Beverly W. Harrison, "Feminist Ecumenical Theory Takes Its Cues from Women's History," *National Catholic Reporter* 20 (April 13, 1984), p. 18.

[4]Katharine Doob Sakenfeld, "Feminist Uses of Biblical Material," in *Feminist Interpretation of the Bible*, ed. Letty M. Russell (Philadelphia: Westminster Press, 1985), p. 55; hereafter cited as *FIB*.

[5]Letty M. Russell, "Introduction," in *FIB*, p. 12.

[6]Russell, *FIB*, pp. 12-13. See the volume Russell edited, *The Liberating Word: A Guide to*

Nonsexist Interpretation of the Bible (Philadelphia: Westminster Press, 1976).

[7]Russell, *FIB*, p. 14.

[8]See Barbara Brown Zikmund, "Feminist Consciousness in Historical Perspective," *FIB*, p. 21.

[9]Zikmund, p. 22.

[10]Ibid.   [11]Ibid., p. 23.

[12]Elisabeth Schüssler Fiorenza, *In Memory of Her: A Feminist Theological Reconstruction of Christian Origins* (New York: Crossroad, 1983), p. 13. Cf. Carol P. Christ, "The New Feminist Theology: A Review of the Literature," *Religious Studies Review* 3 (1977), p. 207.

[13]See *The Original Feminist Attack on the Bible: The Woman's Bible*, ed. Elizabeth Cady Stanton, facsimile edition (New York: Arno, 1974) and *Women and Religion A Feminist Sourcebook of Christian Thought*, eds. Elizabeth Clark and Herbert Richardson (New York: Harper & Row, 1977), pp. 215-224 for selections from *The Woman's Bible*.

[14]Christ, p. 204.

[15]Fiorenza, *Memory*, p. 7.

[16]Ibid., p. 11.   [17]Ibid., p. 8.

[18]Ibid., p. 11.

[19]*The Woman's Bible*, 1.12 cited in Fiorenza, *Memory*, p. 12.

[20]Fiorenza, *Memory*, p. 13.

[21]Zikmund, p. 26.

[22]Ibid., p. 26.   [23]Ibid., p. 27.

[24]Zikmund, p. 27. Cf. the account in *Womanspirit Rising A Feminist Reader in Religion*, eds. Carol P. Christ and Judith Plaskow (San Francisco: Harper & Row, 1979), "Introduction: Womanspirit Rising."

[25]Beifuss, p. 3.

[26]Zikmund, p. 27.

[27]The essay originally appeared in *The Journal of Religion* (April 1960) and is reprinted in *Womanspirit Rising*, pp. 25-42.

[28]In *Womanspirit Rising*, p. 27.

[29]Mary Daly, *The Church and the Second Sex* (New York: Harper & Row, 1968).

[30]Mary Daly, "The Courage to See," *The Christian Century* (September 22, 1971), p. 1108 cited in Deane William Ferm, *Contemporary American Theologies: A Critical Survey* (New York: Seabury Press, 1981), p. 80. On Daly see also Lonnie D. Kliever, *The Shattered Spectrum: A Survey of Contemporary Theology* (Atlanta: John Knox Press, 1981), pp. 81-85 and Fiorenza, *Memory*, pp. 22-26.

[31]Mary Daly, *Beyond God the Father* (Boston: Beacon Press, 1973).

[32]For this see Daly's, *Gyn/Ecology* (Boston: Beacon Press, 1978).

[33]See Christ and Plaskow, *Womanspirit Rising*, p. 8. Harrison refers to these women as "post-Christian feminists." See Harrison, p. 18.

[34]See the section "Creating New Traditions" in *Womanspirit Rising*.

[35]See for example, Starhawk, "Witchcraft and Women's Culture," in *Womanspirit Rising*, pp. 259-268.

[36]Christ and Plaskow, *Womanspirit Rising*, pp. 10-11. Cf. Christ, "Why Women Need the Goddess: Phenomenological, Psychological, and Political Reflections," *Womanspirit Rising*, pp. 273-287.

[37]See Naomi R. Goldenberg, "Dreams and Fantasies as Sources of Revelation: Feminist Appropriation of Jung," *Womanspirit Rising*, pp. 219-227 and her *Changing of the Gods: Feminism and the End of Traditional Religions* (Boston: Beacon Press, 1979). Cf. Patricia Wilson-Kastner, *Faith, Feminism, and the Christ* (Philadelphia: Fortress Press, 1983), pp. 20-23.

[38]Harrison, p. 18.

[39]On these see *Womanspirit Rising* and Donald K. McKim, "Hearkening to the Voices: What Women Theologians are Saying," *The Reformed Journal* 35 (1985), pp. 7-10.

[40]See Christ and Plaskow, *Womanspirit Rising*, pp. 7-8. The "Revolutionary/Reformist" rubric is now a standard designation in literature on feminist theology. A more sophisticated

and helpful typology was offered by Mary Potter in a lecture at the University of Dubuque Theological Seminary on April 22, 1985 when she spoke of the various perspectives as: Evangelical Christian, Neo-Orthodox Christian, Liberal-Revisionist Christian, Political (Liberation) Revisionist Christian, Transcendental Post-Christian and Inductive Post-Christian.

[41]Anne Carr, "Is a Christian Feminist Theology Possible?" *Theological Studies* 43 (1982), p. 282.

[42]Ibid.   [43]Ibid.

[44]Harrison, p. 18 cites this from the title of a collection of essays on feminism and nonviolence edited by Pam McAllister (1982).

[45]On these see McKim, pp. 8-10 and the account by Ferm, pp. 83ff.

[46]Beifuss, p. 3.

[47]Beifuss, p. 3. Ruether writes that "the uniqueness of feminist theology lies not in its use of the criterion of experience but rather in its use of *women's* experience, which has been almost entirely shut out of theological reflection in the past," *Sexism and God-Talk: Toward a Feminist Theology* (Boston: Beacon Press, 1983), p. 13.

[47]Beifuss, p. 3.

[48]Rosemary Radford Ruether, "Feminist Interpretation: A Method of Correlation" in *FIB*, p. 116.

[49]Letty Russell, "Authority and the Challenge of Feminist Interpretation" in *FIB*, pp. 140-141.

[50]Ruether, "Correlation," p. 115.

[51]Ibid., p. 116.

[52]Elisabeth Schüssler Fiorenza, "The Will to Choose or to Reject: Continuing Our Critical Work," in *FIB*, p. 129.

[53]Attention here is paid only to those "reformist" Feminist theologians who wish to work with traditional Christian materials in some fashion.

[54]Ruether, "Correlation," p. 117.

[55]Margaret A. Farley, "Feminist Consciousness and the Interpretation of Scripture" in *FIB*, p. 49. She develops the notions of equality and mutuality as presuppositions for a feminist hermeneutic of Scripture.

[56]Mary Ann Tolbert, "Defining the Problem: The Bible and Feminist Hermeneutics," *Semeia* 28 (1983), p. 119.

[57]Phyllis Trible, *God and the Rhetoric of Sexuality* (Philadelphia: Fortress Press, 1978), p. 7. Cf. p. 203.

[58]See Tolbert, p. 119.

[59]Ibid., p. 122.

[60]Tolbert, pp. 122-123 delineates three positions as: (1) prophetic tradition; (2) remnant standpoint and (3) reconstruction of biblical history. Sakenfeld's model is: (1) Looking to Texts About Women to Counteract Famous Texts Used "Against" Women; (2) Looking to the Bible Generally for a Theological Perspective Offering a Critique of Patriarchy and (3) Looking to Texts About Women to Learn from the History and Stories of Ancient and Modern Women Living in Patriarchal Cultures, pp. 57-63.

[61]Tolbert, p. 119.

[62]Sakenfeld, p. 57. Cf. Leonard Swidler, *Biblical Affirmations of Women* (Philadelphia: Westminster Press, 1979) for collections of biblical texts dealing with women.

[63]See Trible, *God and the Rhetoric of Sexuality*, p. 4 and *Texts of Terror* (Philadelphia: Fortress Press, 1984). Cf. Fiorenza, *Memory*, pp. 19-21 on Trible's method.

[64]Sakenfeld, p. 59.

[65]Ruether, "Correlation," p. 117 and her chapter, "Biblical Resources for Feminism: The Prophetic Principles" in *Sexism and God-Talk*. Cf. Fiorenza, *Memory*, pp. 16-19 on Ruether's method.

[66]See Ruether, "Correlation," pp. 119ff.

[67]Russell, "Authority," p. 138.

[68]Ibid.

[69]See Fiorenza, *Memory*, pp. 15-16 on Russell's method. Cf. the section on Russell in

ENDNOTES

Stanley T. Sutphin, *Options in Contemporary Theology* (Lanham, Maryland: University Press of America, 1977), pp. 50-64.

[70]Russell, "Authority," p. 138.

[71]Ibid.

[72]Ibid., p. 144.   [73]Ibid., p. 146.

[74]Tolbert, p. 123.

[75]Fiorenza, *Memory*, pp. 35-36; cf. p. 92. This approach was developed also in her " 'You Are Not to be Called Father': Early Christian History in a Feminist Perspective," *Cross Currents*, 29 (1979), pp. 301-323.

[76]Fiorenza, "Continuing Our Critical Work," p. 130. Cf. her "Toward a Feminist Biblical Hermeneutics: Biblical Interpretation and Liberation Theology," *The Challenge of Liberation Theology A First World Response*, eds. Brian Mahan and L. Dale Richesin (Maryknoll, New York: Orbis, 1981), pp. 91-112 and her *Bread Not Stone: Introduction to a Feminist Interpretation of Scripture* (Boston: Beacon Press, 1985).

[77]Fiorenza, "Continuing Our Critical Work," p. 135.

[78]Fiorenza, "Continuing Our Critical Work," p. 135. She also writes: "A feminist theological hermeneutics having as its canon the liberation of women from oppressive patriarchal texts, structures, institutions, and values maintains that–if the Bible is not to continue as a tool for the patriarchal oppression of women–only those traditions and texts that critically break through patriarchal culture and 'plausibility structures' have the theological authority of revelation. The 'advocacy stance' of liberation theologies cannot accord revelatory authority to any oppressive and destructive biblical text or tradition. Nor did they have any such claim at any point in history. Such a critical measure must be applied to *all* biblical texts, their historical contexts, and theological interpretations, and not just to the texts on women," *Memory*, p. 33.

[79]Fiorenza, *Memory*, p. 33.

[80]Fiorenza, "Continuing Our Critical Work," p. 135.

[81]Sakenfeld, p. 62.

[82]Fiorenza, *Memory*, p. 34.

[83]Phyllis Trible, "Postscript: Jottings on the Journey" in *FIB*, p. 149.

[84]Ibid.

Index of Names